A SPECIAL CORPS

A Special Corps

The beginnings of
Gorkha service with the British

A.P. Coleman

The Pentland Press
Edinburgh – Cambridge – Durham – USA

First published in 1999 by
The Pentland Press Ltd
1 Hutton Close,
South Church
Bishop Auckland
Durham

ISBN 1–85821-606–0

Typeset in Minion 12/15
by Carnegie Publishing, Carnegie House, Chatsworth Road, Lancaster
Printed and bound by Bookcraft Ltd, Bath

Dedication

The first edition of this book has been published through the generosity of Mr and Mrs Ean Ramsay, close friends of the author. Ean Ramsay is the great-great-great-grandson of Major-General Sir David Ochterlony Bart. GCB (1758–1825) who, in 1815, first recruited large numbers of Gorkhas and other hillmen into the East India Company's Bengal Army. In so doing he founded what was to become the British Indian Army's Gurkha Brigade, and, after 1947, the British Army's Brigade of Gurkhas and the Gorkha units of the Army of India. In 1850, during the Governor-Generalship of Lord Dalhousie, Chief of the Clan Ramsay, the Nasiri Battalion raised by Sir David Ochterlony was brought into the regular Bengal Army as the 66th or Goorka Regiment

Ean Ramsay is a greatly respected honorary member of the Regimental Association of the 1st King George V's Own Gurkha Rifles (The Malaun Regiment) which derived from the Nasiri Battalion. Ean and Lydia Ramsay share Sir David Ochterlony's great admiration for Gorkha soldiers, so much so that, with the author's whole-hearted agreement, they have requested that proceeds from the sale of this edition be donated to the Gurkha Welfare Trust, a most worthy charity to which they have already made generous endowments.

Contents

Appendices

Colour Plates

Illustrations

Maps

Tables

Introductory Commendation

by Major General D.G.T. Horsford CBE DSO

I launched the Gurkha Welfare Trust as Major General Brigade of Gurkhas in 1969 although much of the detailed work had been done by my predecessor. I have worked very closely with the author since 1974 because I am the President of the 1st Gurkha Rifles Regimental Association and he is the Honorary Secretary – a most efficient and capable Secretary and a very close friend.

He has paid a well-deserved tribute to the Gurkhas, with whom we have served, and it is fitting that the proceeds of the sale of the first edition of this book should be devoted to the Welfare of Gurkha ex-servicemen of the Crown, especially now that the strength of the Brigade of Gurkhas has been so drastically reduced resulting in so many men being returned to their homeland before their service has expired.

I had the honour of commanding a battalion of the 1st Gurkhas throughout the 1944/45 campaign in Burma and so I have seen at first hand their soldierly skills, their courage and their proud bearing. Everyone, soldiers and civilians alike, who has met Gurkhas is impressed with their discipline, their good manners and their delightful sense of humour. Even those who have never seen Gurkha soldiers, speak of them with an affection which, by long tradition, seems ingrained in our national spirit.

Gurkhas are indeed special. Unfortunately too few people appreciate the great debt we, the British, owe to them for their unswerving loyalty over nearly two centuries.

The Gurkha Welfare Trust (Charity no.1034080 registered with the Charities Commission of England and Wales) is helping to repay this debt. Through its twenty-four Welfare Centres in Nepal and one in India it dispenses financial, medical and community aid to alleviate hardship and distress among needy Gurkha ex-servicemen and their dependants.

As the complete first edition of this book had been funded by Ean Ramsay (whose Gorkha connections are noted in the Dedication), the proceeds from each sale will be donated to the Gurkha Welfare Trust. Those buying copies are therefore contributing directly to this very worthwhile cause.

Foreword

by Professor Rodney Needham, All Souls College, Oxford

> As fighters … [Gorkhas] possess not only the dash which determines
> the fortune of the attack, but the stubborn pluck which knows how to
> endure punishment without becoming demoralised.[1]

Captain Coleman's monograph combines two sorts of importance: it
is a first-rate historical investigation, and its subjects are superb
soldiers. The skill and professionalism of the author match those of
the Gorkhas. The product derives its authority from his years of
personal acquaintance with men of the 1st King George V's Own
Gurkha Rifles, in the Indian Army before independence, together with
a longer period of original literary research, especially among family
papers and in the archives. No work in the extensive bibliography of
the Gurkha Brigade and the history of Nepal, with regard to the
beginnings of Gorkha service with the British, has achieved such a
pitch of detail, cogency and expository excellence. Every factual statement is supported by reference to accessible sources, the majority of
these being recondite and now brought to light by painstaking and
resolute examination of a daunting mass of evidence. The presentation
of the argument is in a prose that constantly pleases by its unpreten-
tious clarity and consequence. From the hand of a practising historian,
A Special Corps would be received as a masterpiece: that it is the
work of a retired private gentleman makes it all the more admirable.
By the same token, however, its high qualities cause abashment at an
invitation to contribute a foreword. As a rule, a preliminary assessment
of the kind ought not to be attempted unless one is an expert in the
field and has something new to say about the particular case. In the
present instance, some justification (doubtless not sufficient) has been
sought instead under two rubrics: first, the ordinary capacity of an

academic in the humanities to form an appraisal of a work of intellectual art; second, an obligation, and even a debt of honour, to the regiment (1 G.R.) and its men, and hence a desire to be of service to an author who was once a fellow officer in it. Such, at any rate, are considerations that impel certain plain responses to Captain Coleman's history.

The book can be seen under two aspects that stand in contrast. One is that the main events are on a large scale; they pertain to a kingdom in its relations with India, China and Britain. The other is that the course of these events was decided in the field by just a tiny number of remarkable men; most notably, David Ochterlony, Peter Lawtie, Robert Ross, Frederick Young and William Fraser. The setting was a collision of interests between Nepal and the East India Company; this confrontation brought into play the needs and personages from which was formed the Corps of Gorkhas in May 1815. The immediate background to this formal recognition of the Gorkha battalions is the subject of a famously received idea, and Captain Coleman brings a basic correction to bear on it. On 21 February 1815, a large force of locally recruited irregulars numbering more than 3,000 men, under the command of Lieutenant Young, was defeated and broken up in panic by probably not more than 200 Gorkhas. A persistent tradition has it that Young was captured and that the victorious Gorkhas asked him why he too had not fled. 'I have not come so far in order to run away,' he is said to have replied; and at this his captors are supposed to have declared in admiration, 'We could serve under men like you.' This makes indeed a brave tale, a paradigm of mutual esteem between Gorkha and British. It has been repeated until very recently by one writer after another (though Captain Coleman declines to do so), with the subsequent story that Young learned Nepali and Gorkha customs during his time as prisoner of war. Caplan has commented doubtfully on this tradition, which he cannot trace back earlier than 1923, when it seems first to have been published in a biography of Young by his daughter.[2] It is Captain Coleman who has finally put an end to the matter. As he delicately phrases the issue, the account that Young was taken prisoner 'seems to conflict with documentary evidence' (below, p. 96); but his report of the correspondence between Young and Fraser, reproduced in full at Appendix B, makes it clear that actually there is no contemporary evidence that Young was captured or was quartered with his Gorkha opponents.

As to the forces in contention, the presence and actions of the Nepalese government are not problematic; that Scots and English were on the scene has to do with international commerce and the expansion of empire, enterprises that called for far-sighted plans and, in their execution, a cool intrepidity. In apprehending these factors, the presumptions of the day have to be taken as they were made; e.g. the casual arrogation in Ochterlony's announcement to the Cis-Sutlej Sikh chiefs, on 9 February 1809, 'informing them that they had been brought under the protection of the British'. In the prosecution of such ventures, enormous consequences derived from the courage and astute judgement of individuals serving these purposes and subscribing confidently to the ideals of the day.

The substantive theme of the present book is warfare, as conducted by men who engaged themselves as mercenaries, 'hired to kill', in the telling phrase of John Morris (3 G.R.),[3] in the service of the British. It would be pointless to inveigh against war, the most characteristic activity of man, or to recoil from the narrative because of the death, mutilation and misery perpetrated by Gorkhas in their chosen profession. Given the subject, and its atrocious manifestations, there comes under scrutiny the paramount factor sustaining the campaigns described by Captain Coleman: the character of the Gorkhas who did the fighting. The epigraph above provides a summary intimation of its qualities, but it is far from adequate. An ideal epigraph would contain, in a peculiarly apposite formulation, the essence and extension of the entire work that it heralded. In the case of Gorkhas, and the virtues that led to their lengthy incorporation into the Gurkha Brigade, this is not feasible, and very numerous attempts at summation demonstrate as much. It is arguable – and indeed there appears to be no counter-argument – that never has an exotic people attracted, so constantly and for nearly two centuries, such a paean of affectionate laudation as have the Gorkhas. A virtually universal admiration, first on the part of those who were their opponents in the war against

Nepal, has led to encomium and eulogy and panegyric such that no epigraph could compact so much within it. Wingate, it is true, made a notorious exception, but he had mishandled Gorkhas under his command and then compounded his own failings by disparaging them. The praise of Gorkhas vastly carries the day, and it is a phenomenon that illuminates the historical narrative.

About the bravery and endurance and martial skill of Gorkhas there has never been any doubt. As to their character in other respects, there has been an unfailing recognition of their 'sunny nature', from the very first personal meetings with them; their irrepressible high spirits have been reported again and again, and it has been well said that the most memorable expression on the face of a Gorkha is his easy smile. It is easy to understand that, as the author repeats below (p. 197), there should have existed from the start a 'special empathy' between British officers and their men. Lieutenant Lawtie, who was the first British officer to lead Gorkha troops in action – which the author rightly calls a privilege and an honour – was also among the first to testify to this quality; he found that everything the Nasiri contingent (later to become 1 G.R.) did, was done with cheerfulness and good humour (below, p. 122). It is a startling fact that, so many years after 1815, this sentiment should be still recognisable and acknowledged.

But even a universal testimony is not necessarily true, and the concomitant empathy has been called into question. An anthropological commentator, in a challenging and otherwise salutary monograph on Gorkhas, has recently queried the recurrent motif of a warmth of feeling between British officer and Gorkha. According to him, 'it is precisely the social and cultural gulf between officer and soldier which this rhetoric attempts symbolically to bridge' (Caplan, op. cit., p. 120). This is a contention that could be set aside as a typical expression of the literary fashion known as deconstructionism, a movement which, taken strictly as the theory it purports to be, has already proved tenuous and little convincing. Moreover, the proposition itself can hardly withstand a sceptical and more informed examination. The substantive matter is a sentiment that has been abundantly testified to by those who have felt it, and the integrity of this evidence is not to be gainsaid; we have to accept that they who avowed the sentiment, from Lawtie onwards, were not under a compulsion to volunteer as much, and that, whatever the variations, the constant burden of the testimony stands as a matter of responsive fact. To concede that there tend to be standard terms and turns of phrase in which the testimony is couched does not mean that this is rhetorical, i.e. that the language is designed to persuade or impress and is hence insincere. Rhetoric, in any case, cannot itself attempt anything at all, let alone symbolically bridge a social and cultural gulf; only the parties to the relationship could be in a position to attempt to do so, and there is much evidence that they did just that. The tacit premiss to the criticism is that a gulf of the kind evokes a warmth of feeling between those who are separated by it; but in general this is certainly not true, so it then has to be explained why this feeling, as a matter of direct witness, has prevailed when Gorkhas in particular are involved. It is surely far more reasonable, therefore, to give up the literary theory and to turn for commentary to an exceptionally gifted observer who has placed on record what he found especially impressive about a Gorkha battalion on active service.

Graham Greene, namely, was the guest, apparently for some three weeks, of a unit identified merely as 'Gurkha Rifles' (actually 2/7 G.R.) when in 1951 it was engaged in operations against terrorists in Malaya, and he accompanied one of its patrols in the forest. He was no man to be taken in by any regimental rhetoric, and his report was unambiguous:

> In return for their pay the Gurkhas give their British officers absolute loyalty, and their officers return them a quality of love you will not find in any other unit. Officers of the British Army complain that their colleagues in the Gurkhas never stop talking of their men. Their men are their passion.[4]

There is no extravagance in this passage, and it discerns with a precise phrase (probably for the first time in such terms) what can be regarded as the moral influence that runs throughout Captain Coleman's history: it isolates, as it were, the heart of the matter.

There is an important corollary to this demonstration, namely the effect on the officer himself. Tuker (2 G.R.) has enjoined, 'Let any enquirer be assured that if he seeks to understand the meaning of courage and selfless devotion, then he should soldier with a Gurkha regiment.' These are familiar and sincere allusions, not to be disputed, but then Tuker goes on: 'He will return an enlightened and a better man for the experience.'[5] This latter point identifies a consequential factor: that an officer who serves with Gorkhas stands to gain in his conscience and may become more worthy by their impress upon him. Patrick Davis (8 G.R.) well understood this and has stated the outcome plainly. 'It was always a pleasure, and often a joy, to be among them'; and not only this, but 'We grew better for being with them.'[6] To this finding too there is a corollary, and one that virtually anyone who has served in the Brigade has probably been seized by: namely that the inspiration can be counterbalanced, or even undermined, by the officer's realisation of how far he fell below what his men deserved. This is instructive, as well as chastening, and part of the remembrance of Gorkhas consists in a recurrent reassessment of one's own worth against the standards they set. It is an admirable people indeed of whom so much can be said by those best in a position to judge both Gorkhas and themselves.

With this consideration we are returned to the personages of Lawtie, Ross (1 G.R.) and Young (2 G.R.), and from them down through the tradition embodied in the Corps of Gorkhas and afterwards in the Gurkha Brigade, of which formations they and their men were the founders, as is engrossingly recounted by Captain Coleman in the narrative that follows. Political manoeuvres and commercial transactions can be left somewhat out of account, as contingent interests and particular circumstances. What is more constant, and what identifies the 'Special Corps', is Gorkha character, for all the variety and disparity among tribes and clans and individuals. From a moral point of view (not ethnic or military), it can be claimed that it is this factor that confers unity and continuity on the history. The character is also shown forth by individual acts on the part of one or another Gorkha, and these must last in profusion in the recollections of officers who remain indebted to them. Within this context of grateful appreciation, it may perhaps not be bad form therefore to mention that two Gorkhas were decorated for having on separate occasions, once on exercise and then in battle, saved the life of the writer of the present foreword; and these were not the only such occasions, any more than they were unexpected of such steady and careful soldiers. There can be no end to such thankful recollections as are evoked by Captain Coleman's history of the beginnings of Gorkha service with the British, but the memories themselves prompt some reflection on the wider recognition of indebtedness.

Repeatedly in the history below one finds directors, politicians, and bureaucrats looking for ways to pay Gorkhas less or even to disband them altogether. It is a familiar situation, after all, that soldiers, once the hazardous need is past, are treated as expensive encumbrances: the accountants take over, the men are returned to the hills. In 1923, Ralph Turner commented wryly that, after a century of close alliance with Nepal, there was still   no Khaskura dictionary – for 'lack of funds'. (It is pleasing that Brook Northey and Morris, in their general survey of Gorkhas, chose to cite Turner not as professor of Sanskrit – as which he was to be placed in renown alongside Sir William Jones and Sir George Grierson – but as Captain R.L. Turner MC [2/3 G.R.]; the regiment comes first.)[7] He continued, with deliberate loyalty: 'The British public at large have no clear realization of what the inhabitants of that ... country [Nepal] have done for us.'[8] Whether this public, or more generally modern generations in western civilisation, have today any clearer a realisation must be something of a question. What is not to be queried is the vital and unrequitable service rendered to the British, and through them to the great causes in which they have been implicated, by the Gurkha Brigade: most deplorably, 20,000 casualties in the First World War, more than 23,000 in the Second. The imagination blenches at such a toll of loss and suffering, and then at the consequences in grief and hardship for the families bereaved or burdened. The casualty figures may not seem severe when set beside those of the Somme or Kursk, but for a kingdom of small compass and scanty population they are terribly heavy. Against this scale, moreover, it is the more hurtful to appreciate that each digit represents the life or haleness of a Gorkha enticed into extreme danger by the very tradition, shared with the British, that Captain Coleman has, with proper detachment, so convincingly traced. It is intrinsic to his scholarly enterprise that such melancholy reflections should be inseparable from admiration of the superlative qualities of the Gorkha soldier. Tragedy is the inevitable counterpart to the moral example, and its shadow hangs over the entire history. It is thus a further high merit, and again in a moral sense, that the narrative which follows displays so clearly the foundations of British indebtedness to Gorkhas and to the government of Nepal.

An appropriate compliment to this achievement would be that the history be resumed, to cover the period from 1850 down to the present day. In parallel, there is to be hoped for an expansion of more exact knowledge of the Gorkhas in their native environment. Local or tribal ethnographies were not practicable until well after the Second World War, but already much has been accomplished, notable in such studies as that of the Gurung by Pignède and of the northern Magar by Oppitz.[9] It is ironic, no doubt, that a schoolarly understanding of the traditional social life of Gorkhas should be attained, at last, at a time when the demise of the Brigade of Gurkhas can be foreseen as perhaps even imminent, together with the end of a signal form of companionship between peoples. What will then have been lost will call for a profound analysis, and one that cannot be pre-empted. For the present, it is still concision that may best evoke the depth of the relationship. One phrase that returns, to wonderment and gratitude at all it implies, is that of a batman gently shaking his officer awake in the night and softly whispering, with good-humoured solicitude, 'Sir, the enemy have come.' To someone else, a familiar memory may be that of the almost conversational voice in which orders were given, to be followed nevertheless by a cracking alacrity of execution. To yet another, the perfect decorum of men who had been dancing all night, as *maruni* in women's clothes, with their officers, yet confronted these at morning parade with never a trace of recognition, let alone familiarity. These few instances may recall to those who know, and intimate to those readers who do not, something of the style of Gorkha company in the service of the British. The tone of this relationship animates, and alone would justify, Captain Coleman's graphic and original narration of what he rightly calls the extraordinary beginnings to the recruitment of Gorkhas. It was they who were extraordinary, as was appreciated by the British from the very first, and all else began from that character.

R.N.

All Souls College,

Oxford[10]

I am very grateful to the following for their comments on this foreword: Mr George Aitchison (1/4 G.R.); Dr John Gurney (1/2 G.R.), Fellow of Wadham College, Oxford; Lieutenant Colonel Peter Reeve, R.A. (4/1 G.R.).

Notes

1. 'The Highlandmen of Nepaul,' *The Navy and Army Illustrated*, vol. 11 (1900), pp. 337–9.
2. Lionel Caplan, *Warrior Gentlemen: 'Gurkhas' in the Western Imagination* (Providence, Oxford: Berghahn Books, 1995), pp. 115, 124–5 n. 44.
3. John Morris, *Hired to Kill: Some Chapters of Autobiography* (London: Rupert Hart-Davis, 1960).
4. Graham Greene, 'Malaya, the Forgotten War,' *Life*, vol. 31, no. 5 (1951), pp. 59–62, 65; quotation at p. 59; repr. in idem *Ways of Escape* (London: Bodley Head, 1980), p. 48.
5. Francis Tuker, *Gorkha: The Story of the Gurkhas of Nepal* (London: Constable, 1954), p. ix.
6. Patrick Davis, *A Child at Arms* (London: Hutchinson, 1970), pp. 97, 258.
7. W. Brook Northey and C.J. Morris, *The Gurkhas: Their Manners, Customs and Country* (London: John Lane, The Bodley Head, 1928), p. viii.
8. John Morris, 'The Gorge of the Arun', *Geographical Journal*, vol. 52 (1923), pp. 161–73; comments by R.L. Turner, pp. 170–3.
9. Bernard Pignède, *Les Gurungs: une population himalayenne du Népal* (Paris and The Hague: Mouton, 1966); Michael Oppitz, *Onkels Tochter, keine sonst: Heiratsbündnis und Denkweise in einer lokal Kultur des Himalaya* (Frankfurt am Main: Suhrkamp, 1991). The former work is a straightforward description by a gifted amateur ethnographer; the latter, by a professional social anthropologist, is (despite its apparently rather trivial title) the finest and most comprehensively detailed account of any people from whom the Brigade of Gurkhas has traditionally recruited. On the Limbu, see Lionel Caplan, *Land and Social Change in East Nepal: A Study of Hindu-tribal Relations* (London: Routledge & Kegan Paul, 1970), though the scope is narrower.

10. In November 1841, the 4th (Gorkha) Regiment garrison at Charikar, near
    Kabul, was overwhelmed and its commandant, Captain Christopher Co-
    drington, Bengal Army, was killed (below, p. 207). This officer was a collateral
    kinsman, in the junior branch of the family, of Christopher Codrington
    (1668–1710), Fellow of All Souls and sometime colonel in the campaigns in
    Flanders, commemorated as the founder of the magnificent Codrington
    Library of All Souls College, Oxford. (*Transactions of the Bristol and Glouces-
    tershire Archaeological Society*, vol. XXI, 1898, p. 345.)

Preface

The word 'Gorkha', used in the title and throughout the text of this book, is derived from the Nepali word गोर्खा, the correct pronunciation of which involves an 'o' sound similar to that in the French word *bientôt*, followed by the rolled Scottish 'r'. This, being beyond the facility of Anglo-Saxon lips and tongue to form, has resulted in the flat and more easily managed pronunciation 'Gerker' and the anglicised spelling 'Gurkha' which is still used in the British Army. In the early nineteenth century, attempts by East India Company army officers and civil servants to write what they imagined they heard, produced variations such as Goorka, Goorkah, Goorkha – some of which were further adulterated by misspelling (e.g. Ghoorka, Ghurka). The official English records are littered with such variety.

The recruitment of Gorkhas [1] and other hillmen [2] by the British into the East India Company's Bengal Army began in a most extraordinary way. In November 1814, Gorkhas formed the core, although numerically not the major part, of the Nepalese Army at war with Britain.

In April 1815, Major-General David Ochterlony gave Lieutenant Peter Lawtie, his aide-de-camp and field engineer, the honour of being the first British officer to lead a volunteer body of captured Gorkhas and other hillmen into action against their former masters. Lawtie's report on the military skills and soldierly qualities of these men operating in steep mountainous terrain, was made to enable Ochterlony 'to judge the value of a new and so peculiarly [i.e. specially] formed a Corps'. The report, strongly supported by Ochterlony, received the unhesitating *post-facto* approval of Lord Moira, Governor-General and Commander-in-Chief (a general in his own right) for the embodiment of these men into the Bengal Army. At Ochterlony's request they were called Nasiris.

The reason why such a corps was formed was remarkable. Ochterlony, a brilliant military strategist, perceived that to fulfil his orders from Lord Moira he needed troops highly trained and experienced in mountain warfare. He was aware that no such expertise existed in the Bengal Army. The opportunity to test and embody Nasiris and to use them to 'win over' more Gorkhas and other hillmen not only solved his immediate problem but helped to bring about the elimination of the Nepalese Western Army. In May 1815, Kaji Amar Singh Thapa's forces which had fought heroically at Malaun and Jaithak were driven to honourable surrender. About 450 fighting men returned to Nepal with Kaji Amar Singh Thapa and his son, Ranjor Singh Thapa. More than ten times as many remained and were recruited into the Bengal Army. How many of these were Gorkhas has never been established.

From military and political experience gained in the north-west of Hindustan, Ochterlony was well aware that, having defeated Kaji Amar Singh Thapa and wrested from the Nepalese large tracts of hill territory east of the river Sutlej, the British would be faced with the difficult task of defending this territory against potential trans-Sutlej incursions. His solution was to raise two battalions of Nasiris and to base them strategically in key hill forts. In the event four such battalions of irregular hill troops were raised in 1815, the precursors of the 1st, 2nd and 3rd Gurkha Rifle regiments of the Indian Army.

The war with Nepal, the first frontier war in the history of British India, was long neglected by scholars, a fact to which Edward Thompson, the eminent historian, drew attention in 1943:

> Another flaw in British–Indian historical writing is the way in which our want of interest in anything Indian has allowed such interest as we have felt occasionally to concentrate on one or two episodes, notably the mutiny, to the almost complete neglect of other events. The outstanding example of this is the war with Nepal.[3]

A century and a half after the war with Nepal, John Pemble produced his well-researched and documented Ph.D. thesis 'The Invasion of Nepal: John Company at War'.[4] It seems, from the abstract of his thesis, that he had two main interests in the war with Nepal: first, the

Bengal Army's need for a 'structural rationalisation' in the face of its increasing involvement in remote and difficult theatres of war; and second, 'British incapacity', because of the system of advancement by strict seniority, to produce the type of leader to meet these new demands. Ochterlony, whom Pemble acknowledged to have been 'a brilliant commander', was an exception to the general theme. So too were some of the young British officers with him in the far west.

However, Pemble made no more than passing reference to another important aspect of the war with Nepal, the creation of an embryonic Gurkha Brigade which, unlike the Bengal Army, was to survive the disaster of 1857.

This book addresses the subject of how the mainstream of Gorkha service with the British began in 1815 and evolved up to 1850 when a Gorkha battalion first joined the Bengal Line.

September 1998   A.P.C.

Sir David Ochterlony Bart. GCB (1758–1825)

Although the official records provide much evidence of Sir David Ochterlony's military and diplomatic career, they include tantalisingly little about his private life. His grandson, Sir Charles Metcalfe Ochterlony recorded that 'Sir David's papers were dispersed at his death.' Unfortunately, so far, very little of his private correspondence has been traced.

In the course of his researches for this book, the author has accumulated material with a view to writing a more detailed account of the life of Sir David – one of the great men in British Indian history.

Descendants of the beneficiaries of the estate of Sir Isaac Heard (1730–1822), Sir David's stepfather, with whom he corresponded over many years, may have letters or memorabilia. So may descendants of Sir David's married daughters: Henrietta Frances Ochterlony, who married Henry Fisher Salter, an officer in the Bengal Native Cavalry; Mary Anne Ochterlony, who married Henry Johnstone Middleton of the Bengal Civil Service; and Joanna Matilda Ochterlony, who married John Henry Middleton of the Bengal Army.

The author would be grateful to receive from them, or anyone else, information which might enable him to gather further evidence about Sir David Ochterlony's private life.

Beaminster
West Dorset   A.P.C.

Acknowledgements

As the author of this book I take sole responsibility for any errors. I am, however, anxious to acknowledge my good fortune in receiving the unstinting assistance of many. First and foremost I have benefited enormously from the invaluable guidance and advice of Professor Peter Marshall, formerly Rhodes Professor of Imperial History, King's College London and currently President of the Royal Historical Society, to whom I am particularly grateful.

I am most grateful to Major General D.G.T. Horsford CBE DSO for his Introductory Commendation.

To Professor Rodney Needham, All Souls College, Oxford, a former fellow officer of the 1st King George V's Own Gurkha Rifles (The Malaun Regiment) I am indebted for reading the typescript, for his helpful comments and suggestions, and for writing a Foreword.

The book itself would not have been possible without the kind permission of Malcolm and Kathy Fraser to research into their private collection of Fraser family papers. To them I am greatly indebted.

I am also greatly indebted to my friend Ean Ramsay who kindly made available Ochterlony family papers and memorabilia.

To two other close friends, and fellow former officers of the 1st King George V's Own Gurkha Rifles (The Malaun Regiment), Sir Michael Scott (Ambassador to Kathmandu, 1974–7) and Lieutenant Colonel John Cross (a privileged resident in Nepal), I owe much for their knowledge and enthusiastic advice. I am grateful to them not least for smoothing my path in Nepal and for making introductions to distinguished scholars. Among these scholars are Professor K.K. Adhikari, Professor P. Banskota, Dr T. Manandhar and Dr L.F. Stiller S.J. of Tribhuvan University, Kathmandu, and Brigadier-General (Retired) S.P. Sharma of the Royal Nepalese Army – to all of whom I am grateful.

I gratefully acknowledge the value of Sir Michael Scott's own researches into the India Office Collections of the British Library.

I am also grateful to Major General D. Banerjee, formerly Colonel of the First Gorkha Rifles (Indian Army), and to Brigadier R.P.S. Negi, formerly Commandant, 14 Gorkha Training Centre, who made me most welcome in Delhi and Subathu respectively in the furtherance of my research; and to Major R.S. Rawat, of the First Gorkha Rifles, who escorted me on my tour of Subathu and the Simla hills (once known as the Cis-Sutlej hills) including Malaun.

I must also record my gratitude to regimental friends: to the late Ian Henderson and to Gerald Wheatley for their encouragement and help at the inception of my research; to Peter Reeve for his support in the concluding stages; and to Keith and Rhona Macleod.

To another scholarly friend, David Harding (formerly of the 10th Princess Mary's Own Gurkha Rifles), I acknowledge my debt for his assistance in a variety of ways, for his keen interest and specialist advice.

Among numerous others who in one way or another have so willingly assisted me, I feel I must thank Professor P. S. Gupta and his wife, Dr N. Gupta (in Delhi); Anthony Farrington, Dr Richard Bingle, Dr Andrew Cook, Tim Thomas and the Reading Room staff – all of the British Library's Oriental and India Office Collections; Andrew Broom, formerly of the Scottish Record Office; Leslie Thompson and Anita Sawyer.

I owe much gratitude to my family for their support, especially to my sister, Brenda Pearson, for her secretarial assistance, and to my son-in-law, Dr Rolf Meigh, for invaluable help in word processing, and countless hours spent in amending and reprinting several drafts. Most of all, I am grateful to my wife, Peggy, for her patience and tolerance throughout the whole lengthy enterprise.

I gratefully acknowledge permission to reproduce plates, illustrations etc. as follows:

Plate 1	By courtesy of the National Portrait Gallery, Edinburgh.
Plate 3, 4	By courtesy of Buddhiman Gurung.

Illustrations 2, 3, 15, 18	By courtesy of the National Portrait Gallery, London.
Illustration 4 and Map 3	By permission of the British Library.
Illustrations 8, 9, 10, 11	By courtesy of Frank Morley (1 G.R.).
Illustration 12	By permission of the Commandant, 14 Gorkha Training Centre, Subathu.
Illustration 14	By permission of the Syndics of Cambridge University Library.
Illustration 16	By permission of the British Museum.
Illustration 17, 19	By courtesy of David Harding (10 G.R.).
Appendix I	By permission of the Archivist, Lincolnshire Archives.
Map 8	By permission of the Trustees of the Gurkha Museum, Winchester (to whom the map was presented by the 10th Gurkha Rifles Regimental Association).

Glossary

birta	pension specially granted for distinguished government service; paid by the assignment of land revenue
coss	a variable measurement of distance, approximately two and a half miles in north India in the early nineteenth century
dhamakah	disciplined bearer of a superior form of matchlock
doab	tongue of land between two rivers
firelock	soldier bearing a European musket, generally with flintlock ignition
fusil	firearm of shorter barrel and smaller bore than a musket
havildar	sergeant
jagir	grant of right to receive land revenue while employed by the state
jagirdar	holder of a jagir
jat	tribe or sub-tribe
jemadar	company officer (Indian or Gorkha)
jhara	system of tax on labour
Kaji	the highest rank normally given to a commander in the Nepalese Army who was not a member of the royal family
killadar	commandant of a fort or garrison
killat	robe of honour
kukri	curved Gorkha knife
matchlock	Indian form of musket, with long barrel suited to sniping, seldom fitted with a bayonet

musket	firearm designed for European tactics, fitted with a bayonet, and at this period with flintlock ignition
nagi	non-commissioned officer
naik (naick)	corporal
najib	militia armed with Indian-made matchlocks
nesanchi	colour bearer
pahari	hillman
pajani	system of annual recruitment, discharge, or assignment to reserve
parbatiya	hill tribes of western Nepal
puttee	reinforcement group
sal forest	dense hardwood forest in the Terai
sath pagari commander	perhaps the Nepalese equivalent of a battalion commander
sipahi (sepoy)	ordinary soldier
sirdar	senior commander
sohra havildar	perhaps the equivalent of a platoon or section commander
suba	provincial governor
subedar	company commander (Indian or Gorkha)
vakil	agent, representative, ambassador
zamindar	landlord, tax farmer paying revenue direct to the government

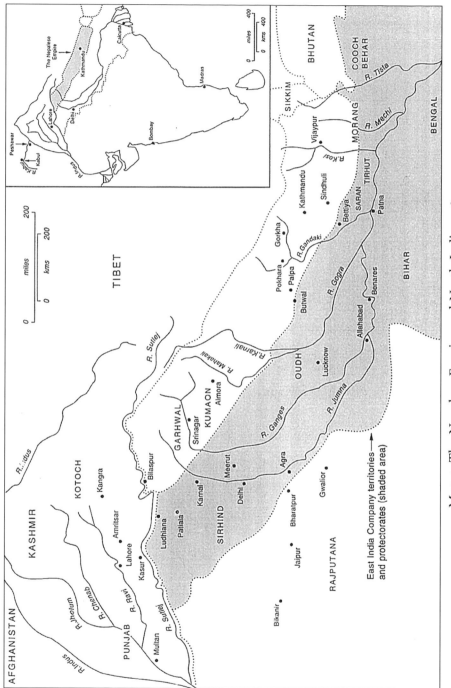

Map 1. The Nepalese Empire and North India c. 1814

East India Company territories
and protectorates (shaded area)

Part I

The origins of an Anglo–Gorkha relationship

PLATE 1. Major General Sir David Ochterlony
– by Arthur William Devis.

PLATE 2. William Fraser – attributed to Robert Home, Calcutta, *c.* 1806.
(*Private collection*)

PLATE 3. Kaji Amar Singh Thapa – by Alok Gurung.

PLATE 4. Bhakti Thapa – by Alok Gurung.

CHAPTER 1

Prologue

The country of Nepal, as it was before the creation of the Nepalese empire in the late eighteenth and early nineteenth centuries and, with minor variations, was again after the treaty of Segauli which ended the Anglo-Nepal War in 1816, covered an area south of the great Himalayan range approximately 550 miles long and 100 miles wide. To the north lay the high plateau of Tibet. Westwards, across the Mahakali river, was the hill state of Kumaon. The kingdom of Sikkim formed the eastern boundary, while along the southern border were territories administered or protected by the East India Company. From its southern border northwards Nepal comprised four distinct regions of increasing elevation: the Terai; the Inner Terai; the hills; and the mountains. The Terai, at an altitude of no more than 300 feet above sea level was a sparsely populated malarial region of swamps and jungles at the northern edge of the Gangetic plain.[5] The Inner Terai,[6] rising to about 3,000 feet above sea level, and including foothills of the Churia and Sivalekh ranges, was a hot, dry, malarial region of sal forests and low river valleys. Divided by broad fertile valleys such as those of Kathmandu and Pokhara and by smaller valleys, it was irrigated by tributaries of the three main river systems of the Karnali, Gandaki and Kosi. The mountain region included a large part of the main Himalayan range with glacial valleys and some trans-Himalayan territory.

Successive waves of immigrants from Tibet and India settled in the hill region of Nepal in the course of many centuries. These immigrants belonged to two major language divisions, the Tibeto-Burman and the Indo-Aryan. The Mongoloid Tibeto-Burman speakers, identifiable by their epicanthic eyelids,[7] are for example represented by the Gurungs and Magars of western Nepal; the Rais, Limbus and Sunwars of eastern Nepal, and the Newars of the Kathmandu valley. The Indo-Aryan speakers, who came from the hills and plains of north India, brought Hinduism and its hierarchy with them. One scholar has aptly likened these immigrations to ethnic tidal waves whose meeting in the hill districts of western Nepal caused a cultural, religious and social 'rip-tide' [8] resulting, through inter-marriage and dispersal, in a highly complex social mosaic.

It is not necessary to enter deeply into the ethnography of Nepal. [9] However, it has been established that one of the Indo-Aryan groups, the Khas (whose language was closely allied to Sanskrit) settled in the hill regions of Garhwal, Kumaon and what is now western Nepal and, in the eleventh, twelfth and thirteenth centuries, founded an empire which included a large part of western Tibet. [10] These Indo-Aryans were ranked in the Hindu tradition as low-caste Sudras having neglected caste rules. However, other early immigrants to Nepal, high-caste Brahmans from the plains of north India, elevated the Khas to the high order of Kshatriya and accorded their own offspring by local Khas hill-women the same distinction. From these Kshatriyas there developed the complex and widely distributed class which became known as Chhetri. [11]

High-caste Mallas (Chhetris) migrated to the Central valley of Nepal where they ruled from the thirteenth to the eighteenth century and introduced orthodox Hinduism with its hierarchy to a predominantly Buddhist people. Noble Rajputs of the Hindu Kshatriya order, escaping from the fifteenth-century Mogul invaders of North India, also settled in the western hills of Nepal and founded the Shah dynasty at Gorkha.

The Mongoloid Magars in their lowland hill kingdom [12] were for long in subservient association with the Chhetris and, through the inter-marriage of Chhetri men and Magar women, acquired the Chhetri's Indo-Aryan language without losing their own Tibeto-Burman language. [13] Although the offspring of such marriages [14] were also allowed to wear the sacred Hindu thread, in general the hill people of Mongolian ancestry were regarded by high-caste Hindus as the equivalent of Sudras. In the higher hills of Lamjung and Kaski, the Gurungs were less influenced by the Brahmans and Chhetris, preserving many of their own customs and seldom inter-marrying with non-Gurung women.[15] Hodgson, British Resident in Kathmandu in the early nineteenth century, noted that 'From lending themselves less early and heartily to Brahmanical influences than the Khas [Chhetris] they have retained, in vivid freshness, their languages, physiognomy and, in a less degree, their original habits.'[16] Chhetris, Magars and Gurungs living in the hills of western Nepal were destined to play a pioneering part in the late eighteenth-century evolution of the modern state of Nepal.

The modern history of Nepal began in the mid-eighteenth century when the term 'Nepal' signified the valley of Kathmandu with its three kingdoms of Kathmandu, Patan and Bhadgaon.[17] Between the Kathmandu valley and the state of Kumaon to the west were forty-six minor principalities grouped in two loosely-linked confederations. Of these the Chaubisi (Nepali for twenty-four) were in the vicinity of the Gandaki river, and the Baisi (Nepali for twenty-two) were in the Karnali river basin. To the east of the Kosi river was the homeland of the fiercely independent Kiranti people.[18]

Gorkha, one of the Chaubisi states, about sixty miles west of Kathmandu, rose to prominence in the mid-eighteenth century under the strong leadership of Prithvi Narayan Shah, a Rajput who became king of Gorkha in 1742 at the age of twenty. A man of great ambition and statesmanship, Prithvi Narayan Shah first took control of the Chaubisi group of minor states and then sought to extend his kingdom eastwards into the Kathmandu valley. He took with him his Rajput-Chhetri officers and the hardy hill tribesmen – Chhetris, Magars and Gurungs – from his enlarged Gorkha kingdom. From these, he raised five companies of regular troops[19] and armed them with weapons and ammunition, some of which were manufactured in Gorkha. Prithvi Narayan Shah's initial attempts to conquer the Kathmandu valley kingdoms not only failed but brought him into conflict with the British.

The influx of Indo-Aryans which brought Hinduism from the Gangetic plain into the Kathmandu valley also established a flourishing trade between India and Nepal. By 1767 the East India Company had become responsible for the civil administration of the territories bordering Nepal, and was anxious to develop trade not only with Nepal but with Tibet and western China through Kathmandu.[20] When, therefore, the king of Kathmandu, Jaya Prakash Malla, sought British help against Prithvi Narayan Shah's invading troops, the East India Company took the opportunity to promote its own commercial interests.[21] A proposal by the Governor of Bengal, Harry Verelst, that the British should mediate, was flatly refused by Prithvi Narayan Shah who, instead, laid claim to Bettiya in the East India Company's border territory. Believing that an expedition 'might be undertaken with great security as well as with the best prospect of success', the Bengal government sent Captain George Kinloch with a force of 2,400 men to assist the king of Kathmandu.[22]

Kinloch's own account of his expedition, which set out on 26 August 1767, shows that British optimism was totally unfounded.[23] Difficulties in transporting troops and guns over swollen rivers and through dense jungle were aggravated by misleading intelligence, unrelenting heavy rain, the ravages of fever, desertion of porters, and desperate lack of food. Kinloch's diary peters out on 17 October 1767, after recording thirteen successive days of famine, and a state of mutiny. As if this was not enough, Kinloch sustained casualties on 19 September 1767 when five companies of his force were beaten off by Prithvi Narayan Shah's troops armed with bows and arrows, long curved swords and knives shaped 'something like a bill-hook' (the Gorkha kukri). Kinloch described his attackers as 'generally robust men with features between the Chinies [*sic*] and Malays'. On 27 September 1767, Kinloch was confronted by 'great numbers of Gurkhas in blue uniforms with matchlocks [muskets]'. Royal Nepalese Army chronicles reveal that all five of Prithvi Narayan Shah's Gorkha companies – perhaps 700 men in all – blocked Kinloch's path at Sindhuli.[24] Overwhelmed by a multiplicity of disasters he was forced to withdraw with the remnant of his force. No doubt heartened by their victory over the British, Prithvi Narayan Shah's troops moved north, and, fighting against resolute defence, captured Kathmandu on 20 September 1768, Patan on 6 October 1768, and, after the sternest resistance, Bhadgaon on 13 November. Prithvi Narayan Shah thus became the first Gorkha king of the entire Kathmandu valley.

By their support for Jaya Prakash Malla, the British did not endear themselves to Prithvi Narayan Shah who, not surprisingly, was highly suspicious of their intentions. He was well aware of the pattern of British control of Indian states through trade and subsequent political domination. His suspicions were deepened further when Kinloch, retreating from Sindhuli, occupied Nepalese territory in the Terai, with the Company's approval, as compensation for the loss sustained in the expedition.[25] Prithvi Narayan Shah's ambition was to establish a unified state of Nepal by annexing the Kiranti country to the east of the Kathmandu valley and by subjugating the Terai to the south and all the principalities to the west. Having conquered the Kathmandu valley, however, he seems to have decided to consolidate his greatly increased kingdom and to define further military and political strategy.[26] Uncharacteristically, he left others to lead his army eastwards. And, once the key town of Vijaypur had been captured and the Morang overrun (see map 1), he treated the fiercely resisting Kiranti tribes with unexpected moderation.

In December 1774, shortly before he died on 10 January 1775, Prithvi Narayan Shah summoned his household, family, nobles, and closest friends and advisers to Nuwakot and addressed them thus: 'When an old man dies, his words die with him, so they say. What you who are gathered here will hear from me, pass on to your children, and they to theirs; and the kingdom will endure.'[27] His Dibya Upadesh (instructions) took the form of Upranta (new trains of thought) which were recorded. With great prescience and wisdom he outlined his foreign and military policy in the following terms:

> The kingdom is like a yam between two boulders. Maintain friendly relations with the emperor of China. Great friendship should also be maintained with the emperor beyond the southern seas [the British] but he is very cunning. He has kept India suppressed and is entrenching himself in the plains. One day the army will come. Do not engage in offensive attacks, fighting should be done on a defensive basis. If it is found difficult to resist in the fight, then every means of persuasion, tact and deceit should be employed.[28]

On the matter of trade, he instructed 'Do not let the merchants of India come to our country, they will leave the people poor' and 'Forbid the use of cloth made in India. Show samples to those who know how to make the cloth. Teach them and begin to make clothing. If this is done our money will not go abroad.'[29]

Prithvi Narayan Shah was particularly explicit regarding the army:

> An important point is that soldiers required for the king should be given their house and land and that they farm it, so that they can support themselves by both means. Then without concern for their family's welfare, whether they are in the capital or in the field, they will be stouthearted. In the annual pajani make up companies of one hundred rifles. Appoint as commander of them one who tested himself in four or five battles. In choosing a sat pagari commander, chose one who has been successful in several battles. In placing his sohra havildar, let him appoint a man he has tested as a man of courage. The sohra havildar should choose soldiers whom he knows to be courageous. In their own companies enlist Khas, Magars, Gurungs, and Thakuris, and only these four jats.[30]
>
> With a company of 100 rifles, the work will be easy. With such a company of 100 rifles I can resist 1,000 men. Placing one company at each fort, divide the ridges, maintain reserves.[31]

In propounding the policies expressed in his Dibya Upadesh, Prithvi Narayan Shah was no doubt concerned at the speed with which the British had expanded in north India during the twenty-six years it had taken him to conquer the Kathmandu valley. When he set out from Gorkha in 1744 the British had little influence in the politics of India. By 1770 they had acquired the diwani (revenue authority) over Bengal, Bihar and Orissa, and were building up their influence in Oudh. During the same period, the East India Company's Bengal Army had grown from a small and unimpressive garrison of some 500 Europeans and half-castes in Calcutta, to a disciplined and well-equipped army of 4,000 Europeans and 26,000 sepoys,[32] supported by European artillery and strategically deployed. It was abundantly clear to Prithvi Narayan Shah that if the lightly equipped Gorkha forces had to face such overwhelming power it must be in the hills where terrain, mobility and harassing tactics would afford some compensation.[33]

The accumulation of British power in India was indeed attributable to the growing might of the army. The outbreak of war with France in southern India in 1744 brought about a change in attitude by the British Government and the Court of Directors of the East India Company. For the first time they were both able and willing to spend the very large sums of money needed to establish and maintain strong European forces in India.[34] Hitherto their policy had been the peaceful pursuit of commercial interests, avoiding the need for force and the expense of war. Now they were ready to resist apparent political and military threats from French intervention. Initially their intention was to limit the use of the new forces, which included King's regiments, to defeating the French in India. However, owing to distance and the time taken (upwards of a year) to exchange communications, control from England of events and actions in India was impossible. Moreover, trade was still important to the Company and demands on Indian rulers for trade concessions were made all the more insistent by the private interests of Company servants and licensed Free Merchants. With the military means of coercion available there was a strong incentive to use them. Although the British persuaded themselves that force could be used for limited objectives without compromising the independence of Indian rulers, repeated demands for concessions had this very effect.[35]

The cost of the army grew with its increasing size, to the extent that only by getting Indian rulers to pay for the major part could the Company hope to remain solvent. From the mid-eighteenth century, the British provided troops for the protection of Indian states on the basis that the cost would be met from state revenue. When rulers failed to pay, the temptation to take control was irresistible. Inevitably the Company was drawn into the administration of Indian states and thence into the formulation of their foreign policy.[36]

While Prithvi Narayan Shah and his successors[37] were preoccupied with creating a unified state of Nepal, the Bengal Government made further attempts to establish trade links with Tibet and China. Warren

Hastings, who arrived in 1772 as Governor of Bengal, was instructed by the Court of Directors of the East India Company to explore the prospects for markets in Bhutan and Assam.[38] The outlook was far from promising. The Bhutanese were already wary of British intentions following Kinloch's seizure of part of the Nepalese Terai, and there was a state of tension along the Company's north-eastern border. In 1765 the Bhutanese, who were anxious to maintain Cooch Behar as a buffer state between Bengal and the hills, had disputed the succession to the Cooch Behar throne. In response to an appeal from the Cooch Beharis for help, the British sent a detachment of troops under Lieutenant Morrison to Cooch Behar, thereby making the Bhutanese even more suspicious. In 1767, a new Deb Raja had come to power in Bhutan and had embarked on a series of armed raids into neighbouring countries in the course of which a Bhutanese force advanced as far as the river Tista in Sikkim. In 1771, the Bhutanese abducted the Raja of Cooch Behar and appointed their protégé in his place. An appeal from the Cooch Beharis in 1772 for help in restoring their Raja to his throne, gave Hastings a chance to pursue his aim of opening up trade routes with Tibet and western China.[39]

Hastings sent a force, under Captain Jones, which drove the Bhutanese out of Cooch Behar. This so alarmed the King of Nepal that he sent a mission to Tibet to warn the Panchen Lama in Tashilhunpo (modern Shigatse) of the dangers to Tibet if the British occupied Bhutan. The intervention of the King of Nepal and the Panchen Lama enabled Hastings to conclude a treaty on 23 April 1774 restoring the Raja of Cooch Behar to his throne and opening up prospects for trade.[40]

In the meantime in Britain the Regulating Act of 1773[41] recognised the political and economic importance of Calcutta and appointed Warren Hastings as the first Governor-General in Bengal with supervisory powers over the Bombay and Madras Presidencies.

In 1774, Hastings sent George Bogle, of the Bengal civil service, to open trade communications with Tassisuden, the winter capital of Bhutan, and thence, if possible, with Lhasa and other parts of Tibet. His instructions were to secure a treaty of 'amity and commerce' with Tibet and 'to open a mutual and equal communication of trade' between Nepal and Bengal. He was also to enquire into the resources of Tibet and to study its trade markets; and to look into the relations between Tibet and China.[42] Bogle arrived in Tashilhunpo in December 1774 and established friendly relations with the Panchen Lama. He failed, however, to conclude any trade agreements. The Bhutanese were obstructive, and Bogle received no reply to his request for the right to trade between India and Tibet. Alexander Hamilton, an assistant surgeon of the Company who had accompanied Bogle, fared no better on missions to Bhutan in 1775 and 1776. A further mission planned for Bogle to visit Tibet in 1779 with the specific aim of opening communications with China, did not take place. Bogle's friend the Panchen Lama died in Peking in 1780 and Bogle himself died in India in 1781. Yet another opportunity seemed to offer itself to Hastings in 1782 in sending Captain Samuel Turner to Tashilhunpo to offer congratulations on the reincarnation of the Panchen Lama. It was to no avail. The route to China by way of Bhutan and Tibet was firmly closed by Chinese representatives in Llasa.

A lingering suspicion in the eastern Himalayan region that the Bengal Government was more interested in gaining territory than in trade, seems to have been shared by the British House of Commons. In 1782 it passed a resolution to the effect that it was totally opposed to territorial expansion. Clause 34 of Pitt's India Act of 1784 contained the words: 'And whereas to pursue schemes of conquest and extension of dominion in India are measures repugnant to the wish, the honour, and the policy of this nation … it shall not be lawful for the said Governor-General and Council to declare war or commence hostilities, or enter into any treaty for making war, against any other prince or state than such as shall be actually committing hostilities or making preparations as aforesaid.'[43] To this end the India Act 1784 established a Board of Control in London to keep a check on the affairs of the East India Company. The Board of Control comprised a President and two Commissioners, the Chancellor of the Exchequer, a Secretary of State, four Privy Councillors and three salaried staff. It was supported by a Secretary and a small body of permanent clerks in the Revenue, Military, Political, Judicial and Public Departments. At the same time, the India Act gave the Governor-General increased powers and responsibilities of control over all three Presidencies in India.

Lord Cornwallis, who became Governor-General in 1786 sought to make the avoidance of war his primary aim. Save for the Mysore War of 1790, he succeeded.

Prithvi Narayan Shah's successors completed the campaign of unification in 1786, by which time the state of Nepal stretched westwards to the Mahakali river and the Gorkha Army had increased from five to twenty-nine regular companies, nineteen of which had been involved in subjugating the Chaubisi and Baisi principalities.[44] The twenty-nine companies were recruited from the Chhetri, Magar, and Gurung hillmen of western Nepal.[45]

Thus far the Nepalese Government, following Prithvi Narayan Shah's precepts, maintained its dual policies of isolationism and of friendly relations with China and Britain. However, once a unified state of Nepal had been created, the Nepalese Government began to turn its attention to expansion beyond its natural borders. In 1787 its army invaded Sikkim, and in the following year, ignoring Prithvi Narayan Shah's advice, made incursions into Tibet, a vassal state of China. Sikkim resisted stoutly but was eventually forced to surrender territory to the west of the river Tista. Tibet concluded a treaty with Nepal in 1789, but, when hostilities were resumed in 1791, appealed to China for help. This brought an army of 70,000 Chinese within twenty miles of Kathmandu in 1792.[46] Although, in the meantime, Nepal had raised a further eleven companies of regular troops[47] making forty in all, perhaps amounting to 5,500 men, its army was no match for so huge a Chinese force. The Nepalese therefore offered the British a commercial treaty in the hope of obtaining military assistance. The Governor-General, who was well aware that the East India Company's paramount interests lay in preserving Chinese friendship and co-operation, sent Captain William Kirkpatrick to mediate between Nepal and China.

Kirkpatrick, the first Englishman to visit Kathmandu, arrived in 1793 after peace had been established between Nepal and China. He stayed long enough to conclude a modest commercial treaty (which did not refer to Tibetan trade), and to gain some insight into Nepal and its resources.[48] Kirkpatrick deduced that the principal strength of the Nepalese Government lay with the high-ranking 'Brahmanical and Chetree Orders' and consisted 'for the most part of the Khus [*sic*] and

Maugur [*sic*] tribes of the Chetree class and of the Pande and some other caste of Brahmins'.[49] He also observed that 'the expenses of the military establishment of this country [Nepal] are for the most part discharged by assignments of land' [jagirs]. These were made according to rank, land being much preferred to other forms of payment.

Kirkpatrick gained few details of the Gorkha Army, pointing out that it was 'not prudent to have appeared inquisitive and perhaps not easy to have obtained accurate information'.[50] He observed nevertheless that irregular militia were generally armed with bows and arrows and hatchet swords. Regular troops were armed with muskets and 'clothed in the slovenly manner of the Purgunnuh Sepoys formerly in the East India Company's service'. They had no uniform but wore clothing of different colours. Kirkpatrick wrote: 'This regular force consists at present, I understand, of from 50–60 companies of unequal strength but containing, on the average, not less than 140 firelocks each commanded by a Subedar and an indeterminate number of jemadars and other inferior [non-commissioned] officers.'[51]

The 'Rajah of Nepal's guards' were distinguished from other companies by having more officers and by carrying 'a war standard in yellow embroidered with the figure of Hunniman'.[52] As to ordnance, 'some European adventurers would seem to have promised much and to have performed nothing'.[53]

Kirkpatrick was evidently not impressed by the bearing of the Gorkha troops, who 'neither march nor carry their arms in a style anything superior to that of the rabble ordinarily dignified with the title of sepoys in the service of the Hindustan powers, nor would their discipline appear to be much stricter'. However, he admitted that 'with all their defects, I am disposed to think they are on the whole no bad soldiers. They are brave, sufficiently tractable and capable of sustaining great hardships.'[54] The description 'no bad soldiers' proved to be a gross understatement; and Kirkpatrick's conclusion 'I do not see how artillery could be advantageously employed in such rugged country as that in which the military operations [take place]' was to be disproved in the Anglo-Nepal war of 1814–16.[55]

In 1790, the Nepalese Government had begun a major campaign of expansion westwards. In January 1790 Nepalese troops under the

1. The Khookeri [56]

command of Kaji Jagajit Pandey and Sirdar Amar Singh Thapa (who was soon to be appointed army commander in the west) crossed the Mahakali river and within a month captured Almora and annexed the kingdom of Kumaon. It may well be that this Nepalese force included not only Parbatiya troops from the hills of western Nepal but recruits from the Baisi states in the far west whose language and ancestry were more closely akin to those of the Kumaonis on the west side of the river.[57] Nepalese success was swift and absolute.[58] The acquisition of heavy taxes through land allocation, and grain from the fertile valleys and gentle hill-country of Kumaon helped fuel a Nepalese drive farther westward into Garhwal. However, here, a land of forts as the name implies, the Nepalese faced a more difficult task in wild and craggy terrain. In the event their plans were interrupted by the urgent need to reinforce Nepalese troops engaged in the war with Tibet and China.

In 1793 Lord Cornwallis left India and was succeeded by Sir John Shore, a Bengal civil servant. Having failed in its attempts to establish links with Tibet, the Bengal Government sought to follow up Kirkpatrick's commercial treaty with Nepal. In 1795 Maulvi Abdul Qadir led a British trade mission to Kathmandu. This too ended in failure.

The politics of Nepal during the late eighteenth and early nineteenth centuries were dominated by factional conspiracies and intrigues at Court. This state of affairs was largely attributable to the fact that from 1777 to 1832 successors to the Nepalese throne were minors. The country was virtually governed by regents or prime ministers whose interests lay in securing their own positions rather than in training the young kings in regal responsibilities and statecraft. As a result, when they came of age they were self-indulgent and incompetent rulers.[59] Such a king was Rana Bahadur Shah, who was born on 25 May 1775 and succeeded to the throne on 17 November 1777 on the death of his father. During the long years of minority, his mother, Rajendra Laxmi, and uncle, Bahadur Shah, served as Regents. Rana Bahadur came of age in 1793, at a time when Nepal was recovering from the war with China and was in need of strong and efficient government. Instead, in February 1799, Rana Bahadur announced his abdication in favour of his son Girbana Yuddha Bikram Shah, who was then one and a half years old. In May 1800 Rana Bahadur arrived with his retinue in Benares, in self-appointed exile, ostensibly to live a life of prayer and penance.[60]

Despite the many calls for his attention, Wellesley (who had succeeded Shore as Governor-General) perceived an opportunity to further the East India Company's interest in establishing trade links with Nepal. In 1800, he sent Captain Alexander Knox on a mission to Benares to attend the exiled Rana Bahadur Shah. On learning of the arrival of Wellesley's emissary in Benares, the Nepalese Government were so fearful of British intentions that they felt obliged to offer a new commercial treaty and, very much against their wishes, the exchange of Residents.[61] Wellesley instructed Knox that it would be 'advisable to exclude from the treaty such stipulations as might by any latitude of construction be considered to operate as a defensive engagement against the power of the Chinese'.[62] Before taking up his appointment as Resident in Kathmandu, Knox was instructed by Wellesley to use the utmost circumspection in order to endeavour to acquire the confidence of the Nepalese Government. He was 'not even to endeavour to acquire information with regard to the resources of Nepal'. However, he was 'to avail himself of every favourable

opportunity to do so'. Knox's primary object was to bring into operation the treaty of commerce concluded by Kirkpatrick in 1793,
broadening its scope to include trade with Tibet.

Francis Buchanan Hamilton, who accompanied Knox to Kathmandu in 1802, discreetly gathered information on 'the civil and
military administration of Nepal, the extent of its resources, the
number, description and discipline of its troops, its connections and
alliances, its external and internal defences, revenues, manufactures
and commerce'.[63] The treaty was completed in October 1801 but, after
Knox's arrival in Kathmandu in April 1802, the Nepalese Government
failed to meet its commitments in full. Knox decided to leave Nepal
with his party at the end of March 1803, and in January 1804 the
Governor-General dissolved both the 1793 and 1801 treaties with
Nepal.[64] Hamilton did, however, update Kirkpatrick's account of
Gorkha troops, 'The military force among the petty chiefs was always
large . . . but consisted of a rabble totally undisciplined and ill-armed.
Much order has since been induced by the chiefs of Gorkha although
both in arms and discipline the soldiers are still very far behind the
Europeans.'[65] Hamilton recorded that each company had two flags, a
band of ten musicians, and a number of artificers. All soldiers wore
'red uniforms with peculiar [special] facings'. They were 'little versed
in tactics', and used swords (being better suited to the terrain than
bayonets) and kukris.[66]

The failure of the East India Company to obtain a commercial treaty
with Tibet through Nepal, and to establish a permanent representative
in Kathmandu, meant that by 1803 little information had been gleaned
by the British about Nepal and its resources. Such as there was had
been obtained on missions to Kathmandu by Kirkpatrick in 1793, and
Knox and Hamilton in 1802. Based on the isolationist foreign policy
of Prithvi Narayan Shah (who died in 1775) successive Nepalese governments retained deep suspicions of British intentions while affecting
an outward show of friendship. Thus it was in 1803, when the Nepalese
Army was preparing to invade Garhwal and the British, having advanced almost to Delhi, were about to embark on the second war with
the Marathas. They were moving westwards on parallel courses.

CHAPTER 2

Delhi: protagonists meet, 1803–6

The unpromising relationship which existed between the East India Company and the Nepalese Government at the turn of the century held out little prospect of a trade agreement, still less of an exchange of representatives in Calcutta and Kathmandu. The notion of the Company employing Gorkha and other Himalayan hillmen in its Bengal Army can hardly have been contemplated. And yet between 1803 and 1806 political and economic changes gave an initial impetus to just such a possibility. Foremost among these changes were the establishment of a Residency at Delhi, in the far north-west of the East India Company's territory, at a time when the Nepalese Army was advancing westwards along the Himalayan foothills to the north; and the coming together at the Residency of two highland Scots: David Ochterlony, an officer of the Bengal Army, and William Fraser, a Bengal civil servant. They were to become close friends and to have an important influence over British frontier policy, and in the eventual recruitment of Gorkhas and other hillmen into the Bengal Army.

At the beginning of the nineteenth century Garhwal suffered a series of misfortunes. In 1801 the fertile Dehra valley was plundered by marauding Marathas from Saharanpur. In 1803 the state capital, Srinagar, was devastated by an earthquake, and later the same year the Nepalese Army returned to annex the country. In January 1804 the young Raja of Garhwal was killed leading a brave but futile counter-attack. His sons fled to India and the protection of the East India Company.[67] Untutored in the art of colonial administration, the Nepalese compounded the internal strains on Garhwal by introducing heavy taxation and demanding intolerable rents from grants of land (jagirs). Garhwali reaction led to ruthless repression and large-scale emigration.

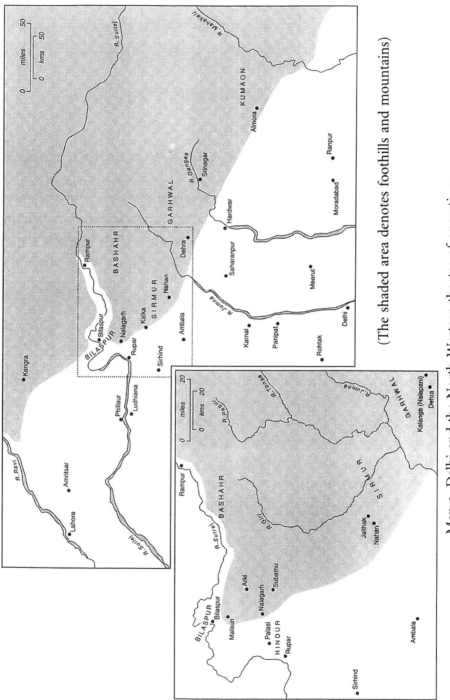

Map 2. Delhi and the North-Western theatre of operations.

(The shaded area denotes foothills and mountains)

During Rana Bahadur Shah's exile in Benares, the young commander of his bodyguard, a little known Chhetri-Thapa named Bhim
Sen, became his trusted adviser. As part of a plot to enable Rana
Bahadur to return to Kathmandu, his senior Queen Rajarajeshvari
Devi re-entered Nepal in 1803 and, being well received in the capital,
assumed the powers of Regent to Girbana Yuddha Bikram Shah when
the former Regent to the young king fled. Damodar Pande, whose
long and distinguished military service had brought him to the fore
in the struggle for power among the noble families, switched his
allegiance to Rajarajeshvari and was made Prime Minister.[68]

In 1804, Rana Bahadur Shah, accompanied by Bhim Sen Thapa,
returned to Kathmandu and, having ruthlessly had Damodar Pande
put to death, declared himself Prime Minister in February 1806. Soon
after, Rana Bahadur was himself assassinated and Bhim Sen Thapa
became Prime Minister – a post he was to hold for the next thirty-three
years. At the same time, and with Bhim Sen's support, one of Rana
Bahadur Shah's other queens, the twelve-years-old Tripura Sundari,
was established as Regent. This ensured Bhim Sen's control over access
to the child monarch. To secure his own position, Bhim Sen instituted
a comprehensive purge of his potential rivals on the spurious grounds
that they had conspired in the assassination of Rana Bahadur Shah.
Ninety-three people died, including Rajarajeshvari Devi.[69]

Bhim Sen Thapa made his authority even more secure by executing
the Raja of Palpa and then sending his own father, whom he promoted
to the English rank of general, with a large force to occupy Palpa.[70]
From there Bam Shah, Prithvi Narayan Shah's brother, was banished
to administer Kumaon, while General Amar Singh Thapa assumed
the functions of Governor of Palpa. Another relative of Bhim Sen
Thapa, also Amar Singh Thapa by name, was promoted to the rank
of Kaji and given command of the Nepalese Army in Garhwal. Kaji
Amar Singh Thapa had spent a lifetime soldiering and had earned a
reputation for leadership. Aged almost sixty he was yet keen to extend
the borders of the Nepalese empire still farther west, perhaps as far
as Kashmir.[71] This prospect found favour with Bhim Sen Thapa who
was intent on expanding and modernising the Nepalese Army based
on his observations of the Bengal Army's organisation and discipline

while he was in Benares. He otherwise had a low opinion of the British and their political methods.[72]

By the end of 1804 Kaji Amar Singh Thapa and his army had advanced beyond Garhwal into the Cis-Sutlej hills, a relatively small tract of country subdivided into thirty states ruled over for several centuries by Rajput families from north India. Of these thirty states, four had become predominant: Sirmur, immediately west of Garhwal; Hindur, lying partly in the hills and partly in the plains; Bilaspur, astride the river Sutlej north of Hindur; and Bashahr further north (see map 2). The capitals of these four states were respectively, Nahan, Palasi, Bilaspur and Rampur. Separating Bashahr from Bilaspur were twelve very small states collectively known as the Twelve Lordships (Bara Thakuri) with Thakuri (Chhetri) overlords.[73] The other fourteen states were scattered in the valleys of the Tonse, Pabur and Giri rivers. The major battles in the Anglo-Nepal War of 1814–16 were to be fought in Sirmur, Hindur and Bilaspur territory. All thirty states owed tribute to the Mogul emperor in Delhi. However, in practice the strongest states exacted from their weaker neighbours tribute which seldom reached the imperial treasury. As military service was widely accepted in lieu of taxes, these small hill states often maintained disproportion- ately large armies.[74] Kaji Amar Singh Thapa, drawn into a power struggle [75] between the Rajas of Hindur and Sirmur, sent 700 men to support the Raja of Sirmur. The Nepalese force was encircled by the Hinduris at Jampta (near Jaithak) in May 1804 and was forced to withdraw. In October 1804 the Kaji crossed the Jumna and defeated the Hinduri troops at Ajmaigarh, capturing the forts of Ramgarh and Nalagarh (see map 1). Sirmur became a vassal state of Nepal, its Raja a mere puppet. Having thus become involved in the affairs of two of the major hill states, Kaji Amar Singh Thapa allowed himself to be persuaded to take up the cause of a third, the Raja of Bilaspur,[76] against the powerful Raja of Kotoch who had annexed Bilaspur territory west of the Sutlej and, in his impregnable fortress of Kangra, had ambitions to rule over a confederation of hill states (see map 2). He was thus an obstacle to the Kaji's aspirations for a Himalayan empire. He was also a potential hindrance to the rising power of Ranjit Singh, the Sikh

Raja of Lahore, who had plans to unite the Sikh chieftains and to extend his kingdom throughout the Punjab plains and into the hills on both sides of the Sutlej. In April 1806, the Kaji crossed the Sutlej with his main army, reaching Kangra in July.[77] Having failed to take the fortress by assault, he resolved to capture it by siege. The siege was to last three years.

The Nepalese Army was well suited to mobile mountain warfare but was neither equipped nor trained for the capture of large fortresses. Of the fourteen regular companies involved all except one were of seasoned troops.[78] Two other regular companies were raised for garrison duties in Kumaon.[79] An unrecorded number of irregular troops were engaged, with little or no remuneration for their services, under the Jhara system of recruiting which, according to one Nepalese scholar, seems to have been followed throughout the period of what came to be known as the unification of Nepal.[80] Such obligatory service under Chhetri officers was imposed on males between the ages of twelve and eighty, who were required to report for duty with two months' rations and their own weapons.[81] There was also the Pajani system of annual recruitment under which many soldiers went on retirement (Dhakree) subject to re-enlistment. This ensured a large reserve of trained soldiers who could be mobilised when required. There were in consequence constant fluctuations in the strength of the Nepalese Army.[82]

Yet another factor ensured that by the time Kaji Amar Singh Thapa reached Kangra in 1806, the constitution of his army had changed. Whereas until the invasion of Kumaon its regular companies were composed almost entirely of Gorkhas, once they had moved into and beyond Garhwal the distance from Nepal made it difficult to obtain reinforcements and replacements. The Kaji therefore began to conscript and train suitable young recruits from within the conquered hill territories, especially Kumaon and Garhwal. Major Young writing from his personal experience of the Anglo-Nepal War (in the course of which he raised the East India Company's Sirmoor Battalion)[83] recorded the methods adopted. Boys were conscripted and attached to individual officers and soldiers. In return for board they 'carried baggage and arms on the march and performed all the menial offices of camp followers, thus rendering the Goorkah Army independent of carriage'.[84] Such apprentice boys were 'extremely useful in action and their services indispensable when it was found necessary to throw up a stockade'. They were generally well treated, frequently becoming adopted and provided with wives. Young pointed out that 'it never was the custom of the Chiefs of the Goorkah army on the North-West frontier to entertain raw recruits'. Instead trained boys were enrolled as soldiers having learned on active service the importance of discipline and the skills of hill and mountain warfare and having become as hardy and resolute as their instructors. Young even went so far as attributing 'the superiority of the Goorkah Army over any other with which the British power has come in contact to proceed from these circumstances'.[85]

The inhabitants of the hills of Kumaon and Garhwal had for long been more exposed to Indian influence than those of western Nepal. They were mainly Khasiyas whose limbs and bodies were generally of lighter build than the sturdy frame of the Tibetan Bhotias in the mountains to the north. In the southern hill parganas (sub-districts) the Khasiyas tended to be tall and spare with sallow complexions. Those in the northern hill parganas were fairer-skinned, shorter, more thick-set and capable of carrying heavy loads all day without sustenance.[86] Such hillmen conscripted into the Nepalese Army were distinguishable from Gorkhas by language, customs and physiognomy. The capacity for obtaining from conquered lands not only food and military stores but highly suitable recruits, made the Nepalese Army in the west a formidable, skilled and mobile force able to move easily and fight well in hilly terrain. However, its lack of siege guns and expertise in siege tactics brought the advance to a halt and prolonged the siege of Kangra until 1809.

While the Nepalese Army was advancing westwards into Garhwal in 1803, British armies were engaged in a second war against the Marathas. The Commander-in-Chief, Lord Lake in the north, and the Governor-General's brother, Arthur Wellesley (later Duke of Wellington) in the south, achieved a series of major victories against the forces of Sindhia and the Maratha confederacy which included French mercenaries under the French General Perron. Not least among these victories was that at Patparganj south of Delhi on 11 September 1803. Under the treaty of Sarji Arjangaon (1803), the East India Company acquired from the Marathas the Delhi territory comprising the city of Shahjahanabad (also known as Dehli, later spelt Delhi) and extensive surrounding territory. The Governor-General, Lord Wellesley, reported to the Court of Directors: 'All the attempts of the French and others in the interests of Daulet Rao Scindia to deter His Majesty [the Mogul Emperor, Shah Alam] from accepting the protection of the British Government were, however, frustrated by the signal and decisive battle of Delhi on the 11 September 1803. Immediately after that event the Commander-in-Chief was apprised of the Emperor's earnest desire to place himself under the immediate protection of the British Army.'[87]

The capture of Delhi and the alienation of the Mogul emperor from the Marathas had been the principal object of the war. Lord Lake had already assured the Governor-General that 'every possible mark of honour and respect shall be paid to His Majesty and the royal family consistent with the security of his person'.[88] Shah Alam retained jurisdiction over his palace in the city. When about to move with his army to Agra, the Commander-in-Chief wrote to the Governor-General:

I have the honour to acquaint your Lordship that I have appointed Lieutenant Colonel Ochterlony, the Deputy Adjutant General, to remain with His Majesty Shah Allum and to take command of the troops that remain for the protection of Delhi. I have selected Lieutenant Colonel Ochterlony for the duty from the knowledge I have of his ability as well as his zeal for the public service in which I place a firm confidence. Though I can ill spare the services of Colonel Ochterlony at this moment, from the impossibility there exists of finding throughout that Army any person calculated for this particular duty, which your Lordship will readily perceive requires an officer of no mean abilities, I have been induced to leave this officer whatever private inconvenience may result to myself in his absence. I have entrusted to this officer the temporary management of the newly acquired territories which I trust will meet with your Lordship's approbation.[89]

Thus Ochterlony, recently promoted to lieutenant-colonel, was charged not only with a difficult military command in Delhi but also with heavy civil responsibilities as British representative there. Lying on the route from Calcutta to the Punjab, Delhi had the strategic importance of a frontier town and served the British as a link with Rajputana (see map 1).[90] The strategic and political importance of Delhi with control over the Mogul Court were clearly recognised by both the Commander-in-Chief and the Governor-General. The Marathas, who had also recognised this, were yet determined to wrest Delhi and Shah Alam from the British.

David Ochterlony, who was later to play a crucial role in relations between Britain and Nepal, was born on 12 February 1758 at Boston, Massachusetts. His father, second son of the Laird of Pitforthy in Scotland, was a captain in the merchant service who died insolvent at St Vincent in August 1765. David's mother, who came from a well-to-do New England family, saw to his education at the Latin School in Boston until 1770 when she brought him and his two younger brothers to England. In the same year, she married Isaac Heard who, in 1759 after an adventurous early life had entered upon a distinguished career in the College of Arms and who for thirty-eight years before his death in 1822 at the age of ninety-one, held the influential office of Garter Principal King of Arms.[91] David Ochterlony's deep affection for his stepfather was reciprocated by Heard who had no children by either of his marriages. They corresponded frequently during almost all of Ochterlony's service in India where, as an East India Company Army cadet, he went in 1777 and where in 1825 he died. During the period 1770 to 1776 the young David Ochterlony travelled among his father's family in the highlands of Scotland, a country for which he felt an abiding love and yearning. On joining the East India Company's Bengal Army he was appointed ensign with the 31st Native Infantry on 7 February 1778 and promoted to lieutenant later the same year.[92]

In 1781, while with the 24th Bengal Native Infantry Ochterlony joined Colonel Thomas Deane Pearse's force of five regiments which marched 1,100 miles from Bengal to Madras to reinforce Lieutenant-General

Sir Eyre Coote's army after the disastrous defeat of Colonel Baillie at Parambakam in 1780. Pearse's force played a prominent part in the operations against Haider Ali, Sultan of Mysore, and the French under de Bussy during the Second Mysore War. At Cuddalore in June 1783 the force distinguished itself as the first trained and disciplined Indian troops to engage in hand-to-hand fighting against European troops. The French were defeated with severe losses. Ochterlony, in the thick of the battle, was wounded and taken prisoner. He was released on the declaration of peace in 1784 following Haider Ali's death. He had seen for himself the qualities of the trained Bengal Native Infantry and had time to ponder the vital importance of careful planning in avoiding disaster. Ochterlony's military prowess did not escape the notice of higher authority. Perhaps to enable him to recover from his wounds and captivity, he was appointed to the staff as Deputy Judge Advocate General for a division of the Bengal Army. He was promoted captain in April 1796, major in April 1800 and lieutenant-colonel on 18 March 1803 when, on the orders of the Commander-in-Chief, Lord Lake, he relinquished his staff appointment on assuming command of the 2/12th Native Infantry. His skilful leadership at the capture of the forts of Sasni, Bejaigarh, and Kachoura in the Doab, caused Lake to appoint him Deputy Adjutant-General of his army on the outbreak of the Second Maratha War. He was with Lake at the battles of Koil (29 August 1803), Aligarh (4 September 1803), and the capture of Delhi (11 September 1803) when the Maratha forces under Courguin were defeated with heavy losses in men and guns.

In 1804, when the Nepalese Army, under the command of Kaji Amar Singh Thapa, moved into the Cis-Sutlej hills with their eyes turned westward, the attention of the British in the East India Company's Bengal Presidency was focused in the same direction. Holkar, the Maratha Chief, was again on the rampage with a large army. In August 1804 at Delhi, Ochterlony wrote: 'Every native account seems to suppose that he [Holkar] will come this way, but if we have not crippled ourselves by the supposition of the impossibility of the attempt I hope there will soon be an army in the field that will induce him to recross the Chambah. We ought to have been raising more regiments just at the time we turned off 10,000 sepoys, and when I contemplate what has been done and the means we had, I feel more and more grateful that the Lord was on our side. To talk of more regiments is treason!' [93]

Ochterlony's resourcefulness was soon to be tested to the full. Holkar, flushed with the success of having ambushed and wiped out a small British detachment under Colonel William Monson, during 24–29 August 1804, was marching on Delhi. Ochterlony had under his command a small garrison with which to hold seven miles of crumbling city walls. Lord Lake had left him the 2nd Battalion and the 4th and 5th companies of the 11th Native Infantry together with 'a body of matchlockmen which are raising under the superintendence of two enterprising young men who quitted Sindhia's service on the first appearance of hostilities'. [94] Not surprisingly Ochterlony was less sanguine than Lake that this small force would be 'fully adequate for the protection of the City and Fortress of Delhi and its environs and to ensure the safety of His Majesty's person from any attack'. He noted, somewhat ruefully 'which of our plays says any man can do [wonders] with money but your true genius lives without it? Any man might conquer with the troops and the proper mussalah [resources]. We manage without these aids.' [95] Nevertheless Ochterlony's tactics in the face of a large enemy force were determined and skilful. He organised with all speed the repair of walls and the fortification of strong defensive parapets and called in Lieutenant-Colonel Burn [96] from Saharanpur, Major Harriett from Rohtak, and Lieutenant Birch [97] from Panipat (see map 2). Burn, who arrived on 5 September with his troops after forced marches of nearly thirty miles a day, assumed command of all troops including the two newly recruited najib [militia] battalions of matchlockmen under Lieutenants Birch and Woodville. Burn took up defensive positions outside Delhi but, on the approach of the Maratha army, the najib battalions mutinied and some of the irregular cavalry deserted. On 7 October Ochterlony called Burn into Delhi and for nine days within the city walls a force of some 2,500 men and eleven guns withstood an enemy army of 18,000 men and 160 guns. Attempts by the Marathas to undermine the walls were halted by news of Lake's approach with a relieving army. On 13 October a final

Maratha assault was repulsed and two days later the siege was abandoned.

Throughout the siege Burn displayed the greatest skill and fortitude, for which he was thanked in a General Order of the Commander-in-Chief dated 24 October 1804. The same General Order expressed the 'highest approbation for Ochterlony's wise and timely precautions, energy and decision' and for his assistance to Burn. The unsung heroes were the Indian infantry who, despite the threat of overwhelming numbers and of brutal atrocities, lived up to the very high opinion in which Ochterlony held them.

The value of Ochterlony's services was recognised by his permanent appointment as Resident at the Court of His Majesty Shah Alam in Delhi. Edmonstone, Secretary to the Government in Calcutta, wrote to Ochterlony on 11 November 1804:

> In nominating you to this important station His Excellency the Governor-General in Council is desirous of affording public testimony of his approbation of your conduct during your Residence at the Court of His Majesty under the immediate authority of His Excellency the Commander-in-Chief, and especially of manifesting the high sense which the Governor-General in Council entertained of the judgment, firmness and activity displayed in your conducting the arrangements for the late successful defence of the City and the Fortress of Delhi against the numerous forces and artillery of the enemy under circumstances of peculiar difficulty and disadvantage. His Excellency in Council is happy to learn that your conduct in the provisional discharge of duties of British Representative at the Court of Delhi has conciliated the approbation and confidence of His Majesty Shah Alam added to a conviction that you possess the qualities necessary for the due discharge of the duties, supplies an additional motive for your permanent appointment to that high and important station.[98]

Ochterlony may not have been aware that on 25 February 1804 Colonel William Scott had been appointed to succeed him as Resident at Delhi. It was following the death of Scott on 27 September 1804, *en route* from Lucknow to take up his new post, that Ochterlony was appointed Resident at Delhi on a permanent basis from 7 November 1804.

British victory over the Marathas in 1803 had brought them into contact with the lowland Sikhs in the Cis-Sutlej area, and at the same time had provided the opportunity of exerting influence. Although the Governor-General, Wellesley, was content for Delhi to be defended with a line on the Jumna, raids into Delhi territory caused him to take Karnal and Jinjannu, gateways to the hills. The appointment of a British Resident at Delhi therefore carried with it responsibility for the security and administration of a large tract of land not only surrounding Delhi but extending far to the north-west. Ochterlony was quick to perceive that the defence of this territory stretching across the plains to the northern foothills would be far from easy. In December 1804, Ochterlony proposed that the British should establish a more defensible boundary on the Sutlej either by annexing the Jumna-Sutlej Doab or by bringing the Sikh chiefs in this territory under British protection. This was rejected, the Chief Secretary, John Lumsden, arguing that the Sikhs were untrustworthy and that the British should have no dealings with them. Further recommendations by Ochterlony that the British should establish complete control by partitioning the whole territory between the four paramount chiefs, or by exacting tribute, as Perron had done before, were also rejected. In a letter of 13 January 1805 to Ochterlony, Edmonstone, the Chief Secretary to the Government set out the principles of Government policy.[99] Edmonstone explained that the subjection of the territory to the authority of the British Government was out of the question: 'His Excellency's [the Governor-General's] views in that quarter are limited to the secure and tranquil possession of the territories in the Douab and the right bank of the Jumna ceded to us by the Treaty of Peace with Dowlut Rao Scindia or which may be acquired in the course of existing hostilities with Holkar and the Rajah of Bhurtpore.'[100]

Partition was held to be as unjustified as annexation. Moreover the Government would not enter into any of Ranjit Singh's schemes for conquest nor assist the Raja of Patiala or any other Sikh chieftain against Ranjit Singh. In short it was the Governor-General's desire 'to maintain a system of perfect neutrality'. Lake's subsequent hot pursuit of Holkar across the Sutlej into the Punjab inevitably brought the British into confrontation with the Raja of Lahore, Ranjit Singh. A treaty was negotiated with him in January 1806 whereby Ranjit Singh undertook not to give aid to Holkar and the British agreed not to enter the Punjab.[101]

While Ochterlony was distinguishing himself at Delhi, another Scot of ancient highland lineage, William Fraser, was showing great promise in Calcutta. They were destined to meet, become firm friends and to play predominant parts in the eventual recruitment of Gorkha and other hillmen into the Bengal Army. William Fraser had been accepted into the Honourable East India Company's civil service on the nomination of Charles Grant, Scottish Director of the East India Company, and was appointed as a writer to the Bengal service in 1801. He sailed on the Comet in September of that year and arrived in Calcutta on 9 February 1802. At the College in Fort William he won a gold medal in 1803 and a prize of £500 (which he sent home to his father), and a medal of merit in 1804.[102]

William's family, the Frasers of Reelig,[103] a branch of Clan Lovat, established a connection with India early in the eighteenth century. His grandfather James Fraser (1712–54; eleventh of Reelig) resided there for seventeen years as a young man, and acquired a good knowledge of Arabic, Persian, and Indian languages.[104] William's father, Edward Satchwell Fraser (1751–1835; twelfth of Reelig) who was born at Easter Moniack (now known as Reelig) on the family estate near Inverness, did not go to India. After schooling at Charterhouse he was commissioned into the 1st (Grenadier) Guards in 1777 and served in America throughout the American War of Independence as ADC to General Simon Fraser, 12th Lord Lovat, his Clan Chief. Edward Satchwell Fraser, having greatly improved the family estate, unwisely mortgaged it in order to invest in sugar plantations at Berbice in Guiana. The instability of the sugar market and the vagaries of climate were such that the plantations themselves had to be mortgaged and eventually sold in 1817 when their market value was at a low ebb. Against this background of crippling debt, at a time when many less adventurous Scottish landowners were hard-pressed to make ends meet, Edward Satchwell and his wife Jane (1749–1847) raised a family which included a daughter, and five sons: James Baillie (1783–1856); William (1784–1835); Edward Satchwell (1786–1813); Alexander Charles (1789–1816);

and George John (1800–1824). The five sons were given a good education and, although James spent his early life vainly endeavouring to
salvage Fraser interests in Berbice, were despatched to India to help
retrieve the family fortunes. James alone survived to return to Scotland.[105] William was assassinated. Edward, having been appointed to
the Honourable East India Company's civil service, soon became ill,
eventually dying in St Helena where he had been sent to recuperate.
George, an officer in the Company's 1st Bengal Cavalry, died at
Aurungabad, also without fame or fortune. Alexander, whose appointment as an Assistant to the Resident at Delhi failed to fulfil early hopes
of advancement, was dogged by illness and accident and died of
tuberculosis. He was the desk-bound family scribe, relaying news of
the brothers to his father and mother in frequent letters which also
touched on aspects of Indian politics and society. Among the Fraser
of Reelig papers,[106] Alexander's clearly written letters and diaries are
an important record supplementing those of James (who did not arrive
in India until January 1814) and William whose illegible scrawl he
sometimes transcribed for the benefit of his parents.

In 1805 William wrote to his father: 'my standing in College though
moderately good does not entitle me to the first appointment'.[107] He
added: 'there is only one situation I should have preferred to any
other, viz. to be placed under Mr. Edmonstone in his office – this
directly points to the diplomatic department but indirectly to any
other' where, William pointed out, he would be 'in the Government
eye' with 'insight into business transactions of Government'. Nevertheless he wisely determined to abide by Lord Wellesley's pleasure
regarding his appointment. No doubt he recalled informing his father
that under Lord Wellesley as Governor-General 'Secrecy is the word
here and people are afraid to open their mouths. It is indeed necessary
for many reasons, for the public welfare and your own safety and
advancement. Lord Wellesley has established, if I may use the expression, a most active police. Nothing can be said or done of which he
is not informed. This lays a heavy restraint on the community; they
are afraid of expressing their sentiments, become envious of one
another, and friendly intercourse and communication is checked.'[108]

Wellesley refused him his first choice, but, impressed by William's linguistic skills and administrative potential, gave him a priority list at the head of which was the appointment of Assistant to the Resident at the Court in Delhi. William chose Delhi. 'After looking over the whole [list]', he wrote, 'none appeared more eligible than this which is my destination. I am happy to say that all my friends and particularly my patron, Mr. Edmonstone, approve perfectly of my choice.'[109] William's father who was delighted at the news, wrote to remind William: 'Colonel Ochterlony is the very intimate and early friend of our favourite friend Colonel Grant Lochletter ... I am happy to find you placed under a man I must have so high an opinion of from being Lochletter's friend – if he were not an able man he would not have been selected by Lord Wellesley for such a station.'[110]

An early indication of William Fraser's political outlook is clear from a letter written in May 1805 to his father: 'What do they think at home of our expanding dominions? It may be argued that the power of Britain and her superiority over other nations arises solely from her extensive commerce ultimately producing a race of sea-bred warriors at once her pride and her protection, . . . but were we to give overweight to trade this would lead to excessive luxury and we would sink like the Dutch and become prey to an enterprising enemy.'[111]

William Fraser, like Ochterlony, was well aware of the propaganda advantages of military victory and the widespread dangers from news of defeat. He wrote: 'Our good old Commander-in-Chief [Lord Lake] has done honour to himself and country . . . [His] masterly pursuit and overtaking of Holkar and his cavalry, putting them to rout and completely scattering of them has struck the minds of the natives with more force than any other circumstance could have done, and I trust will have great effect.' [112]

William Fraser was, however, aware that news of Lake's disastrous failures to take the Jat fortress of Bharatpur, with the loss of 100 officers and 3,100 men, would spread throughout north India strengthening the resolve of the Marathas and raising in the minds of Indian states fresh notions of British vulnerability. These disasters following upon Monson's retreat in July-August 1804 caused William to write to his father: 'What will they [the East India Company's proprietors] feel on hearing of Monson's retreat and our three repulses at Bhurtpore.

Holkar, I suppose, in their imagination will already be plundering
Benares, Patna and Moorshadabad and be rapidly advancing to Calcutta.'[113]

En route to join Ochterlony, William wrote: 'we must humble our
enemies before we can expect to rest secure'.[114] He was soon to discover
how far removed Delhi was from Calcutta. A circuitous and dangerous
journey which he envisaged would take three months, in fact took
twice as long: 'This morning (15 January 1806) ended my journey by
breakfasting with Colonel Ochterlony in Delhi, six months and a day
since I left Calcutta.'[115]

Fraser's father, writing in response to William's report from Cawn-
pore (Kanpur) dated 21 October 1805, assessed the importance of his
appointment:

> I conclude that your occupation will be that of an Ambassador's Sec-
> retary, and your time may, with propriety and advantage to your office
> and to yourself, be very well filled by the duties and ceremonies incident
> to it. You will in point of etiquette and ceremonial have I suppose to
> attend the Emperor's Court, visit and receive visits from the Courtiers
> and the Ambassadors of other native princes and of all Eastern poten-
> tates. You will of course have a part of important duty to obtain
> intelligence and make observation upon all the transactions, movements
> and state of all neighbouring powers in Hindoostan . . . In this way
> you will be gradually inducted into diplomatic knowledge.[116]

Although William Fraser was well equipped for administration and
for gathering intelligence, his temperament did not fit him at all times
for the finer points of diplomacy. His brother Alexander, who knew
him well, described him as 'proud, fiery and impetuous' and 'too fond
of exposing himself to danger'.[117] This was certainly true. William, a
keen and accomplished horseman, liked nothing better than to hunt
tigers on horseback, unless it was to hunt them on foot. On learning
of William's apparent recklessness his father wrote to him: 'what would
be our consolation to know that you had braved and killed 50 tygers
[*sic*] or lions and finally were maimed or killed'.[118] This reproof
brought the assurance from William that 'I borrow an elephant when
I wish to shoot. By your desire I have given up wholly pursuing tygers

on foot or horseback.' [119] It did not, however, cure him of an insatiable quest for danger. On 25 November 1814 he narrowly escaped death from an arrow in the neck when in the forefront of the assault on Kalanga fort, at which General Gillespie was killed. [120] This time the reproof came from Charles Grant, then Chairman of the East India Company's Court of Directors in London, who wrote to William's father: 'I cannot well pardon the young man for so unnecessarily exposing himself and the interest and happiness of his family.' [121] William's courage did not, however, go unnoticed in India. Alexander Fraser, forwarding letters from William to his mother, added: 'we have the satisfaction at least of a most flattering public note of his gallant conduct, by Lord Moira [the Governor-General, later known as the Marquess of Hastings]'. [122] As further evidence of William's courage, there is in his diary a laconic account of an attempt on his life by a Jat assassin armed with a sword. Unarmed and alone William was wounded in the head and, in attempting to fend off his attacker, sustained further cuts to a foot and a hand. He was saved from death by the arrival of a servant and by the swift retribution of a Gorkha orderly. William walked to his tent, bled himself and bound his own wounds. [123]

William Fraser had two ambitions: to become a Resident, preferably at Delhi; and to be granted a military commission. He wrote that an 'active political and military life is the strongest stimulus to existence'. [124] His father, who did not approve of his military pretensions, wrote in August 1815: 'He may be rewarded by the applause of India and his own conscience. But I see no chance of other acknowledgement or of fruit from travelling out of the records, as lawyers say, or departing from his civilian course, in the warmth of his zeal, to exercise military duties; and the perils are not of any ordinary cast even for a soldier.' [125]

In the meantime, William had informed his brother Alexander: 'The Government have accepted my services in a military command for the next campaign.' [126] In August 1815 he was offered a commission as a major with Skinner's Horse or as a lieutenant-colonel unattached to any particular corps. [127] He unhesitatingly accepted a majority with his great friend Lieutenant-Colonel James Skinner and his 'Yellow

Boys'. However, Ochterlony warned him: 'I think there will be no call for your military services, my dear William, in any shape or form'.[128] It was not until September 1817 that William wrote to his brother James: 'Hastings allows me to join the corps if I can be spared from Delhi.'[129] The following month the Resident at Delhi, Charles Metcalfe, sent a formal letter to William conveying the Governor-General's permission for him to join Skinner.[130] In December 1817 James Fraser wrote to his father: 'William and I are quite well. He accompanies the army of General Ochterlony on the march to Jeypoore.'[131] When active military service ceased, William turned his attention to prospects for an active political life: 'I see no present probability of the Jypore Residency but I know nothing of what Lord Hastings' intentions may or may not be. I shall not stay with the Army longer than the end of January.'[132]

Having refused an offer of the Residency at Holkar's camp in 1818,[133] he returned to work at the Delhi Residency. In the political field he saw fit to decline other opportunities which, but for his forthright nature, might have led to a Residency. He was for a time Agent to the Governor-General in Delhi in 1825, and in 1828 acted very briefly as Resident at Delhi when handing over the appointment to Francis Hawkins following Sir Edward Colebrooke's dismissal from office. From 1832 – when the office of Resident at Delhi was abolished – until his death in 1835 William Fraser was Agent and Commissioner in the North-West Provinces. Alexander Fraser summed up his brother's character thus: 'William's delight is in surmounting great difficulties, braving dangers, performing duties of which the beneficial effects are vast and rapid in operation. His mind is remarkable rather for capacity and decision than acumen and precision. Willie would make a better statesman than a lawyer, a better teacher of morality than of metaphysics. The enthusiasm and ardour of his character are rather adverse to the effectual fulfilment of duties which require patient application rather than energetic but somewhat irregular exertions.'[134]

It was perhaps surprising that such a man should find a rapport with the calm and careful Ochterlony, twenty-six years his senior. Yet they were lifelong friends. Fraser wrote in 1819: 'I look upon it to be one of the most fortunate events of my life that my official career, commencing in 1806, has been spent under four, I may safely say of the most distinguished characters of the Bengal Service in General Ochterlony, Mr. Seton, Mr. Elphinstone and Mr. Metcalfe.'[135] William Fraser's initial service under Ochterlony lasted little more than three months. Ochterlony was summarily replaced by a civil servant, Archibald Seton, who took over as Resident on 27 April 1806. The instruction from John Adam, the Deputy Secretary to the Government in Calcutta was uncharacteristically brief and terse to the point of rudeness: 'I am directed to inform you that the Honourable the Governor-General has been pleased to appoint Mr. A. Seton to be Resident at Delhi and to desire that you will deliver over the charge of the Residency to that Gentleman immediately after his arrival at Delhi.'[136] This bolt from the blue surprised William Fraser as much as it shocked Ochterlony. William wrote to his father: 'You must have learnt from me before of the removal of Colonel Ochterlony. It was an act of the present Government for which of course it must have had its reasons though they never were assigned to himself. I was exceedingly sorry for it, at the time, chiefly however as it hurt the feelings of an excellent veteran officer.'[137]

Ochterlony had time to brood upon the unwelcome news. It was not until 5 June 1806 that the Governor-General in Council appointed him to command the fortress and station of Allahabad, halfway between Delhi and Calcutta.[138] Lord Lake and Shah Alam had protested strongly at Ochterlony's removal from Delhi, but to no avail. The courtly manners and tact of Ochterlony as well as his gallantry had won Shah Alam's respect and affection. Moreover Ochterlony's appointment as Resident at Delhi had done much to erase the sense of slight felt by the Mogul emperor at the removal of Major James Browne whom Warren Hastings had sent as British Agent to the Court at Delhi in 1783.[139] From 1785 to 1803 the gathering of information on the affairs of Delhi was left to the British Agent at the Court of Daulat Rao Sindhia who, as Vakil-i-mutlaq (Regent Plenipotentiary) exercised complete control over Shah Alam. Shah Alam died on 19 November 1806 and was succeeded by his eldest surviving son, Prince Mirza Akbar Shah, whose domestic problems caused considerable difficulty for Seton.[140] Lake wrote to the Governor-General:

His Majesty [Shah Alam] when I was about to depart, mentioned with the strongest emotion that he had heard with equal grief and surprise a report respecting the removal of Colonel Ochterlony from his present station. He dwelt much upon the conduct of that officer since his first appointment every part of which he extoled [*sic*] in the highest manner. The character of the Colonel, Shah Aulum said, might be read in his happiness and that of his family and in the prosperity of the city of Dehli and that surrounding countryside; and concluded by observing that he knew not the reasons which dictated change but that it had evidently been made without any consideration for his feelings as these alone would have been gratified by increased favours being bestowed upon an individual to whom he was deeply indebted.[141]

Barlow wrote to Lake a long rambling letter which contrasted starkly with the brevity of Adam's letter of 27 January 1806 to Ochterlony. Barlow sought to explain that the special circumstances of Ochterlony's appointment by Lake 'to the charge of the Residency at Delhi' having been superseded by an ordinary system of administration, a civil servant should take over. In no sense was this to be seen as a reflection on Colonel Ochterlony's conduct: 'It originates exclusively in my sense of the augmented importance of that situation under the progressive system of our proposed arrangements.'[142] The following belated testimonial to Ochterlony's service as Acting Resident and Resident at Delhi did little to sweeten the pill:

The Governor-General avails himself of the occasion to express the high sense which Government entertains of the merits and services of Lieu-tenant-Colonel Ochterlony. The zeal, integrity and ability uniformly manifested by Lieutenant-Colonel Ochterlony in conducting the ardu-ous duties of Resident of Delhi and especially the firmness, energy and activity displayed by him during that crisis of difficulty when the city of Delhi was besieged by the collective force of Jaswant Rao Holkar, commanded by the chieftain in person, and during the prevalence of warfare, tumult and disorder in the surrounding districts established that valuable officer's claims to the recorded approbation of the British Government: and the Governor-General in Council discharges a satis-factory part of his duty in combining with the notification of

Lieutenant-Colonel Ochterlony's appointment to the command of Allahabad this public acknowledgement of the value of his services and of the distinguished merits of his character and conduct.[143]

Ochterlony may have reflected on the reference to 'arduous duties' and wondered whether, at forty-eight, he was considered too old for such active service. Or he may have concluded that the new Governor-General was bound to favour a fellow civil servant. In any event Ochterlony's abrupt and unexplained removal from Delhi was to sour his attitude to Calcutta for the rest of his life. He wrote to William Fraser in 1820 regarding his own offer to move from Delhi to make way for his dear friend Charles Metcalfe: 'It does not seem to me improbable that they [the Government] may not avail themselves of the strict tenor of it to place a favoured civilian where a soldier has been found so inconvenient.'[144]

Nevertheless, Allahabad, a holy city at the sacred confluence of the Ganges and the Jumna, was not without its attractions. William Fraser, *en route* for Delhi in 1805, had found the Allahabad fort enchanting in the early sun.[145] Reginald Heber, Bishop of Calcutta, on tour in northern India in September 1824, recorded that 'Allahabad stands in perhaps the most favourable situation which India affords for a great city, in a dry and healthy soil, on a triangle . . . capable of being fortified so as to become almost impregnable.'[146] Its buildings 'in the Oriental style and containing noble vaulted rooms' would have appealed to Ochterlony. Arrangements were made to ensure that he did not suffer financially from his new posting.

As to William Fraser, he soon found Seton, another fellow Scot, a congenial successor to Ochterlony as Resident at Delhi. He informed his mother: 'I am not the less happy notwithstanding under Seton, and as my duties are more defined, more independent.' He added: 'there is no man in the world I would sooner see an inmate at Moniack than Seton . . . He has a paternal estate in Stirling and Inverness, Touch and Reelick very commonly engross most of our leisure hours.'[147] To his father, William Fraser described his official duties as follows: 'What I do is mostly judicial and political correspondence besides doing much judicial business superintending police and frequently out in the adjacent country to intimidate by threats or soothe by persuasion and assurances of protection and assistance the unfortunate inhabitants of the *ci-devant* Mahratta tract now thank God under our lenient and excellent Government.' [148]

Despite the brevity of their initial collaboration, Ochterlony and William Fraser were destined to spend much of their service in close association under the governor-generalships of Lord Minto (1807–13) and Lord Hastings (1813–23). When they were not together, they corresponded. William Fraser also kept in touch with two of Ochterlony's closest aides, Robert Ross and Peter Lawtie, who were also 'cronies' of Alexander Fraser.[149] That Ochterlony and William Fraser did not always agree was an inevitable reflection of their different personalities and backgrounds. William wrote to his brother James in 1818: 'I never see the General. We have quarreled upon Sikh boundaries'.[150] Such quarrels were soon repaired. In a personal letter to Charles Metcalfe, then Secretary to the Government, regarding William Fraser's career, Ochterlony wrote: 'I have had a long conversation with Fraser whose inclination would lead him to take charge of a district but who, were it otherwise, would in the spirit of our old affection, now happily restored, make a sacrifice for my indulgence.' [151] William Fraser's affection for Ochterlony is shown in a letter to his father around the same time: 'I expected to have effected an exchange of appointments between Middleton, Ochterlony's son-in-law and myself, an arrangement which would have placed me at Hansee and kept him at Delhi. I wished this for the General's sake that he might have his daughter and son-in-law with him at Delhi, but Government would not agree.' [152]

The Fraser papers provide ample evidence of the close and abiding friendship between William Fraser and Ochterlony. Ochterlony's last letter to William, undated but probably written in 1824 when his health was deteriorating rapidly, bears eloquent testimony:

Considering all the circumstances I think it improbable we should meet again. Take then with you the assurance that wherever I may be my sincere wishes for your health, happiness and success will ever be with you, and shall, from

> Your truly affectionate
> Da. Ochterlony.[153]

The friendship between Ochterlony and Fraser is all the more remarkable at a time when there was a good deal of antipathy between the Company's civil and military servants in Bengal. In 1832, Mountstuart Elphinstone wrote: 'The great problem there [the Bengal Presidency] has been always to maintain the subordination of the military power to the civil, and to prevent clashing between the Governors and the Commanders-in-Chief.'[154]

Of the lowest levels in the Bengal military service, Alexander Fraser noted in his diary:

> The cadets on arrival are immediately sent to a place called Barraset, about 15 or 18 miles from Calcutta, where they form a company under certain regulations of military discipline and learn (if they please) the languages and their military science, and are commanded by officers for the purpose. They are not (regularly) allowed to join the army until they attain certain proficiency in their studies. This institution, worse if possible than the Calcutta [Fort William] College, generally sends the young men into the army plunged in debt and shattered in constitution. Some who have sense and fortitude in an unusual degree, profit by the place. The young men at Barraset conceive themselves hardly used on seeing the liberty allowed to writers and the more ample allowances they receive; and from this source springs a jealousy unworthy of all.[155]

James Fraser, writing to William from Inverness about Edward Fraser's voyage to India in 1811 to take up his appointment as a writer, drew attention to the rift between the Civil and Military: 'It appears that Sir George [Nugent, Commander-in-Chief, India] has taken little notice of him and that in consequence of a line being distinctly drawn between the civil and military people.'[156] Lady Nugent, on tour with Sir George in 1813 at Saharanpur, observed: 'At this station as well as most others we found the civil and military authorities a little at variance.'[157]

Why then were Ochterlony and William Fraser such good friends? There were at least three underlying reasons. Firstly, they liked each other and spent much of their service in close association at Delhi or in the extensive surrounding territory. Far from the Government, military headquarters and society in Calcutta, they relied on each other and on a few European colleagues for gathering and exchanging intelligence and for general conversation. Secondly, the bond of friendship was strengthened by sharing in disappointments. William's first disappointment was not long in coming. Charles Theophilus Metcalfe was appointed First Secretary at the Delhi Residency over his head on 15 August 1806. In their respective careers Ochterlony and William Fraser were in and out of favour, and both were prone to a sense of frustration and moods of depression. Both tilted at authority: Ochterlony being charged with insubordination; William Fraser narrowly avoiding a charge of interfering in military matters during the Anglo-Nepal War. Thirdly, they shared an interest in Indian culture and society which went beyond official requirement. Off-duty, both wore a modified Indian dress. William went so far as to wear Indian-style beard and moustachios. In the manner of eighteenth-century East India Company officials, both kept Indian 'bibis', women who bore them natural children.

This chapter has traced the westward drive of a Nepalese Army which, under an elderly but experienced and ambitious Gorkha commander, had developed into a skilled and highly mobile fighting force augmented and supplied locally as it advanced through the Himalayan foothills of Kumaon, Garhwal and the Cis-Sutlej states. Its weakness lay not so much in its military limitations (it lacked adequate artillery and was ill-equipped and untrained in siege tactics) as in its failure to provide sound civil administration in the lands it conquered. As a result of harsh repression and heavy taxation it left in its wake populations diminished by wholesale emigration and hostile to their Nepalese overlords. As the southern perimeter of the expanding Nepalese empire was co-terminous with the northern borders of the East India Company's territory – borders imprecisely defined across difficult terrain – there was a growing risk of cross-border incidents and encroachments. British interests in the defence of the Company's north-west frontier led them to establish a Residency at the Court of Shah Alam in Delhi.

The Residency at Delhi was regarded by the Government in India as of the greatest political and strategic importance. The first Resident, Lieutenant-Colonel David Ochterlony, was joined by another Highland Scot, William Fraser, as his Assistant at a time when the Nepalese Army, comprising Gorkhas and other hillmen, had reached the northern Punjab where Ranjit Singh, Raja of Lahore, was expanding his influence into the same territory and with the same objectives as the Nepalese. The association of Ochterlony, a brilliant military commander with a penchant for diplomacy, and Fraser, a forceful diplomat with a hankering for military command, produced a formidable partnership. Both became political agents to the Governor-General and did not hesitate to approach him direct. In addition, Ochterlony had sympathetic access to the Commander-in-Chief through the Adjutant-General, and William Fraser had good relations with John Adam who, as the Political Secretary to the Government in Calcutta, was a powerful influence with both the Governor-General and the Council. With their Scots ancestry, Ochterlony and William Fraser shared a love of hill country and a strong fellow-feeling with hill people. They were keenly aware of the vital importance to the defence of northern India of the city of Delhi, its surrounding territory, and the hills of the then North-West Frontier. Events and their joint experience were to lead them to pay special attention to the Cis-Sutlej hills and to the Nepalese Army's Gorkha and other hillmen.

CHAPTER 3

The North-West Quarter of Hindustan, 1807–12

The arrival of Lord Minto in July 1807 to succeed Sir George Barlow as Governor-General was to shape the careers of both William Fraser and David Ochterlony and to cause them to take a special interest in the hills of what became known as the North-West Quarter of Hindustan. Minto, erstwhile President of the Board of Control, came with authority to send diplomatic missions to Tehran, Sind, Kabul and Lahore with the aim of establishing treaties of collaborative defence against a possible French invasion of India via the North-West Frontier.[158] The general purpose of the missions to Kabul (Afghanistan) and Lahore (Punjab) was 'that of encouraging the states of Caubul and Lahore to resist or impede the progress of the French Army which may endeavour to traverse the territories of these states'. [159] The Kabul mission was to be headed by the Hon. Mountstuart Elphinstone, a cousin of John Adam, with William Fraser as his Assistant. The mission to Lahore would be led by Charles Metcalfe, with David Ochterlony in support. Fraser and Ochterlony were chosen for their respective roles because of their knowledge and experience of the Company's north-western territories. Although the alleged French threat did not materialise, the North-West Quarter of Hindustan remained an area of great concern to the Government in India. By 1812 the Cis-Sutlej territories to the north-west and north of Delhi had become centres of contention between the British and the Raja of Lahore, and, so far as borders were concerned, between the British and the Government of Nepal.

Two inter-related factors brought Cis-Sutlej territories into contention. These were the trans-Sutlej incursions of the Sikh Raja of Lahore, Ranjit Singh, into the lowlands of northern Sirhind; and, farther north, the trans-Sutlej withdrawal of Kaji Amar Singh Thapa and his army to consolidate their possession of the hills following defeat by Ranjit Singh's army at Kangra. Measures to contain Ranjit Singh to the line of the Sutlej forced the British also to face up to boundary problems with the Nepalese along an ill-defined border. The movement of Nepalese troops into fortified positions close to British protectorates was a cause for concern. Continuing encroachments onto what the British held to be their territory led to argument with the Nepalese Government and raised the possibility of war. The involvement of Ochterlony and William Fraser in political missions gave them insight into the particular problems of mountain warfare. It also suggested the need for trained hillmen in the Bengal Army.

Elphinstone's mission to Kabul left Delhi on 12 October 1808 and, travelling via Bikanir, Multan and the Indus, arrived in Peshawar on 25 February 1809. It got no farther. A rebellion against Shah Shuja-ul-Mulk had been inspired by his nephew and was being led by Mahmud, a tribal leader with a 'cruel and vicious reputation'.[160] Shuja, who held the north and east of Afghanistan while Mahmud held the south and west, was far too pre-occupied with the starkly real dangers of civil war to concern himself with remote and dubious threats from elsewhere. William Fraser noted in his journal for 27 March 1809: 'We are in a curious position between two parties. God send us well out of it.' [161] William Fraser was far from happy with his new role. He regarded Elphinstone as a 'cool, frostbitten character'.[162] In a letter dated 29 January 1809 to his brother Alexander, he wrote that when Elphinstone knew that William was to accompany him his manner became formal 'and we have ever been since that cool and indifferent. If there is anything to do he sends it and I do it; he never speaks to me on any sort of business. Thus we go on and shall go on.' [163] In forwarding William's letter to his mother, Alexander explained that William's views on Elphinstone were 'three fourths fancy' as William had been 'spoilt by Seton'. Elphinstone may indeed have had doubts about William's diplomacy, for Alexander added that William, while in Peshawar had 'behaved very ill' having 'risen in rage at a feast for being stared at by his Afghan hosts'.[164] William had earlier complained that 'dipping our fingers and whiskers in poached eggs and honey' had been humiliating.[165] Although kept in ignorance of political affairs, William informed Alexander: 'We have heard nothing of the French or their manoeuvres in Persia, but doubtless they gain strength daily. We shall I fear too certainly have a grand struggle, for their daring disposition is indisputable. But with so strong a frontier as we possess it will be a tough business and we shall have large armies and large supplies of men and money from home.' [166] He also wrote to his father: 'I consider the present superiority of Russia and their ascendancy over Persia in power and arms as dangerous to Indian interests and prejudicial to our superiority and power.' [167]

On 6 March 1809, Edmonstone sent Elphinstone new instructions severely limiting the terms of any treaty which might be made with Shah Shuja. The Spanish uprising against the French had made a French invasion of India seem highly unlikely, and a defensive alliance with Afghanistan was therefore unnecessary.[168] A treaty of perpetual friendship was however concluded in three simple clauses, and ratified on 17 June 1809. On 3 April 1809, William Fraser noted in his journal: 'Our treaty is I believe signed by the King and if the French are beaten at home and driven out of Persia we shall return I think immediately. If the French still remain in Persia and are also able to hold up their heads at home in spite of Spain, Germany and Russia, we cannot lay aside alarm nor can this embassy be withdrawn.' [169]

On 7 May 1809 he wrote that the King's army in Kashmir had been destroyed; many had joined the rebels and the remainder could not be trusted.[170] His entry for 21 May 1809 records that Kabul having been seized by the rebels 'the Embassy think of retiring to Attock as a place of security and to avoid suspicion of favouring either party'. He added: 'We have already obtained all that is at present necessary, and Government will probably await further intelligence from home before proceeding to carry on its plans of defence against French intrigue and influence at this Court.' [171] On 18 June 1809 William Fraser wrote to Seton from Attock 'you cannot think how tired all but Strachey and Elphinstone are of this country and life'.[172] However, on 26 June 1809, Elphinstone received orders to withdraw, marching via Rawalpindi through the Punjab towards Lahore.[173]

William Fraser found Afghanistan a 'miserable, uninteresting place' of 'hot, barren sameness'.[174] He noted in his journal on 3 April 1809: 'It would be very unpleasant to be left here almost at the mercy of the surrounding country.'[175] Uninformed of Elphinstone's plans or of the mission's progress, he had little to occupy his active mind other than to study the countryside and its people and to write his journal and long letters home. He wrote on 12 April 1809 to his father: 'Had I not to write to you and carry on my journal I do not know how I might manage time.'[176] However, the fact that Shah Shuja, to whom he was presented on 6 March 1809, forbade communication with the inhabitants of Afghanistan, did not deter him. Indeed it was from Peshawar that William had written to his brother Alexander a long letter dated 6 February 1809 strongly recommending, *inter alia*, 'a personal intercourse with natives of all denominations to acquire idioms, dialect, manner, local knowledge, religion, internal arrangements, ancient hereditary habits and distinguishing characteristics'.[177] Following talks with a village schoolmaster, William wrote to Alexander on 12 April 1809 about the local hillmen: '[They] are very like the people of the highlands in personal customs but not in the laws of the community or feudal dependence; besides that they have the advantages of a written language and able teachers – yet the hospitality, kindness, openness and wild bravery with devoted fondness to their country and native place they are like our countrymen.'[178]

In his journal for 25 January 1809, William Fraser had written: 'There are great preparations in our part of northern Hindoostan in consequence of an expected war with the Seiks.'[179] By 16 July 1809 he noted that 'The Seiks have been extremely civil and kind, naturally enough jealous but covering that feeling with cordial expressions of the usual hospitality. Ranjeet [Ranjit Singh, Raja of Lahore] has been very civil and sent men to conduct us by the best and quickest way; at least so they say.'[180] In fact Ranjit Singh, who did not share British fears of a French invasion, and had his own ambitions for Kashmir, was suspicious of British intentions in Afghanistan. His ambassadors kept an eye on events in Peshawar and Attock.[181] William Fraser made light of 'a small skirmish' west of the Jhelum river, in which a soldier of the Kabul mission's escort was killed and an officer wounded. He thought the Sikhs were civil but 'semi–independent'.[182] The mission otherwise passed safely through the Punjab, arriving at Ludhiana on 19 August 1809 where William Fraser would have met Ochterlony before moving on. On 14 March 1810 the Governor-General ordered the Kabul mission to be wound up and responsibility for relations with Afghanistan returned to the Resident at Delhi. Shuja's army was finally routed at Peshawar on 12 September 1810, whereupon he fled to join his family at Ludhiana under British protection. Elphinstone's report, based largely on Afghan informants, was published in 1815.[183] William Fraser made his own report when he returned to Delhi. Alexander Fraser noted from this, on 11 September 1809, that in William's view 'the Cabul mission was indeed frustrated of almost all its objects . . . by events which could not be foreseen' and that 'the journey of the British envoy has been however, far from destitute of interest'. 'The survey of country has been extensive and may eventually be most useful – wars are highly probable on our north-western frontier.'[184] On this prospect Ochterlony would have agreed. He would also have agreed with William Fraser that 'It is our military force alone which keeps them [the warlike people of upper Hindustan] in subjection and that subjection and that force is kept up by making the profession of a soldier the most happy and profitable a native can pursue.'[185] It was Ochterlony's letter of 15 August 1809 which assured William Fraser 'your name still stands on the strength of the Delhi Residency'.[186]

The Governor-General regarded the Kabul mission as of more diplomatic importance than the mission to Lahore.[187] Elphinstone and the Commander-in-Chief did not agree with Minto. They regarded the Punjab as a more natural and defensible frontier.[188] Charles Theophilus Metcalfe, son of a director of the East India Company, had, since his arrival in India in January 1801, been groomed for responsibility.[189] In sequence, he had been appointed Assistant to the Chief Secretary to the Government, Assistant to the Governor-General in Wellesley's private office, then attached to Lake, the Commander-in-Chief, before becoming First Assistant to the Resident at Delhi on 15 August 1806. Having already met and befriended Ochterlony, he now became acquainted with William Fraser. Like them he had experience of the North-West Quarter. In 1805 Metcalfe wrote a 'Memoir of Hindoostan West of the Jumna' [190] in which he observed: 'The Sikhs can scarcely be considered as one nation since they have no bond of association among themselves. They are well mounted and armed with matchlocks and are continually involved in dissenting with one another. Runjeet Singh of Lahore appears of late to have acquired a considerable ascendancy among them. When Lord Lake pursued Holkar into the Punjab, alliances were concluded with many of the Chiefs but no more intimate connection has yet been formed between them and our Government.' [191]

Writing to Edmonstone in June 1809, Metcalfe pointed out that since the beginning of 1806 Ranjit Singh's power had 'increased in an extraordinary manner' and that he had 'tasted the sweets of Empire beyond [south of] the Sutlej'. [192] His freedom to do so rested on the Treaty of 1806, article 2 of which assured him of British neutrality so long as he did not consort with the enemies of Britain. [193] His expeditions into Malwa were ignored by the British as none of their business, and any British misgivings about his first crossing of the Sutlej to plunder Nakodar were allayed. [194] His second crossing of the Sutlej, in 1807, brought him more booty which he distributed among the Sikh chiefs in return for their acceptance of his suzerainty. With virtual supremacy over Malwa and Sirhind, Ranjit Singh dominated many of the Sikh chiefs of the Cis-Sutlej lowland area. In March 1808 Sikh chiefs who went to meet Seton in Delhi seeking British protection were refused on the grounds that the British had no quarrel with Ranjit Singh. [195] Metcalfe's objectives for his mission to Lahore specified the avoidance of discussion of the future of the Cis-Sutlej Sikhs, save where this would ensure Ranjit Singh's co-operation against an imminent French attack. [196]

Metcalfe left Delhi on 28 July 1808 and met a highly suspicious Ranjit Singh on 12 September 1808 at Kasur in the Punjab (see map 1). He soon found that 'the habits and dispositions of the Raja [of Lahore] and his government were entirely military and his views exclusively those of conquest and inordinate ambition'. [197] Ranjit Singh was apprehensive about the real intentions of the British missions to Lahore and Kabul. He wanted no part in a defensive alliance which might thwart his plans to annex Kashmir and extend his territory beyond the Indus. He feared disaffection among the chiefs he had subjugated, and saw the British as an obstacle to the further spread of his influence in the Jumna-Sutlej Doab [198] in the cause of which he was about to

2. Charles Theophilus Metcalfe by George Chinnery.

launch a third trans-Sutlej expedition. Having promised Metcalfe, on 25 September 1808, that he would conclude an agreement next day, he broke camp instead and, to Metcalfe's consternation, crossed the Sutlej and enforced his authority over all the Cis-Sutlej chiefs except Patiala, Thanesar and Kunjpara. The Governor-General in Council decided that the proximity of the Raja of Lahore's 'military dominion' to the Company was 'an imminent hazard to tranquility and eventually even the security of the British possessions'.[199] Metcalfe was therefore instructed, on 31 October 1808, 'to extend British protection to the chiefs on the South of the Sutlej, to require the Raja to withdraw his army to the other side of that river, and to establish a military post near the frontier of the Punjaub'.[200] Metcalfe pursued Ranjit Singh tenaciously to deliver the Governor-General's demands. This and the threat of British forces on the Sutlej so alarmed Ranjit Singh that he asked for a treaty.

Ochterlony was swiftly summoned from Allahabad to lead a military detachment to the Sutlej. The fulsome wording of Edmonstone's letter of 14 November 1808 informing Ochterlony of the Governor-General's decision to appoint him to duties 'of a delicate and important character requiring a combination of the talents of the military profession with political qualities, local knowledge and experience'[201] must have pleased Ochterlony immensely. So, too, must the generous financial arrangements set out in a separate letter.[202] The main objects of Ochterlony's assignment were broadly as follows: to collaborate with Metcalfe until his mission left Ranjit Singh's territory; to watch Ranjit Singh and acquire intelligence on the nature of his military resources, and on the temper and disposition, character, condition and military strengths of the Cis-Sutlej chiefs with a view to possible co-operation on military operations to protect them; and to submit regular reports, via the Resident at Delhi, to the Governor-General and the Commander-in-Chief.[203] Having received guidance and instructions on military and political aspects of his duties from the Commander-in-Chief and Seton respectively, Ochterlony set out from Delhi on 27 January 1809, followed by a strong force under Major-General St Leger.

The delicacy of his assignment and the awkward dichotomy of his responsibilities soon caused him anguish. While en route for

Ludhiana, where he arrived on 18 February 1809, his decision to halt his detachment for five days at the request of Ranjit Singh while a headstrong Sikh commander and his army were persuaded to recross the Sutlej[204] brought a charge of insubordination from the Commander-in-Chief and a recommendation that Ochterlony be sent back to Allahabad.[205] The case against Ochterlony was that 'he had failed to take severe disciplinary action against Sikhs insulting British troops'.[206] The occasion, disclosed in Ochterlony's letter of resignation from his new command, was the firing upon British troops unwisely encamped 'under the walls of a fort garrisoned by troops of a prince [Ranjit Singh] with whom the British are seeking amity . . . firing by a few irregulars not worthy of strong reprisals'.[207] Edmonstone handled a difficult predicament with considerable skill, strongly supported by Metcalfe who wrote from Amritsar on 14 April 1809 to defend his friend Ochterlony. Metcalfe assured Edmonstone that the danger of war 'with likely harrassments in Cis-Sutlej country' had been avoided by Ochterlony's action. He added: 'I think it probable that Colonel Ochterlony was in some degree influenced in his conduct by the tenor of the communications which he had had from me during his advance from Putteeala.'[208] The matter was closed with the Commander-in-Chief supporting Ochterlony's retention of his command at Ludhiana.[209] In the meantime Ochterlony had issued a Proclamation to the Cis-Sutlej Sikh chiefs on 9 February 1809 informing them that they had been brought under the protection of the British. And, in March 1809, Metcalfe had been authorised to negotiate a treaty of friendship with Ranjit Singh.

Ochterlony's report, dated 11 March 1809, on the co-operation and resources of the Cis-Sutlej hill chiefs contained a statement of Ranjit Singh's conquests and of the estimated revenue and military establishments of the chiefs between the Sutlej and the Jumna.[210] Ochterlony believed that the British could count on not less than 5,000 irregular cavalry but that a confederacy of chiefs could only be relied on under certain conditions. Ochterlony also considered it necessary to maintain large forces in Meerut and 'to increase the force at the army base in Kurnaul for movement as necessary against hostile advances anywhere in the East and West Hills – or the Punjab'.[211] In his reply (copied to the Commander-in-Chief and the Resident at Delhi), Edmonstone agreed to the promulgation of a Declaration of British Protection to the Cis-Sutlej Sikh chiefs on the basis of a bond of common interest. Ochterlony was authorised to convey the Declaration to the chiefs 'in such mode as you may judge proper' assuring them of permanent protection from Ranjit Singh, exemption from all pecuniary tribute, and the continuation of rights hitherto enjoyed within the limits of their own possessions. In return they were to afford every facility to British troops and to give zealous co-operation in the event of invasion. On the matter of military forces Edmonstone made no comment save that 'The Governor-General wishes it to be known that the advanced post at Ludhiana is not permanent.'[212]

A treaty between the British and the Raja of Lahore was concluded at Amritsar on 25 April 1809 and ratified by the Governor-General in Council on 25 October 1809.[213] Its terms were contained in three articles, the first two of which read as follows:

> 1. Perpetual friendship shall subsist between the British Government and the State of Lahore, the latter shall be considered with respect to the former to be on the footing of the most favoured powers; and the British Government will have no concern with the Territories and subjects of the Raja to the northward of the river Sutluj.
>
> 2. The Raja will never maintain in the territory occupied by him and his dependants on the left bank of the river Sutluj more troops than are necessary for the internal duties of that territory nor commit or suffer any encroachments on the possession or rights of the Chiefs in its vicinity.

The Governor-General evidently made clear that the assertion of supremacy over Sikh chiefs in the Cis-Sutlej hills 'may justifiably be considered a defensive measure and must not be construed into a lust of conquest or of dominion'.[214] Ochterlony was authorised to issue a further Proclamation to the Cis-Sutlej Sikh chiefs on 3 May 1809. This called on them to co-operate with the British in matters of defence and to admit British troops to the area. Another Proclamation of 22 August 1809 gave the British the right to intervene to prevent disputes between chiefs.[215] Ochterlony held firm views about the need to shield them from the disastrous results of 'their own base passions, their universal rapacity and their internal discord'.[216] He also considered it strategically vital to retain Ludhiana as a strong defensive fort as well as a listening post on the Company's north-west frontier. Minto, however, was prepared to retain it only until the Kabul mission had returned.[217] Metcalfe, who agreed with Ochterlony that a certain amount of control over the Sikh chiefs was needed, took up Ochterlony's cause in a letter to Edmonstone: 'The post at Ludhiana cannot be withdrawn without injury.' He pointed out that withdrawal from Ludhiana fort, which lay across the Sutlej from the Sikh fort of Phillaur would suggest to Ranjit Singh a change of plan, and might reawaken his ambition to take the Doab by intrigue if not by direct intervention.[218] Metcalfe went further: 'It is proper to consider the question of retaining or relinquishing the fort at Ludhiana with reference to the possibility of eventual war with Ranjit Singh,'[219] and he added that it was convenient and economical to unite the functions of 'a political advance post' with a military fort to cope with matters not so easily controlled from Delhi.[220] The Ludhiana post was not only retained but upgraded to a Political Agency in 1810 subordinate to the Resident at Delhi. Ochterlony was therefore appointed Agent to the Governor-General as well as military commander at Ludhiana. The Treaty of 1809 put an end to Ranjit Singh's ambition to expand his dominion across the Sutlej. It also secured the Cis-Sutlej chiefs under British protection, and obliged the British to turn their attention to the Nepalese.

The siege of Kangra fortress, begun by the Nepalese Army in 1806,[221] continued for three full years. During this time Raja Sansar Chand and his large garrison survived under great privation, while Kaji Amar Singh Thapa and his Nepalese troops suffered no less through lack of provisions, the ravages of disease, and the constant need to send troops back across the Sutlej to quell disturbances in the newly acquired but unsubjugated territories. Hill chieftains, released from Sansar Chand's oppression, plundered and laid waste the fertile valleys of Kangra until 'not a blade of cultivation was to be seen;

grass grew up in towns, and tigresses whelped in the streets of Nadaun'.[222] In all this time the only reinforcements to make the difficult 500 mile journey from Nepal arrived under the command of Nayan Singh Thapa, Bhim Sen Thapa's brother. This enabled Kaji Amar Singh Thapa to send his ablest and bravest commander, Bhakti Thapa, with 2,500 men to establish Nepalese control in Hindur and in the Bara Thakuri hill states[223] which had banded together and fought fiercely in a concerted effort to retain their territories.[224] Bhakti Thapa reopened supply lines which had been threatened by the sporadic attacks made by Ram Saran, Raja of Hindur, from his stronghold in Palasi. In addition to the fourteen regular companies of the Nepalese Army which fought in the Kangra campaign,[225] there were irregular levies of 'militia' raised largely from Kumaonis and not incorporated with the regular companies.[226]

In 1808, when Sansar Chand's situation in Kangra seemed desperate, Nayan Singh Thapa insisted that the fortress could be taken by frontal assault. His determined attack failed and Nayan Singh Thapa was killed. However, the prospect of a further, and perhaps successful, attack caused Sansar Chand to turn to Ranjit Singh for help rather than accept Kaji Amar Singh Thapa's offer of a compromise by partitioning the Kangra hills and Kashmir between them.[227] Escaping from Kangra fortress by a subterfuge, Sansar Chand entered into a treaty with Ranjit Singh, a move which brought the Sikh Army to Kangra in July 1809 and caused those Cis-Sutlej chieftains who had been supplying the Nepalese Army to switch their allegiance to Ranjit Singh. Cut off from provisions, the Nepalese position was doomed to fail. The ensuing battle forced Kaji Amar Singh Thapa reluctantly to withdraw across the Sutlej having undertaken never to cross the river again.[228] Kaji Amar Singh Thapa's account of what happened is contained in a long letter to Ochterlony received on 15 December 1809.[229] It began: 'Formerly I had written to you two or three letters respecting Kangra; it is probable they were duly received For these fifty years past, friendship has been established between the Company and the deceased Raja Parthi Narain [Prithvi Narayan] Shah Shumsher Jung, and has continued to this day.' The Kaji's explanation of his failure to take Kangra rested on two errors of judgement: his neglect to settle the Cis-Sutlej hill states before crossing the Sutlej; and his decision to allow Sansar Chand to leave the fortress with his family and treasure before the Nepalese Army had occupied it.

Ochterlony forwarded Kaji Amar Singh Thapa's letter to Delhi on 16 December 1809, and in his covering letter wrote: 'The object of the whole is clearly to induce us to advance in cooperation with his design on Kot Kangra.' Ochterlony added: 'I have replied that a Treaty has taken place between the British and the Rajah of Lahore and a 50-years acquaintance with us should convince him it will not be violated on our part.' [230] The 'design on Kot Kangra' was evident from the translation of Kaji Amar Singh Thapa's own words: 'Lately a letter has arrived from the Maharajah [of Nepal] informing me that he has sent troops to my assistance and it is my intention on the arrival of these forces and the reduction of these forts to proceed to Kangra, because leaving this country unsettled in my rear on the former occasion has caused all this trouble.' [231]

The 'reduction of these forts' in the Cis-Sutlej hill states brought the Nepalese Army into close proximity with the British. Moving south, Kaji Amar Singh Thapa occupied and strengthened forts on successive hill ranges, establishing his headquarters at Arki and a depth of defensive positions in Hindur and Sirmur from which to manoeuvre against the British should this become necessary. In so doing he followed the strategy advocated by Prithvi Narayan Shah.[232] Kennedy records that in 1810 Sirmur fell to the Nepalese without a fight, followed by Jubal, Pundur and Bashahr.[233] Hindur also fell with the notable exception of the fortress of Palasi which was close to Ochterlony's forces in Ludhiana. Evidence of the intention 'to proceed to Kangra' is given in a letter from Ranjit Singh received by Ochterlony on 2 September 1811. This reported that Kaji Amar Singh Thapa, having taken Bashahr had begun collecting boats preparatory to crossing into Ranjit Singh's territories of Kulu and Mandi.[234] However the crossing did not take place and Nepalese ambitions of further expansion to the west came to an end. Attention became focused instead on the borders between British territories and the Cis-Sutlej Sikh protectorates and Greater Nepal. With the Nepalese Army so close to the Cis-Sutlej Sikh protectorates, Ochterlony had informed Kaji Amar Singh Thapa in

April 1810 of a 'principle of limitation' which had been adopted by the Governor-General in Council. Under this principle, the British would not interfere in 'the proceedings of Nipaul in the hills' and 'the Nepalese authority should on no account be extended below the hills'.[235] This was hardly likely to appeal to the Kaji or to the Nepalese Government which depended on the lowlands and the Terai for essential materials and supplies for its army. Moreover so broad a definition offered great scope for claims and counterclaims and the grave risk of misunderstandings. A dispute over a Nepalese claim to the Butwal zamindari of Palpa, which had arisen in 1806,[236] led to British complaints about Nepalese occupation of Butwal in 1808.[237] Further problems about lands in Morang (1809)[238] and Bhim Nagar (1810)[239] brought a state of tension between the British and Nepalese along the southern border of Nepal. This was relieved but not entirely dispelled by a directive from the King of Nepal to his zamindars in 1812 to give up the disputed lands.[240]

In the meantime, Bhim Sen Thapa was appointed Commander-in-Chief with the rank of general in 1811, despite the fact that he had had no experience of high military command.[241] Bhim Sen Thapa was not, by nature, a leader of men in the manner of Prithvi Narayan Shah, but an administrator and a skilful politician. As an administrator he set up barracks and cantonments, and arsenals and magazines for manufacturing and storing arms and ammunition, in the Kathmandu valley and in Palpa and other strategic locations in Nepal.[242] As a politician he was shrewd enough to consult widely to ensure that he had strong support before he made important decisions.[243]

Despite the treaty of friendship with Ranjit Singh, Ochterlony, Metcalfe and Fraser had no illusions about the Sikh leader's inordinate ambitions to extend his dominion. All foresaw the possibility of war in the Punjab. Ochterlony gave his opinion that 'Ranjit's ambition is as unbounded as his rapacity.'[244] Metcalfe was convinced that it was vital for the British to retain a stronghold and 'listening post' on the Sutlej at Ludhiana. Fraser, who regarded war as 'highly probable on our north-western frontier', evidently thought that the British might be drawn into conflict further west, and that the extensive survey of

Afghanistan made by Elphinstone's mission might eventually be useful. As Political Agent to the Governor-General, Ochterlony no doubt pondered the implications of British protection for the deposed ruler of Afghanistan and his family at Ludhiana. However, based there as military commander of British forces in the far north-west, Ochterlony had more immediate problems to contend with: how to cope with the particular problems of mountain warfare; how to sustain an aura of British invincibility; and how to obtain intelligence about Sikh and Nepalese armies.

In February 1812 Ochterlony had the good fortune to be invited by Ranjit Singh to attend his son's wedding in Amritsar and to visit Lahore. This gave him opportunities to inspect the fortifications of Lahore and to watch some of Ranjit Singh's troops at exercise. He would have been aware of Ranjit Singh's keen interest in modelling his army on British lines, developing battalions of disciplined infantry under the training and leadership of European officers. Ochterlony may have seen and been impressed by some of the 'Gurkha' hillmen enlisted by Ranjit Singh after the battle of Kangra in 1809.[245] In 1810 Ochterlony, who anticipated the need forcibly to remove Kaji Amar Singh Thapa's troops from the lowland villages they had occupied, had described the 'Gorkhas' (of the Nepalese Army) as 'a body of ill-armed and undisciplined barbarians who affect a wretched imita-tion of the dress, accoutrements and constitution of a British native battalion and who might have been successfully resisted in such country [the plains of Sirhind] by less than a third of their numbers'.[246] This judgement owed more to their being poorly armed than to any knowledge of their fighting qualities, especially in the high hills. As Ochterlony had not yet met with Gorkhas he may have relied on descriptions given by Kinloch, Kirkpatrick and Hamilton[247] about their appearance and discipline. It is possible that news reached him of the brush which William Moorcroft and Haider Hearsey had in 1812 with the Nepalese authorities in Garhwal and Kumaon on their return from an illicit visit to Tibet.[248] Hearsey, of whom more will be written in later chapters, was a half-caste mercenary officer who had served with several Indian princes before 1804, and had subsequently engaged in far-ranging adventures in the Himalayan foothills. Ochterlony would certainly have been interested in the entry for 2 October 1812 in Moorcroft's diary: 'It is worthy of note that two thirds of the troops of Bhacti Thappa [*sic*] consisted of the natives of the subjugated countries.'[249]

While Ochterlony was thus employed from Ludhiana, William Fraser was ranging far and wide from Delhi 'reducing to order and obedience certain of our territory on this [west] side of the Jumna long notorious for the rebellious, refractory and plundering disposition of its inhabitants'.[250] These excursions, took him, accompanied by a military escort, into Gujur, Mewat and Bhutnere. The 'fine moving life' appealed to his adventurous spirit but did not satisfy his ambitions. Seton, who by now had Alexander Fraser as his Fourth Assistant at Delhi, foresaw that William Fraser would become his First Assistant when Charles Metcalfe became Resident at the Court of Daulat Rao Sindhia.[251] Seton had not, however, anticipated that Metcalfe would return to Delhi to succeed him as Resident on 25 February 1811. The loss of Seton, who looked upon William Fraser as 'one of the dearest friends I have on earth',[252] and the appointment of Metcalfe, who had only one year longer service than himself, was a double blow to William. However, he received advice from Seton: 'I think you will act perfectly right in not attaching yourself too exclusively to Delhi as to preclude your accepting another eligible appointment.'[253]

Like Ochterlony, William Fraser was destined to turn his attention to the Cis-Sutlej Sikh states and to the northern hills beyond. Alexander Fraser noted in his diary for 23 December 1810: 'The countries to the north and west of our territories are in possession of a number of petty Seikh Chieftains. The internal government of their territory we leave to themselves, but their political motions are under our control.'[254] When one of these chiefs seized the territory of another, William Fraser was sent with a detachment of troops to settle the affair with a show of force. It was while in the Sikh country that William Fraser made a visit 'to the hills from which the Jumna issues, staying with the [Garhwali] highlanders several days'.[255] There can be little doubt that with his powers of observation and skills as a linguist, he gathered useful intelligence as well as a first-hand acquaintance with the difficulties of the terrain.

Two inter-related factors brought the Cis-Sutlej territories into contention. The first of these was the trans-Sutlej incursions of Ranjit Singh, the Sikh Raja of Lahore, the rising power in the Punjab. The Governor-General, Lord Minto, anxious to contain Ranjit Singh's dominion to the Sutlej, authorised the issue of proclamations taking the lowland Sikh states in the Jumna-Sutlej Doab under British protection. This action was reinforced by a Treaty of Perpetual Friendship between Ranjit Singh and the British in 1809, and by the establishment of a strong defensive position and listening post at Ludhiana. The second factor was the trans-Sutlej withdrawal of Kaji Amar Singh Thapa and his Nepalese forces, following his defeat by Ranjit Singh's army in 1809 at Kangra. The Kaji's subsequent campaign to subjugate the thirty hill states in the Cis-Sutlej region, brought the Nepalese Army up to the northern borders of lowland states protected by the British. Ochterlony and William Fraser became closely involved. Ochterlony, recalled from his command at Allahabad in 1808, was appointed military commander at Ludhiana. In 1810 Ludhiana was made a Political Agency (subordinate to the Resident at Delhi). Ochterlony therefore became Agent to the Governor-General with political responsibilities, as well as military commander, at Ludhiana. While still watching Ranjit Singh from across the Sutlej he was now directly concerned with Kaji Amar Singh Thapa and the Nepalese Army. William Fraser, having returned to Delhi via the Punjab, from a mission to Kabul with Mountstuart Elphinstone in 1808–9, spent much of his time resolving disputes and establishing order in the lowland Cis-Sutlej protectorates. In 1810 he ventured into the hill country of Garhwal. His interest, like Ochterlony's, was turning to Nepalese-held territory in the North-West Quarter, and he and Ochterlony were still in communication.

Border incidents along the southern border of Nepalese territory had occurred sporadically since 1806 and had led to a general state of tension by 1810. This caused the Governor-General in Council to introduce a 'principle of limitation' of which Ochterlony informed Kaji Amar Singh Thapa in April 1810. This principle was broadly that the British would not interfere in the Cis-Sutlej hills if the Nepalese did not intrude in the lowlands. The lack of precise border delineation led, inevitably, to further incidents which, in turn, led to a hardening of attitudes. By 1813 discussion of the 'principle of limitation' and the means of resolving border disputes became of critical importance, for there was a growing prospect of war between Britain and Nepal.

Part II

The war with Nepal

CHAPTER 4

The onset of war, 1813–14

The North-West Quarter continued to attract attention. The Commander-in-Chief, Sir George Nugent, made a tour of the area with Lady Nugent from 19 December 1812 to 24 February 1813, in the course of which they met William Fraser, David Ochterlony, Edward Gardner, and Charles Metcalfe. Fraser and Gardner accompanied them for several days after their stay at the Residency in Delhi. Lady Nugent, who was shocked to find that they had beards and refused to eat beef or pork, reproved them for being 'as much Hindoo as Christian'.[256] The Nugents met Ochterlony in the military base at Karnal, 'a comfortable town transformed from a wild place'.[257] Having moved on to Hardwar, they crossed into 'Nepaul country just to say we had been there'. Lady Nugent wrote that 'the race of people who inhabit Nepaul are called Goorkahs' and added 'we saw some of them at a distance'.[258] Charles Metcalfe, 'an excellent man and exceedingly pleasant', arrived from Delhi to meet them in Meerut on 28 January 1813.[259] Writing early in 1813, Charles Metcalfe still had misgivings about Ranjit Singh's long-term intentions: 'The transfer of sovereignty of Cashmere to Ranjit Singh would be a revolution full of interesting consequences whether we consider the fact of the transfer from the Affghanns to the Seiks or the personal character of the individual into whose hands it would fall, his actual power, his extraordinary rise, his ambition and the use he would make of such an acquisition.'[260]

Ochterlony also was concerned about Ranjit Singh's twenty-five battalions of infantry 'disciplined in our manner. With these and his irregular host of cavalry he doubtless meditates further conquests; but his more immediate object at present is the attainment of Mooltaun.'[261] Both Metcalfe and Ochterlony suspected that the Raja of

3. Francis Rawdon-Hastings, 1st Marquess of Hastings
– by Thomas Mitchell

Lahore, having established himself in Kangra and the Himalayan foothills north of the Sutlej, might turn covetous eyes across the river to the hill country occupied by the Nepalese. These lingering misgivings about Ranjit Singh's ultimate intentions probably had a bearing on the eventual decision to recruit hillmen for the local defence of the Cis-Sutlej hills. Metcalfe and Ochterlony believed that holding a line on the Sutlej was strategically imperative. However, their meetings with Nugent were inconsequential. As Lady Nugent recorded in her journal for 26 May 1813, Lord Moira [Hastings] was coming as Governor-General and there was 'much conjecture about the future'. Hastings held the rank of general in the British Army and, as Lord Rawden, had a distinguished military record in the American War of Independence and in the Revolutionary War in the Low Countries. His appointment to the dual role of Governor-General and Commander-in-Chief was a shock to Nugent and entailed some embarrassment for Hastings who had expected the Nugents to leave for the United Kingdom forthwith. The awkwardness was eventually resolved without undue loss of face for Sir George, whom Hastings invested as KCB, and to whom he gave the specially created post of Commander of the Forces in Bengal.[262] The Nugents finally left for England on 31 December 1814.

In making an appreciation of the major problems he had inherited from Minto, Hastings found that no fewer than seven – including the whole question of border problems with Nepal – seemed to call for a military solution either by intervention or by the threat of intervention.[263] He therefore had no wish to add to his problems by risking offence to Ranjit Singh, for example by offering asylum to Shah Shuja of Kabul.[264] On 1 February 1814 Hastings recorded in his diary: 'In short I see around me the elements of a war more general than any which we have hitherto encountered in India.' [265] Five days later he summarised his general policy as follows: 'Our object ought to be to render the British Government paramount in effect, if not declaredly so. We should hold the other states as vassals, in substance though not in name; not precisely as they stood in the Mogul Government but possessed of perfect internal sovereignty.' [266]

In return for a guarantee of protection, the states would pledge themselves to 'two great feudal duties' (viz. the local supply of troops and general support in time of war); and to 'submit their mutual differences to the head of the confederacy [the British Government], without attacking each other's territories'.[267] Hastings' scheme was not accepted by his Council. With Seton's support, Edmonstone, the senior member of the Council, opposed it vehemently as being totally impractical.[268] In face of this rebuff Hastings turned to Charles Metcalfe whose political outlook, as he was aware from seeing private correspondence between Metcalfe and Adam, closely resembled his own.[269] Hastings was aware that the greatest threats to British paramountcy lay with the Maratha confederacy and with the predations of Pindari hordes who roamed and ravaged the vast breadth of central India. Their subjugation would require massive military operations on a broad front, thereby leaving open to attack the north-western territories held or protected by the British. Not only might the Nepalese decide to move south, but Ranjit Singh might be tempted to cross the Sutlej with his Sikh army while the British were heavily engaged elsewhere. Hastings did not share the 'unqualified homage to the good faith of Runjeet Sing' paid by Edmonstone, who considered that 'nothing could be farther from his [Ranjit Singh's] thoughts than any injurious purpose towards us in his preparing a force on our frontier'. Hastings firmly believed that 'in cases of this nature where error is ruinous, one is bound to form one's deduction from appearances and facts not resting on illusory protestations'.[270] Indeed, Hastings foresaw potential war with the Sikhs: 'I think we ought to take every means of strengthening ourselves at home against the future possible occurrence of hostilities with Ranjit Singh.'[271]

It seems, therefore, in tackling the complexity of the problems which confronted him, Hastings' primary aim was to secure the Company's north-west frontier. To this end, the reliance which Hastings came to place on Metcalfe's advice was to focus his immediate attention on dealing with the Nepalese. It also furthered his respect for Ochterlony.

The continuation of border disputes with the Nepalese is hardly surprising. As Stiller points out, the Western concept of 'boundary lines' was alien to Nepalese thinking and experience. For the Nepalese the control of villages was through military might. Borders were 'rivers, ridges, mountain ranges, and the extent of one's military control'.[272] Moreover as there were no means of identifying boundaries, it was far from easy to determine the extent of possible encroachments. It was also open to unscrupulous zamindars in Company territory to make complaints which had no foundation. As a result magistrates' courts were overwhelmed by a vast accumulation of claims. With two exceptions, it is not necessary to enter into the complexities of individual border disputes.[273] It is however necessary to say something more about the 'principle of limitation' to which reference was made in chapter 3.[274] This British concept of claiming the lowlands, while recognising Nepalese claims to the hills and mountains, paid no heed to the fact that certain of the border hill states annexed by Nepal such as Hindur and Sirmur owned, or claimed to own, lowland territory. As by proclamation in 1809[275] the lowlands had been given British protection, claims were made against the Nepalese Government for encroachment. Not unnaturally the Nepalese regarded their acquisition of Hindur and Sirmur as conveying comprehensive ownership of all the associated land. The occupation in 1813 by Kaji Amar Singh Thapa's troops of four lowland villages formerly belonging to Raja Ram Saran of Hindur (who had been deposed by the Nepalese) brought a protest from the Governor-General informing the King of Nepal that Colonel Ochterlony had been instructed 'after ascertaining that the four villages are, as there is no reason to doubt, situated below the hills, to take the necessary measures for defending them against any attempt to dispossess the proprietor Raja Ram Sing [*sic*]'. The Governor-General added: 'I have communicated these particulars in the firm expectation that you will issue positive orders to Amer Sing Thappa [*sic*], to desist from his attempt on those villages, and to abstain carefully in future from any interference in the countries below the hills.'[276] In his reply the King of Nepal pointed out: 'As the Honourable Company have by the grace of God established their dominion in Hindoostan by the power of the sword, so have I by the same means acquired the possession of the hills together with the lowlands dependent on the territories of former Rajahs, some of whom tamely submitted to my authority, while others were expelled for their conduct.'

While laying claim to the prior possession of the villages (since 1805) the King, 'in consideration of friendship', issued orders to Kaji Amar Singh Thapa to desist from any attempts upon the villages 'in case the villages in question should appear to have been previously held by the Honourable Company'. He was evidently following the precepts of the first Gorkha King, Prithvi Narayan Shah, in avoiding war with the British on the plains.[277] However, the underlying problem remained, for the British and Nepalese positions were irreconcilable. On the one hand the Nepalese firmly believed that the British should yield wherever the Nepalese had first claim on lowlands as the result of their conquest of a hill raja. On the other, the British were intent on denying them access.

Ochterlony had no doubt that the immediate threat to British interests was from the Nepalese Army of Kaji Amar Singh Thapa which now occupied the Cis-Sutlej hills. In July 1813 he proposed that military operations with light field guns were necessary 'to convince Ummer Sing that his hills are not to us inaccessible or his forts impregnable'. By means of road-making, perseverance and exertion, a march on Nalagarh could be made as a punishment for the seizure of the four Hinduri villages by the Nepalese. Ochterlony also observed that a detachment from Karnal could occupy the Kayarda valley to divide forces and take Nahan which 'itself has no other strengths than the difficulty of approach'. This manoeuvre would cut off supplies to Amar Singh Thapa's army. In this respect Ochterlony had asked Captain William Richards in the summer of 1813 to give him full details of his visit (which had the Kaji's permission) into the Kayarda valley ostensibly to obtain timber.[278] However, as yet the Government had no intentions of entering upon extended operations against the Nepalese. On the contrary it wished to maintain friendship with the Nepalese Government through negotiation, while defending its subjects by expelling those who encroached.[279]

It was perhaps in the spirit of this policy that Ochterlony wrote to Adam on 28 October 1813 that as the four Hinduri villages occupied by the Nepalese had been restored to Raja Ram Saran and the Nepalese

seemed anxious not to offend the British, he would comply with Kaji
Amar Singh Thapa's wish for a meeting with him. Ochterlony proposed to take the opportunity to 'skirt along the hills, or as near as
the roads will admit, not only for the purpose of acquiring more
accurate knowledge of the country but to see the villages of Moondlai
and Berowly which are yet occupied by troops from Putteealah, and
thence to Boorial to settle disputes between two brothers'.[280] Ochterlony reported to Adam on 18 December 1813 that, travelling via Rupar,
Palasi and the Punjur valley, he had met Kaji Amar Singh Thapa at
Kalka about a mile from Tucksal fort on 10 December 1813.[281] The
meeting had seemed amicable in that the Kaji had requested that
Ochterlony's son (Roderick Peregrine Ochterlony, who had accompanied him as his Persian interpreter) should exchange 'turbands'
with Kaji Amar Singh Thapa's second son as a token of friendship.
Ochterlony pointed out that his son was not a military man and did
not wear a turban. Instead he presented a 'khillut' (robe of honour)
with turban. Also at the Kaji's request, Ochterlony met Bhakti Thapa
at Punjur on the following day. He noted that the Kaji's finest field
commander was 'attended by a most curious rabble called
troops'.[282] The two incidents had deeper significance. Bhakti Thapa
took the opportunity to explain Ranjit Singh's deception at Kangra
and to seek Ochterlony's advice on a second attack on Kangra fortress
in order to retrieve the credit Kaji Amar Singh Thapa had lost. The
Kaji was convinced that the British intended to take the Punjab and
would therefore ally themselves with the Nepalese. However, Ochterlony made it clear through Bhakti Thapa that an attack on Kangra
was no concern of the British and, in his view, would be unlikely to
succeed. The gesture of exchanging turbans was intended to commit
Ochterlony to arrange medical treatment at Ludhiana for the Kaji's
son who had become 'the adopted brother of Mr. Ochterlony'. The
young 'patient' repeated what Bhakti Thapa had said to Ochterlony.
After the meetings Ochterlony visited the villages of Munny Majra,
Ramgarh, Raipoor, Berowly and Moondlai. He took care to have a
sketch map made of his journey and no doubt observed Nepalese
defensive positions, especially in the far west, perhaps gaining distant
views of stockades (see map 3).

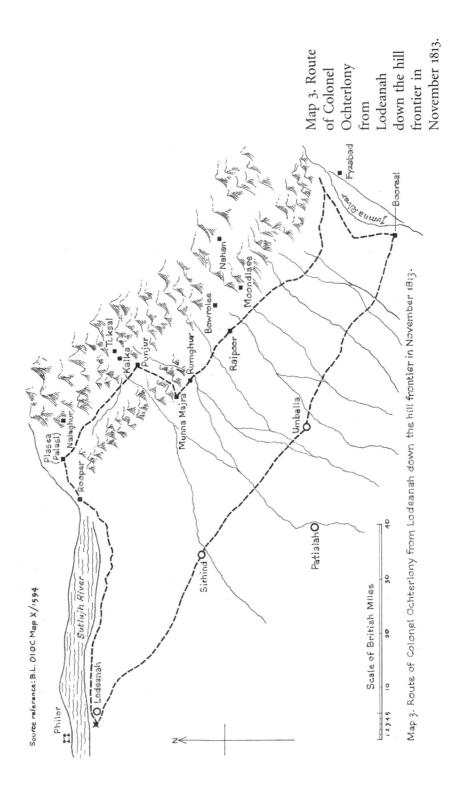

Source reference: B.L. OIOC Map X/1594

Philor

Sutluih River

Lodeanah

Plasca (Patasi)
Rooper
Nalaghur
Tuksal
Kalka
Punjur
Munna Majra
Rumghur
Bowrolee
Nahan
Moondliee
Raipoor
Umballa
Sirhind
Patialah

Fyzabad
Booraal
Jumna River

N

Scale of British Miles
1 2 3 4 5   10   20   30   40

Map 3. Route of Colonel Ochterlony from Lodeanah down the hill frontier in November 1813.

Map 3. Route of Colonel Ochterlony from Lodeanah down the hill frontier in November 1813.

Stockades were a most important feature of Nepalese military tactics. Alexander Fraser writing on New Year's Day 1815 described the stockade as 'a species of fortification which the Gurkhas construct with great art and defend admirably, the jungle which covers the sides of the hills furnishing the materials'. [283] A few days later he gave his father more detailed information supplied by William Fraser:

> The woods furnish strong stakes [and on] the hills plenty of large stones are at hand. The active Goorkhas of these materials form rude but efficient fortifications at the shortest warning. They seem under the strictest discipline and yet seem to possess all the natural spirit of mountaineers. Their stockaded positions are generally areas of different sizes and figures, according to the nature of the ground or the numbers of the people who are to occupy them. Sometimes however a stockade is merely a palisade across a defile. The stockaded enclosures are generally placed on heights whence with musquetry they command the avenues to their forts and towns. These are for a time equal to forts, are stormed with loss and cannot be turned without loss and danger to the rear. But the grand difficulty in truth is the bravery of the defenders – your own great danger arises from stupid security and arrogant confidence.[284]

A letter from Alexander to his mother provides details of the construction of a stockade:

> The enclosure is formed by a double palisade of fir stakes. The space between the pallisades (4 or 5 feet) filled with gabions and the whole occasionally strengthened by a stone wall (probably without cement). Within the enclosure are deep trenches cut in all directions for our shells to sink into and burst comparatively harmlessly, the trenches being covered over with branches of trees and loose earth. Some of the more important stockades have sheds all round the inside of the fence, with sloping roofs whence our shells slide off and burst at a distance from the shed which also affords shelter from the weather. Many of these enclosures are of great extent, capable of holding some thousand men.[285]

The stockade, as a feature of mountain warfare, was to engage

Ochterlony in planning his military operations. In adopting the stock-ade for his own purposes he was not unnaturally keen to recruit some of the hillmen whose expertise in the rapid construction of stockades he greatly admired.

In June 1814 Hastings began a fifteen-month tour of the upper Provinces by boat up the Ganges, the main highway in the absence of all-weather roads. This gave him the opportunity to visit major military depots, such as Dinapur, Kanpur and Meerut, located close to the river. It also enabled him to take the advice of senior local officials whom he invited to stay with his party. Charles Metcalfe spent two long periods with Hastings during which they discussed British policy and Metcalfe presented memoranda on the Indian states.[286] Metcalfe's influence on Hastings was further strengthened by the presence in the party of Metcalfe's close friend John Adam, the Secretary concerned with such matters. Both Adam and Metcalfe were in close touch with Richard Jenkins, Resident at Nagpur, who like them had served in Wellesley's private office. Although Hastings intended to deal once and for all with the Maratha states and to suppress the marauding Pindaris whose predations created such instability in northern and central India, he gave his immediate attention to the Nepalese. The Court of Directors of the East India Company had, in February 1814, already given him authority for 'a recourse to arms for the recovery and protection of the rights of the British Government'.[287]

The fact that Hastings held appointments as both Governor-General and Commander-in-Chief simplified administration, for he also had with him Lieutenant-Colonel George Fagan, the Adjutant-General. Although the diplomatic and military departments maintained separate offices 'in order to keep the records of each distinct and regular',[288] their proximity made for easy communication with each other as well as with Hastings. The presence of Hastings, Adam, and Fagan in an area not far removed from the North-West Quarter was advantageous at a time when the Cis-Sutlej hills were likely to become a crucial theatre in a war with Nepal. Of the Delhi Residency staff, Ochterlony, Metcalfe's great friend and Agent to the Governor-General at Ludhiana, would become an army divisional commander in the Cis-Sutlej hills. William Fraser, First Assistant at Delhi, was destined soon to become Agent to the Governor-General for Garhwal. The Hon. Edward Gardner, Second Assistant, whom Alexander Fraser (Third Assistant) regarded as 'a most gentlemanly well-informed man',[289] would eventually be Resident at Kathmandu. In a letter to his sister, Alexander Fraser explained that 'the society of each station resembles in some measure one family'.[290] This was substantially true at Delhi, where 'sixteen to eighteen normally mustered for dinner at the Residency', of whom 'half or more are Scots, up to a quarter Irish, the rest English'. 'Amusements' comprised 'occasional reading, much conversation and writing.'[291] Among the Scots was Engineer Lieutenant Peter Lawtie (of whom more will be written later).

Brother-in-law to George Fagan, the Adjutant-General, Lawtie was to become a most highly regarded field engineer and ADC to Ochterlony. A close friend of Alexander and William Fraser, he kept in touch with them throughout his short and eventful life on active service. As in most families there were occasional differences of opinion, especially between Metcalfe and William Fraser regarding William's career. Although Metcalfe did his best to preserve their friendship, William's forthright manner sometimes made this difficult.[292] However, evidence of the family atmosphere at Delhi is given in Lawtie's letter of 27 December 1813 to Alexander Fraser in Calcutta: 'we are now all settled at the Shalimar, Metcalfe's house. If you go about the libraries I wish you would look for Gregory's Mechanics and if you find it bring it with you.'[293] In a letter to his father written on Christmas Day 1813 in Meerut, William Fraser made a stark comparison between Delhi which 'has more society than most stations', and Meerut, where 'I suppose we often sit down to dinner at the Residency 100 people . . . I have lived a much more social and comfortable life in a spot where there were perhaps not a dozen people, than here. At Meeruth there is a Playhouse, a Ballroom, frequent concerts and balls, and races once or twice a year. I am however sorry to say that the clergyman is very little attended and no-one would subscribe to build a church although every person did so to the Playhouse and Ballroom.'[294]

The lack of entertainment and diversions at Delhi concentrated the minds of Residency staff on more serious issues. Lawtie noted in a letter to Alexander Fraser 'morning and evening and meals are the times of intercourse'.[295] With Kaji Amar Singh Thapa's army on Delhi district's northern frontier, and the prospect of war with Nepal, the gathering and exchange of intelligence took on an even greater importance, especially as so little was known about Garhwal and the Cis-Sutlej hill country. In February 1814 William Fraser and Lawtie went on a hunting expedition in Rohtak, accompanied by three dragoons and a post-officer, ostensibly on business.[296] In April 1814, William Fraser was in Garhwal. He wrote to his father: 'This letter is written in a most beautiful valley about 14 or 15 miles broad between the first and second ranges of hills which bound Hindustan to the north and having the Ganges and Jumna to the east and west extremities. This, called the Valley of [Dehra] Doon, is very fertile and healthy. I have come hither with Lady Hood.'[297]

Ochterlony had already been gathering intelligence. In particular he had approached Captain William Richards in the summer of 1813 'for information respecting the hill forts and country he had been going through to Nahan'. Richards sent him a long report together with a rough copy of his journal, his notebook on passes and distances and a map.[298] The report included information on roads, forts, towns and villages together with recommendations on the use of artillery, pioneers and porters, and on supplies, equipment and tactics. Ochterlony noted that 'the Goorkhas have but few guns of small calibre which are transported by slings and fired on the ground by a train; they have no carriages' and that elephants could be used to carry British guns. He was already aware of the Nepalese Army's use of stockaded posts which Richards described as 'stronger than stone forts'. Ochterlony also knew that the Nepalese Army was poorly armed and comprised two-thirds Kumaonis and Garhwalis and one-third Nepalese. Richards' comment that 'they are very hardy, endure great bodily fatigue under the greatest privations' and are 'not very nice [i.e. fussy] in what they eat' would have interested him. However two points must have struck him very forcibly. The first was Richards' stress that water was the key to operational planning. The second, even more significant in the light of subsequent events, was Richards' observation that 'a great many of the Nepalese on pay of six rupees a month would take service and form a corps of excellent Hill Rangers. They are remarkably obedient to their officers'. More will be made of this in chapters 5, 6 and 7.

In his 'Report on the Hill Districts occupied by the Goorkhas', Ochterlony estimated that some 7,000 Nepalese including 4,500 to 5,000 regulars 'armed with muskets and clothed in red cloth uniform in imitation of the British' had occupied the whole extent of the hill country between the Jumna and the Sutlej. These troops were divided into companies in strong positions in the hills or in forts, especially in the lower hills towards the Sikh country. Few were in the 'upper country' which was not strongly fortified but elevated and difficult to approach. In the event of war, scattered Nepalese troops would no doubt be gathered to key points.[299] Ochterlony believed that a battering train could be got up to most defensive positions and that none could resist howitzers and field artillery with shrapnel shells. He planned to start his operations at Nalagarh and anticipated that the river Gambar, which ran within six coss (about fifteen miles) of 'the residence of Ummer Sing Thappa [at Arki] might be a road for the guns'.[300]

As to the Hill chiefs, Ochterlony believed that the Thakuris[301] were anti-Nepalese and that the Sikh chiefs might be called on to provide a small body of irregular militia. The Raja of Hindur could supply 200–300 armed men and a greater number of unarmed men to clear roads and carry loads – perhaps 500–600 in all.[302] Ochterlony suggested in July 1814 that 'Kishen Sing, a relation of the Nahan Rajah, an active man and brave soldier who defended Narinegurh against Runjeet [Ranjit Singh], is now, I believe in the service of Patialo, and might be usefully employed as a partizan in his native country.'[303] With some misgiving, Ochterlony now further recommended that if Kishen Singh could be trusted and were given money he should be able to raise a considerable body of men before hostilities commenced. Ochterlony thought his influence might, if the first action were successful, command a great part of the population of the Raja of Sirmur.[304] Ochterlony did not presume to specify the standards to be applied in such recruitment. In the event, failure carefully to select recruits was to prove disastrous. Ochterlony concluded that 'Goorkha power must be completely overthrown to avoid a constant source of trouble and expense.'[305] By now he had no illusions about his adversaries: 'Giving the Goorkhas full credit for the reputation they have acquired, an officer must make up his mind to contend with a hardy and brave people, by no means uninformed in the arts and strategems of mountainous warfare . . . every defensive art of stockade etc.'[306] His admiration for Gorkhas had begun.

Although the crucial battles of the war were to be fought initially in the western hills, the incident which provoked war occurred in the north-eastern Terai. Butwal and the neighbouring Siuraj had come into Company possession by cession from the Nawab of Oudh. However, whereas the Nepalese had occupied Siuraj for sixteen years before it became Company territory, Butwal – a much more fertile and attractive district – had been virtually annexed with the territories of the Raja of Palpa by General Amar Singh Thapa, Bhim Sen Thapa's father,[307] in 1806, since when the Nepalese had collected the revenues. British failure to re-establish Company ownership led the Nepalese to believe they had tacitly recognised Nepalese rights over Butwal.[308] In 1811, the Raja of Bettiya, one of the Company's zamindars in Saran district, had caused an affray by attempting to seize some villages occupied by the Nepalese who claimed them as part of their conquest of the hill state of Makwanpur. A Nepalese civil governor was killed. In order to resolve this and the Butwal issue the British proposed to an angry and reluctant Nepalese Government that the whole border question should be investigated by an Anglo-Nepalese commission. Pending the convening of this commission the Nepalese seized more villages making a total of twenty-two.[309] Major Paris Bradshaw, the Company's chief commissioner, charged with establishing British claims to Butwal and Siuraj, gave the Nepalese representatives cause to break off negotiations in April 1814 in consequence of which the Nepalese Government decided to defend the territories they held.[310] On 22 April 1814, an ultimatum issued in December 1813 by the British for the formal surrender of Butwal and Siuraj, expired and the Magistrate of Gorakhpur sent seventeen companies of native infantry to take possession. Having met no resistance, the troops were forced to withdraw during the malarial season. The defence of the territory was left to a few police posts, three of which were attacked in Butwal on 29 May 1814 by Nepalese forces. At one of them eighteen policemen were killed and seven including the chief police officer were wounded. Having surrendered, the officer was tied to a tree and shot dead with arrows.[311] The Governor-General, ready to declare war as soon as this was practicable, demanded from the King of Nepal a repudiation of the murder of the chief police officer and the punishment of the culprits, failing which the two countries would be at war. The King's reply of 12 August 1814 gave no such undertaking.[312]

In the meantime Hastings gave orders to prepare for war. Hastings, who had been Master General of the Ordnance in 1806, designed carriages for a howitzer which was capable of being dismantled and carried in separate sections,[313] and for a light cannon.[314] He also devised a system of storage depots at strategic locations on the border with the Nepalese. These were to hold six months' supplies and were to be supported by back-up depots holding reserve stocks. However, in the matter of fighting in unknown mountain terrain, Hastings took the view that 'the difficulties of mountain warfare were greater on the defensive side than on that of a well-conducted operation'.[315] Ochterlony alone among his field commanders was aware that mountain warfare called for a new approach to strategy and tactics. The traditional drills of infantry formation fighting, so well rehearsed by the Bengal Army's British and native troops on the plains, were useless in the steep, narrow, rugged confines of the hills. So, too, were cavalry.[316]

From July 1814, John Adam (Secretary to Government) and George Fagan (Adjutant-General) began to gather information essential for the prosecution of war in the Terai and north-western hills. The Surveyor General was consulted regarding maps (of which few existed), the Commissary General about stores, and anyone who had relevant knowledge and experience was pressed for assistance. Among these were Dr Francis Hamilton who had visited Kathmandu in 1801,[317] William Moorcroft[318] and Captain Haider Hearsey, whom Lady Nugent had described as 'a very ingenious but uneducated man who has been making a tour in Chinese Tartary',[319] and who was destined to serve with the Bengal forces in Kumaon. Moorcroft had introduced

Hearsey to John Adam[320] and Hearsey was able from his personal experience to offer useful information about Garhwal and Kumaon[321] and to pass on an account by Lieutenant Frederick Young on Sirmur.[322] Among a number of points of interest, Young noted that hill forts in general had no springs or tanks of water within them, but the garrison had to fetch water from some distance below. Of the hill forts themselves he was dismissive: 'they are built of slabs of stone without any cement, and are not above thirty paces square, above twelve feet high and the stockade which surrounds them is easily destroyed . . . I presume a shell from a four and a half inch howitzer would cause the immediate evacuation of them. They can easily be approached by infantry under cover to within less than musket-shot.'[323] The ill-fated assaults on the small Nepalese fort of Kalanga [or Nalapani] in October and November 1814 were to disprove this.

A letter from Kaji Amar Singh Thapa received by Ochterlony on 6 July 1814 and forwarded to Adam on 9 July for the attention of the Governor-General, complained of British encroachments in Palpa 'which had for a series of years belonged to the Goorka Government'. It also threatened that unless such incidents ceased 'the troops of the Goorkhas, resembling the waves of the ocean, whose chief employments are war and hostilities, will make the necessary preparations to prevent the usurpation of any one place which has been in their possession for years past'.[324] This can hardly have been a surprise. Rumours of military preparations in Nepal had reached the Government by the end of 1813.[325]

Metcalfe and Ochterlony were anxious about the security of the Company's territory in the North-West Quarter against Nepalese encroachments into the lowlands, and the longer-term possibility of an incursion into the Cis-Sutlej hills by Ranjit Singh's army. Metcalfe's influence on Hastings, the new Governor-General and Commander-in-Chief, was a factor in focusing Hastings' mind on tackling border disputes with Nepal as the first among several politico-military problems. Ochterlony realised that mountain warfare called for specialised tactics new to the Bengal Army, and for the hardiness and skills of hill soldiers. Intelligence gained on missions by Moorcroft, Hearsey,

Young, William Fraser, and more especially Richards, caused Ochterlony to change his mind about the fighting qualities of Gorkhas and other hillmen in the Nepalese Army. A suggestion from Richards may have persuaded Ochterlony of the possibility of raising a corps of Hill Rangers from Nepalese soldiers.

In the meantime, border disputes continued, due in large measure to Minto's 'principle of limitation' whereby the hills and mountains were to be wholly Nepalese territory and the lowlands, including the Terai, exclusively British. This was bound to be unacceptable to the Nepalese for whom the Terai was vitally important. Moreover the principle paid no heed to the fact that in the border hill states, territory captured by the Nepalese included not only hills but associated lowlands. Such a border problem involving villages seized by Kaji Amar Singh Thapa's forces was amicably resolved when the King of Nepal ordered the withdrawal of Nepalese troops. The incident caused Ochterlony to meet the Kaji and gave him the opportunity to tour the border country and study Nepalese defences. However, a more intractable dispute to the east in Butwal provided the provocation for war, and led to the possibility of the Bengal Army acquiring the skills of Nepalese soldiers either by capture or through desertion.

CHAPTER 5

The first campaign, a disastrous beginning: 1814

War did indeed break out between Britain and Nepal, but not until the British were ready. During his progress upriver, Hastings was occupied, in his joint capacity as Commander-in-Chief and Governor-General, in 'fashioning a system of military operations and political arrangements, with a view to the commencement of the campaign, as soon as the season should enable the troops to act'.[326] It was recognised that because of the grave risk of malaria in crossing the Terai, operations could not start until the end of October or early November and would need to be completed by mid-May at the latest.[327] In framing his strategy, Hastings was faced with many problems, not the least of which were the length of the Nepalese border and the fact that, in difficult mountainous country, the British were entering upon 'an entirely different species of warfare'.[328] Hastings' intelligence sources suggested that the Nepalese field army under Kaji Amar Singh Thapa, based far to the west at Arki in the Cis-Sutlej hills, did not exceed 6,000 fighting men of whom about 1,800 or 2,000 were regular troops, 'real Goorkas'. The remainder were Kumaonis, Garhwalis and other hill tribes who were 'very indifferently attached to their masters' and might be encouraged to desert.[329] These irregular troops, a great number of whom were Kumaonis, were commanded by Gorkha sirdars and armed, as were the regular troops, with muskets and 'kookerees' (a curved 'formidable weapon of offence' worn in the girdle); some also carried swords and bows and arrows.[330] Captain Raper recorded that 'In point of respectability or personal qualifications, these troops are far inferior to the native Goorkas.'[331] The 'hardy and active tribes' which comprised the regular Nepalese forces in Kaji

Amar Singh Thapa's army were hillmen inured to long marches across mountainous terrain.[332]

4. Ghoorkha Chiefs and Soldiers.[333] The third from the right in this group portrait is Subhir Singh, a Gorkha subedar who commanded a company at Jaithak. The two on the left are from Kaski in western Nepal.

Hastings' plan[334] was for four divisions of the Bengal field army to invade Nepalese territory simultaneously. The principal division under Major-General Marley, based on Dinapur, was to capture the hill fort of Makwanpur and then the Nepalese capital, Kathmandu (see map 4). An associated division commanded by Major-General John Wood was to advance from Gorakhpur, occupy the disputed territory of Siuraj and Butwal,[335] and create a diversion to aid Marley. If possible, Wood was to capture General Amar Singh Thapa's headquarters near Palpa and the town of Palpa itself, thereby cutting the main line of communication between Kathmandu and the west. The second field division led by Major-General Gillespie was to set out from Saharanpur, capture Dehra Dun, the valleys and passes of Garhwal and the land between the Jumna and the Ganges, preventing the Nepalese Army in the west from retreating eastwards (see map 2). The third field division based on Ludhiana under Ochterlony (now promoted to major-general) was, with the co-operation of the second division, to destroy Kaji Amar Singh Thapa's army, which was understood 'to be composed of the flower of the Goorka troops'.[336] Ochterlony's other task was 'the annihilation of the Goorka influence and authority' in the countries between the Jumna and Sutlej. Hastings regarded these as 'objects of primary interest'.[337] In addition, Hastings intended to raise a force for the capture of Kumaon as soon as the Nepalese forces were sufficiently engaged elsewhere.[338] The protection of the northern frontier east of the Kosi was to be entrusted to Captain Latter whose Rangpur Battalion was to be augmented by detachments of regular and irregular troops (see map 1).[339]

In seeking to fulfil his general intention of reinstating the 'ancient chiefs' to their lands, so long as this was the will of the majority of the inhabitants, Hastings appointed political agents. Ochterlony was made responsible for intelligence and negotiations in the Cis-Sutlej Hill States.[340] William Fraser was attached to Gillespie's division and made responsible for political affairs in Garhwal.[341] Edward Gardner was made similarly responsible for Kumaon.[342] John Wood was authorised to conduct political negotiations in his area of military operations;[343] and Lieutenant-Colonel Bradshaw, attached to Marley's division, was appointed Political Agent for the remainder of the eastern sector and for negotiations with Nepal.[344]

Although a formal state of war did not exist until 1 November 1814, the first Nepalese prisoners of war were taken on 25 August 1814 in the course of an attack by Bradshaw's troops on a Nepalese frontier post at Kacharwa in the Terai. However, he was authorised to liberate them as 'there does not seem to be any advantage in detaining them in custody'.[345] Bradshaw reported the capture of further Nepalese prisoners on 25 November 1814 during an attack on the Nepalese post at Baraharwa by the newly formed Champaran Light Infantry. His orders having prohibited the capture of prisoners, these were described as 'fugitives who begged for their lives, or who after the combat came in wounded'. They were sent for disposal to Divisional Headquarters at Dinapur.[346]

In the meantime, Ochterlony had taken ninety-five prisoners on 6 November 1814: seventy-eight at the surrender of Nalagarh fort and seventeen from a hill defence at nearby Taragarh.[347] As a matter of policy as well as of humanity, Ochterlony told the captured Subedar and his men 'everything likely to satisfy their minds of their personal safety, and everything that could conciliate and reconcile them to their captors'.[348] Of considerably more significance, before sending them to Ludhiana under cavalry escort, Ochterlony had 'assured the Subedar and his men of service, at the rate of pay received from their own Government' and had politely declined the Subedar's offer to accompany him saying 'as our acquaintance was so short, it would not be prudent to accept his services at present, but I might soon call on him'. Ochterlony added: 'I should be glad that he could send, or intimate a wish to send, a messenger to the hills, as I am confident the treatment they have received requires only to be known to have good effect.'[349] Ochterlony was given cautious approval by Hastings, who nevertheless pointed out that while it would be politic to adopt any measure which, particularly at the outset, tended to disorganise or break up the enemy's force such 'as that of occasionally entertaining detached bodies of it evidently has', it would be 'extremely hazardous to engage the natives of Goorka Proper' to any great extent.[350] As Commander-in-Chief, Hastings saw danger in 'the unrestricted grant of service to the troops of Nepal, and still more to their employment with ours'. He believed it might be possible to distinguish Gorkhas from the natives of other countries serving with the Nepalese Army. Major Ludlow of the Second Division evidently thought so. In referring to upwards of fifty Nepalese killed in action near Kalanga on 2 December 1814, he noted that all the bodies he had seen were of 'genuine Goorkas'.[351] Captain Raper had observed that 'nature has drawn a very striking difference; for the slender form of the Kumaonese cannot be put in competition with the stout Herculean limbs of the Goorkali soldier'.[352] Hastings himself saw wounded Gorkha prisoners in the hospitals at Saharanpur and wrote in his diary on 30 December 1814: 'Their countenances are absolutely Chinees [*sic*], only on a larger scale.'[353] It was left to Ochterlony's discretion to offer service to enemy troops subject to the ratification of the Commander-in-Chief or the Governor-General.[354] The policy regarding the treatment of prisoners of war does not seem to have been conveyed at that time to the other divisional commanders. Perhaps the Adjutant General saw no immediate need. The two divisions in the Eastern campaign had still not engaged the enemy.

To avoid confusion, it is necessary here to explain the use and likely derivation of the terms 'Goorka' (Gorkha) and 'Goorkali' (Gorkhali).

In *Military History of Nepal* (Kathmandu, 1992, p. 71) S.P. Sharma et al. suggest that the adoption of Gorakh Nath by the Rajput Shah family, who ruled the town and minor state of Gorkha, may have led to Brahmins and Chhetris in their entourage – and perhaps the Shahs themselves – being identified as Gorkhalis or followers of Gorakh. This may indeed have drawn the king and his people together in resisting persistent attacks from the ancient Kingdom of Lamjung.

L.F. Stiller maintains, in chapter 4 of his *The rise of the House of Gorkha* (Patna, 1973), that when Prithvi Narayan Shah set out in 1744 as King of Gorkha to conquer the Valley kingdoms of Nepal, he took with him Gorkhali soldiers in his Gorkhali army. In accordance with his own edicts these Gorkhalis would have comprised not only Chhetris, Magar-Chhetris, and Magars, but Gurungs from the high hills west of Gorkha. It was perhaps convenient to identify his troops collectively as Gorkhalis or followers of the King of Gorkha. This is how they were perceived by their adversaries in the Valley of Nepal.

Once Nepal's western army had crossed the Mahakali river into Kumaon in 1790, its lines of communication became severely stretched. The army therefore began not only to take its supplies from the fertile hills of Kumaon but to conscript and train Kumaoni hill boys as auxiliaries. Although they became soldiers of the Nepalese Army they were not Gorkhalis. Nor were the Garhwalis who were recruited as the Nepalese Army moved further west into Garhwal. By the time the Nepalese western army reached Kangra in 1806 and subsequently settled in the Cis-Sutlej hills, a large proportion of its soldiers originated from Kumaon and Garhwal.

Among the British, much of the confused use of terminology in official records may be attributed to ignorance in Calcutta. For example the word 'Nepal' had several connotations. To this day its early meaning of the Valley of Nepal (or even of Kathmandu itself) is still held by some Nepalis. Small wonder that there was confusion among desk-bound British officials in attempting to distinguish 'Nepal' (the Valley) from 'Nepal' (the unified country between the Tista and the Mahakali rivers) and from 'Nepal' (Greater Nepal, the Nepalese empire). How much more difficult it must have been for officials to understand the distinction between Gorkhalis, whom they had never seen, and Nepalese subjects of other ethnic origins.

On the other hand, Ochterlony and other British officers on active service in the north-west had no difficulty in distinguishing Gorkhalis from Kumaoni and Garhwali soldiers. However, in order to distinguish Gorkhalis from other Nepalese troops in writing despatches and correspondence, British officers sometimes resorted to referring to soldiers from the hills of western Nepal (Prithvi Narayan Shah's Gorkhalis) as 'real', 'proper' or 'genuine' Gorkhas. It was in these Gorkhas that Ochterlony was most interested. Who among the British first used the word 'Gorkha' (in its various phonetic spellings) instead of the term 'Gorkhali' is not known. However, the term 'Gorkhali' which appears occasionally in official records, became superseded by the word 'Gorkha'. The Gorkha war-cry 'Ayo Gorkhali' (the Gorkhas are here) has persisted for more than two centuries. That Gorkhali and Gorkha tend now to be regarded as synonymous is illustrated by Rishikesh Shaha. In volume 1 of his *Modern Nepal: a Political History 1769–1955*, New Delhi, 1990, he makes reference to 'Gorkha troops' and the 'Gorkhali army'; and, alluding to Kaji Amar Singh Thapa, the 'Gorkha commander' and 'Gorkhali commander'. Shaha also wrote: 'Though short in stature the Gorkhali soldiers were sturdy in build and had a keen sense of loyalty and discipline. It was for these reasons that the British decided to recruit Gorkhas into their army.' [355] It appears that just as Prithvi Narayan Shah changed the original concept of 'Gorkha' to a broader meaning of 'Gorkhali', the British did little if anything more than abbreviate 'Gorkhali' to 'Gorkha'.

Rathaur's assertion that 'the inhabitants of the territories west of the Kali river up to the river Sutlej … were considered "Gurkhas" by the British' [356] is questionable. This view may have been held by some

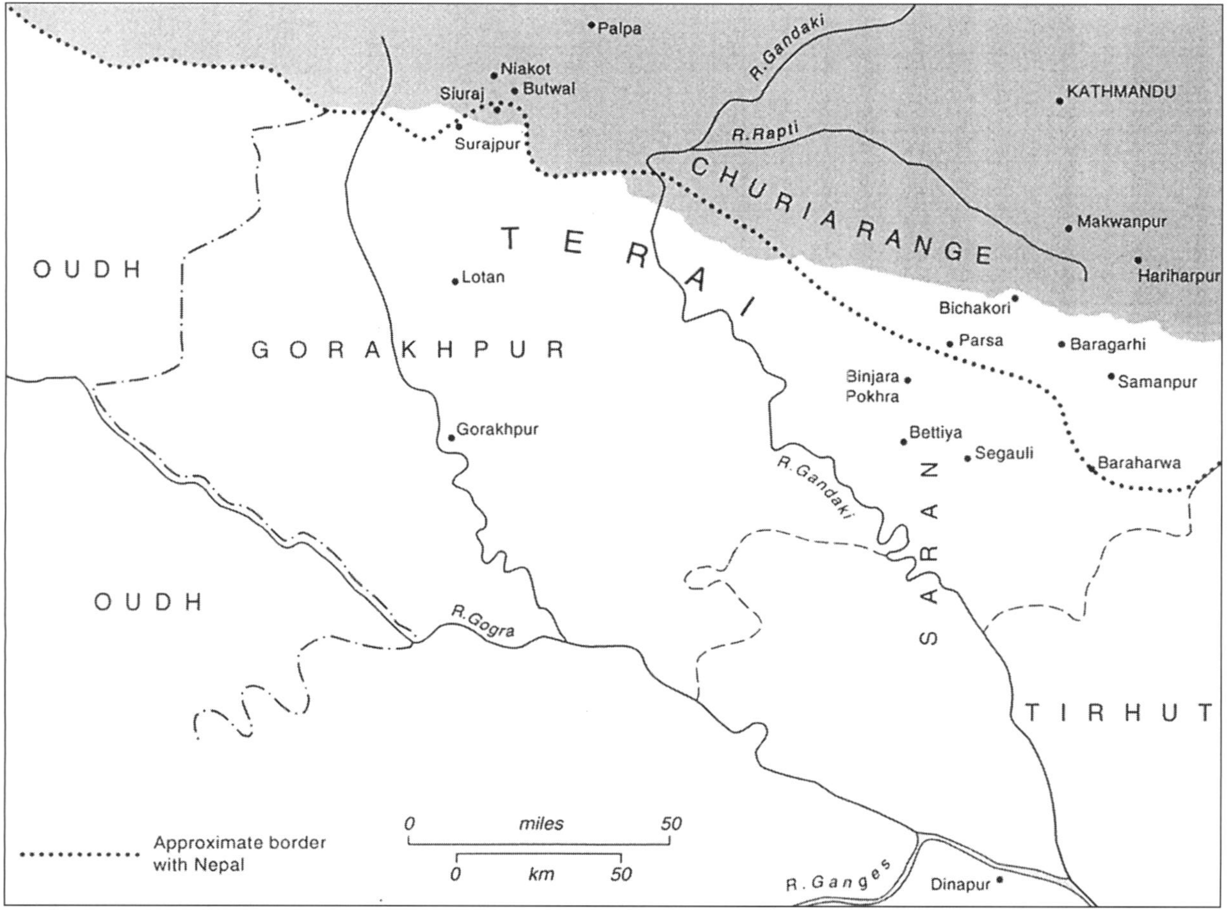

KATHMANDU

Makwanpur •
Hariharpur •

Baragarhi •
Samanpur •
Baraharwa •

Bichakori •
Parsa •

Segauli
Binjara • Bettiya •
Pokhra •

Palpa •

Niakot
• Butwal
Siuraj • Surajpur

• Lotan

Gorakhpur •

R. Gandaki

R. Gaupaki

R. Rapti

CHURIA RANGE

T E R A I

G O R A K H P U R

O U D H

O U D H

S A R A N

T I R H U T

R. Gogra

R. Ganges

Dinapur •

0   50
        miles
        50
        km
0

······· Approximate border
        with Nepal

Map 4.
The Eastern
theatre of
operations,
1814–15.

misguided or ignorant officials in Calcutta. It was not shared by the British officers engaged in the western campaign of the Anglo-Nepal war who had encountered Gorkhalis.

Pemble's view that 'real Gurkhas (as opposed to the Mongolian hill-men whom the British regarded as "real Gurkhas")' were similar to the native Khas [tribe] of Sirmur[357] is also open to doubt.

The offensive in the east proved to be an unmitigated disaster. Major-General Bennett Marley, in command of the main division crossed the Ganges at the end of November 1814 with the object of marching into Nepal through the Bichakori pass near Parsa (see map 4). However, he was reluctant to cross the Terai into the hills without his heavy artillery. By the time this reached Bettiya on 30 December and was ready to move forward to Parsa, news reached him that a strong Nepalese force was threatening his outpost there. Before reinforcements arrived the Parsa detachment of 360 men had been overwhelmed sustaining heavy casualties.[358] Marley then ordered the withdrawal of all his forward troops, but not before the outpost at Samanpur had been attacked and its depot destroyed.[359] Marley became convinced he was opposed by a Nepalese Army of some 13,000 against which his own force was hopelessly inadequate. Having consulted his brigade commanders, he withdrew to Binjara Pokhra, fifteen miles south-west of Parsa, and gave up all thought of advancing on Kathmandu.[360] For failing to obey his instructions Hastings directed Marley to surrender his command to Major-General George Wood. Unable to face this humiliation, Marley disappeared before his successor arrived.

George Wood, anxious to preserve his military reputation, was as reluctant as Marley to take risks. His decision not to move his division into Nepalese territory until the next campaigning season, brought a stinging rebuke from Hastings, who made it clear that by then Wood would no longer hold his command.[361] Having marched half of his division ineffectually through the Terai, George Wood returned to the remainder at Bettiya where he made arrangements to disperse them all for the monsoon period. This done, he left for Dinapur, ostensibly because of poor health.

Major-General John Wood, commanding a supporting diversionary force some eighty miles west of Marley's Division, fared no better. A fastidious man with a King's cavalry background, he lingered in Benares until mid-November 1814 by which time Nepalese troops had appeared on the Gorakhpur frontier causing alarm to the local population.[362] John Wood sent Captain Heathcote with five companies through the jungle and swamps of the Gorakhpur hinterland to Lotan, a village in the Terai south of the Butwal pass (see map 4). He himself arrived with part of his force on 15 November at Gorakhpur town where, joined by other troops, he remained for a month organising his division with paralysing punctiliousness. He was eventually forced to move to Lotan with his force having received an urgent report from Heathcote that about 8,000 Nepalese troops were preparing to attack. Although the attack did not take place, John Wood waited four days at Lotan for bullock carts and stores before he crept at snail-like pace to Siuraj, near Butwal. From there he moved north on 3 January 1815 with most of his force, only to be led into a Nepalese trap by a Brahmin guide who swiftly vanished. Despite the fact that a British battalion successfully fought its way to hold a commanding position before Niakot, the Major-General was unsure what to do. A subordinate officer, whom he consulted advised him to support the battalion or withdraw it. To the consternation of his troops and the encouragement of the Nepalese, John Wood ordered a general retreat. By 20 January be was in Lotan, convinced that the Butwal pass was impregnable. His division crawled aimlessly along the Gorakhpur border until reports of threatened attacks caused him to seek instructions from Headquarters. A disgusted Hastings realised that John Wood was unlikely to cross the Butwal Pass. He therefore ordered him to ensure the safety of Gorakhpur town and to organise a mobile column capable of striking at marauding parties of Nepalese. Mobility was not, however, John Wood's forte. After further inconsequential meanderings he turned his thoughts to the more agreeable process of planning the dispersal of his troops for the rainy season.

In the whole Eastern offensive, Captain Barré Latter alone fulfilled Hastings' intentions, succeeding with his tiny force where divisional commanders had failed.[363] Latter showed great enterprise and skill in both military and political operations in the hills and lowlands east of the river Kosi (see map 1), holding the Nepalese at bay and securing the Company's north-eastern border. Hastings' hopes of bringing the Nepalese Government to terms through the threat of a British army in the Valley of Nepal were dismally unfulfilled.

In the west as in the east the field army made a disastrous start. Gillespie's division, the first to cross enemy borders, was held up for more than a month by three unsuccessful attempts to capture the small hill fort of Kalanga in Garhwal. When, on 30 November 1814, the fort was evacuated after heavy bombardment it was found to contain severely wounded survivors of the garrison. Able-bodied troops from this and other local fortified positions had escaped into the hills. William Fraser, having joined Gillespie's division as a civilian, was soon involved in military activities. He wrote from Dehra to his brother Alexander on 26 October 1814: 'Yesterday myself and two officers spent in reconnoitring. Today Gillespie arrived. We shall probably wait for heavier guns to take Kalunga or Nalapanee,[364] but tomorrow will determine. I go out tomorrow with Major Pennington of the Horse Artillery and Ensign Blane of the Engineers to reconnoitre. I shall be out all day. This is quite a life to my liking. I am deep in politics and war.'[365] Five days later William Fraser was wounded in the second assault and General Gillespie was killed. William wrote: 'We failed in our assault upon Kalunga.'[366] Later he explained: 'The heat, impatience and impetuosity of poor Gillespie our General was the principal cause of our defeat. There were four attacking columns and only one engaged in the assault, which enabled the defenders to give their whole strength against it . . . the other columns were resting on their arms. General Gillespie was shot dead in the act of huzzaing to the men, waving his hat in his left hand and sword in his right hand; and yet not a man would follow him nor advance with him.'[367] He added: 'The Goorkhas fought most bravely and resolutely and if they fight as well in the field we shall have a tough campaign.' William Fraser took it upon himself, despite being wounded by an arrow through the throat and hit five times by stones thrown by women defenders, to report the defeat 'immediately and by express' to the Secretary to Government.[368]

Martindell, who assumed command of the second division on 19 December 1814, was quite unlike Gillespie. Having suffered defeats on 27 and 28 December 1814 in his attempts to capture the lofty fortress of Jaithak (whence Ranjor Singh Thapa had withdrawn his army on the orders of his father, Kaji Amar Singh Thapa), Martindell contented himself with inactivity and a lack of enterprise which drove William Fraser to distraction. In a letter of 31 January 1815 to his brother Alexander, William Fraser complained about Martindell's decision to await reinforcements and about further delay caused by his selection of an impracticable route to Jaithak: 'Such want of decision, arrangements and enterprise I cannot imagine . . . But 12 [i.e. 1,200] or at the very utmost 1500 Gorkahs appal 700 Europeans, 2200 regular native infantry and 3000 irregulars.'[369] In a further letter to Alexander, William wrote in disgust: 'I cannot tell you how much General . . . [Martindell]'s management is scorned and reviled by the army for indecision, want of promptness, energy and enterprise. The garrison [of Jaithak] are very much straitened for provisions but a road left open as if on purpose to enable them to hold out. We might have been as safely and as far advanced a month ago as we are today, and by delay we have lost a position without which the Fort cannot be invested and which must be regularly attacked. I am quite sick of the business. A good General would have laid Jytuk in ashes before now.'[370]

Initially William Fraser's task was to communicate with the inhabitants of the mountainous regions of north Garhwal in the hope of enlisting their help in interrupting Kaji Amar Singh Thapa's line of retreat.[371] His main responsibility was, however, for the civil administration – police, revenue and finance – in territory occupied by the British advancing into Garhwal. He was informed that it was not the Governor-General's intention for him to 'assume any authority, separate or independent of that which must rest in Major-General Gillespie'.[372] The Governor-General had assured Major-General Gillespie that he would find in Mr Fraser 'a cordial disposition to conform, to the extent of his power, to the suggestions and wishes which the Major-General may communicate to him'.[373] In addition to commanding the third division, Ochterlony was to continue to 'exercise the power of Governor General's Agent to the Seikh States, and of Agent for Goorka affairs between the Jumna and the Sutleje'.[374] This was made clear to Gillespie [375] who was also instructed that, once his division had joined forces with Ochterlony's division, Fraser's presence would no longer be necessary west of the Jumna.[376] Martindell, Gillespie's successor, was similarly informed.[377]

As both Commander-in-Chief and Governor-General, Hastings had the highest regard for Ochterlony.[378] He was therefore careful to avoid any misunderstanding. This was a wise precaution. As has already been pointed out, William Fraser rather fancied himself as a military leader. Soon after taking up his appointment, he dared to suggest that 'a very effectual and decisive measure would have been the immediate occupation of Sreenuggur'.[379] In self-defence he added: 'I make this remark as matter of information, stating the practicability of the measures, not by any means suggesting it, which would be completely out of line of my duty, and deviating from the course of respectful and submissive deference.' While he considered that the people in Kumaon were more likely than those of Garhwal to assist and co-operate with the British troops, he sent his representatives into the mountains of northern Garhwal to attempt to form small parties 'to act as light troops, to hang upon precipices, and harass the flanks and rear of flying bodies of Nepalese'. Since the Garhwalis had been deprived of arms by the Gorkhas, these parties were limited to such primitive devices as building obstructions and breaking up roads.[380] Whereas Ochterlony was authorised to rearm the inhabitants of the Cis-Sutlej states before hostilities began,[381] Fraser was not given authority to do so in Garhwal until almost two months later.[382]

The depopulation of Garhwal in 1811 and 1812, when nearly 80,000 people had emigrated,[383] and the news of the British disasters at Kalanga, which had a discouraging effect on the Garhwalis, served to thwart Fraser's immediate ambitions. Nevertheless he seized the opportunity in the interval between Gillespie's death and the arrival of Martindell (at a time when Mawby was in local control of the second division under Ochterlony's command) [384] to press the case for light irregular troops. In a letter dated 25 November 1814 to

Adam, the Secretary to Government, William Fraser wrote that Gillespie had agreed to a suggestion he had made 'of endeavouring to raise some bodies of light irregular troops to push forward into the mountains, for the purpose of giving confidence to the inhabitants, destroying the few detached parties scattered about and to collect the revenue and awe the people, and seizing difficult passes and strengthening them if necessary with stockades or barriers'.[385] Fraser reported that 'principally under the sanction and order of the late General Gillespie, and partly on my individual responsibility' he had begun to raise a corps of up to 1,500 irregulars. These would include Mewattis from the hilly country of Rajputana and mountaineers from Garhwal, as well as Kumaonis and deserters from the enemy.[386] Fraser added that owing to the British failure at Kalanga insufficient men had been recruited 'to answer the common purposes of police and collection for the valley of Dhoon'.[387] In the same letter he explained that 'the dread entertained of the Goorka soldiery is such, their activity, enterprize, hardiness, patience and abstinence so remarkable, that with the knowledge they possess of the country, the cheapness and quantity of provision, the various roads they pursue, their expertness in passing rivers not fordable, . . ., successful opposition to the overpowering force of Ummer Sing (should he think of retreat) by the people of the country, or even harassing his troops by falling back into the mountains and refusing carriage or provision cannot be relied upon'.[388]

Fraser requested the indulgence of the Governor-General 'if I am led to hazard opinions which are obviously expressive of military subjects. Matters thus communicated will, I respectfully hope, be received as simple information, and not considered as interfering, inconsiderate intrusion.'[389] Having thus protested his innocence, William Fraser again referred to the suggestion he had made to Gillespie that advantage 'might be reaped from collecting a force of irregular infantry, calculated to act in a country so inaccessible, mountainous, and unknown, where climate and other physical difficulties might check, restrain or disable a larger proportion of the army than would be calculated upon in a common campaign, and where much fatiguing and harassing duty might be performed equally well by light irregular troops', and to Gillespie's authority to a 'levy not exceeding fifteen hundred men'.[390] He pointed out however that 'it was impossible in a short period to raise people accustomed and equal to serve in the mountains to that extent'.[391]

In his reply dated 30 November 1814, Adam conveyed the Governor-General's approval for the levy as an 'irregular corps' and for Fraser's recommendation that these auxiliary troops should be commanded by Lieutenant Young, when he could be spared from his important duties in the Guide and Intelligence Department under Major Stevenson. With the exception of men retained for revenue and police purposes, the irregulars were to act on Young's orders.[392] The Political Secretary added that the Governor-General was happy to receive from William Fraser any suggestions 'relative to the conduct of the important civilian branch of the public affairs with which your present labours are associated'. Perhaps surprisingly, William Fraser does not seem to have informed, still less consulted, Ochterlony. Indeed the Governor-General appears to have taken the initiative in authorising Ochterlony also to raise a force of irregulars.[393] Fraser did not take the Political Secretary's hint – if hint it was. In forwarding translations of letters which had come into his hands, he advocated an attack on a Nepalese position at Chamur where about 400 men from Kalanga, Nahan, Srinagar and Birat had gathered. Again he 'humbly' relied on 'the indulgent forgiveness of the Right Honourable the Governor-General for touching upon subjects foreign to my situation and duties'.[394] In reply, the Political Secretary conveyed the Governor-General's authority for Fraser to increase his levy of irregulars 'to such extent as you may consider to be advisable' not only from hillmen but from the neighbouring province.[395]

The initial constitution of William Fraser's irregular force, as given by Alexander Fraser in a letter dated 31 December 1814 to his father, was 'a small corps of irregulars raised from the natives of the country who supported the British in the expectation of their ancient Royal family being restored to power'. William had 'officered the corps with rejected chieftains glad of the opportunity to attempt with some chance of success' the rescue of their country.[396] By 20 January 1815, when Alexander wrote to his father again, William Fraser had raised '1,200 irregulars among the mountaineers (always to be distinguished from the Goorkhas); he is daily increasing his levy'.[397] This distinction is of fundamental importance in considering the subsequent separate development of the Gorkha corps.

The following table summarises details in pay abstracts and abstracts of muster rolls, and shows the growing numerical strength of 'the irregular corps entertained by Mr. Fraser'.[398]

Table 1. *The strength of William Fraser's irregular corps*

	Native Officers	Nagies	Sepoys	Non-Combatants	Totals
October 1814	2	—	35	2	39
November 1814	13	—	403	16	432
December 1814	73	—	2,465	96	2,634
January 1815	170	592	4,723	225	5,710
February 1815	217	774	6,206	289	7,486

Note: The first recruits, 2 native officers, 10 sepoys and 2 non-combatants, were enlisted on 26 October 1814

It is interesting to note that in his letter of 2 August 1815 to the Secret Committee of the Court of Directors, giving a narrative of the Anglo-Nepal War, Hastings wrote that the duty of raising these irregulars devolved on Mr Fraser.[399] Moreover, there is a record in the Fraser papers of Young addressing William Fraser as 'Sup[erintendent] of Irreg. Corps' while signing himself 'Comd. of Irregs.'.[400] Fraser's own interpretation of their relationship is given in a postscript to his letter to Young dated 25 February 1815:

To prevent any mistake on the point of authority and the degree of authority which you may consider I am directed to exercise in the general economy of the corps under your immediate command, I beg leave to forward to you extract of a letter from the Secretary to Government in the Secret and Political department of date the 12th ultimo which I had omitted previously to send at the period when you assumed command. To the extent you may consider this authority to apply you will generally acquiesce and on points wherein you wish to exercise exclusive control I shall be happy always to agree to every latitude consistent with the benefit of the public service.[401]

It seems that, in essence, they were Fraser's irregulars who came under Young for operational orders. Unfortunately, as the following figures (included in those given in table 1 above) indicate, disaster befell Young and a large body of the irregulars on 21 February 1815 near Jaithak:

Table 2. *Irregulars who deserted or were discharged*

	Native Officers	Nagies	Sepoys	Non-Combatants	Totals
January 1815	3	11	114	—	128
February 1815	37	202	1,784	39	2,062

The occasion was described by William Fraser in a letter probably dated 24 February 1815 to his brother James:

Three days ago accounts were brought of a party detached from Umr Sing's army; it is supposed with many females of his family and his son's family and treasure, etc. Against this force we sent out irregulars under Young at first about 1500, afterwards nearly to the amount of 2500 or 3000. Yesterday an advanced party of ours came up with the enemy and hemmed them in. The same evening Young with his force came up and invested them more closely. After nightfall a report was conveyed to Young that a covering and reinforcing party had been sent from Jytuck to support the force approaching and defend them from our superior attack. In consequence of this report Young took a position on the road from Jytuck to Chinalgurh, where the enemy stood, to intercept the Jytuck detachment, beat it and afterwards pursue his success against the Ramgurh detachment. The night passed and no party appeared from Jytuck. In the morning Young determined to move down in two columns to attack the Ramgurh party in Chinalgurh, but they anticipated him and advanced against his right column driving it back.

The repulse gave a panic to the whole, and probably not more than 200 Goorkas who had attacked, drove before them over 3000 irregulars like a flock of sheep. Many were not killed for they ran too fast but a number broke their legs and necks by tumbling down precipices. No particular party behaved well – all equally ill. Young supposed the detachment must have been reinforced from the westward and conjectures their strength to have been this morning eight hundred. But that this force even should have beaten 3000 is too bad.[402]

Fraser could not forbear from adding a further criticism of Martindell: 'All our luck is to come and it will not come until [we] get another General, for this old body is worse than none. Had the General supported the irregulars by a party of 300 Native Infantry the result would have been very different. Their presence alone would have inspired confidence and prevented the general flight. To this he was repeatedly and urgently pressed – but without success.'

Tradition has it that Lieutenant Young was captured by 'the Gorkhas' when his large force of irregulars deserted him near Jaithak. In her book about her father's life, Young's daughter, Mrs Jenkins, gave an account of the incident and added: 'How long exactly Frederick Young remained a prisoner, I have no means of stating accurately, but I know that he was treated with every mark of honour as a brave foe and that he usefully employed the time. He became intimately conversant with their language, he studied their religion, their prejudices, their manners and customs, and gained their steady admiration and even friendship as a man among men'.[403] There can be no doubt that Young, who later in 1815 became commandant of the Sirmoor battalion, gained the great respect of his soldiers. However, Mrs Jenkins' account of his being taken prisoner seems to conflict with documentary evidence. William Fraser wrote to Young on 25 February 1815 at Camp Nauri: 'It having come to my knowledge that in consequence of the affair of 21st instant in which the principal part of the Corps of Irregular Infantry under your command was engaged with a strong force of the enemy, a considerable number of casualties have taken place and that a much greater number of desertions ensued.' In order that the Governor-General might be fully informed Fraser requested urgent answers to ten questions together with a descriptive detail of the numbers of men engaged, casualties and desertions, and of those who had requested to be discharged from further service.[404] A copy of the descriptive detail[405] dated 26 February 1815, signed by both Young and William Fraser, is at appendix A. Probably on the same day (the letter is erroneously dated 21 February 1815) Young replied to Fraser's request, question by question, in columnar form, to which Fraser added his comments (see appendix B).[406] Neither Young nor Fraser made any reference to Young having been taken prisoner.[407]

The descriptive detail reveals that in addition to Kishen Singh (chief sirdar) there were two other Sirmuri leaders, and seven Pathan leaders; of the total force of 3,305 irregulars: 1,941 were plainsmen of mixed origins and 1,364 were hillmen (including 481 Paharis, 283 Sirmuris and 600 Mewattis). Of the ninety-six hillmen who deserted, fifty-six were Sirmooris led by Kundaz of the Sirmuri family. The other forty were Mewattis who deserted before the action began. All the plainsmen had applied for discharge.

In his covering letter to William Fraser, Young explained: 'I beg leave to state the Irregular Corps being raised on the spur of the moment to the amount of 4000 men, it was unavoidably open to the fellows of all coasts [*sic*] who could procure arms and the recommendation of a sirdar, whose interest it was to assemble all the men he could as his own rank depended on the number of his followers. As might be expected the Corps was made up in a hurry of every description who offered their services to obtain 6 rupees in advance and the chance of that sum monthly in comfortable quarters.'[408]

Young's answers to Fraser's questions show that he was under no illusions about the need to make a fresh start by raising a local corps of disciplined Paharis armed with fusils and led by two European officers. Such a corps of not more than 1,000 men would, he believed, after six months' training be better for hill service than regular sepoys. From his experience, Young was convinced that mixed bodies of men with 'separate interests and prejudices' were unsuited for hard service in the hills. Properly trained Paharis alone, in Young's opinion, were fit for hill service as they could withstand fatigue and cold and were easier to feed. Young noted that the Nepalese had given up recruiting Sirmuris as being neither brave nor faithful, but had enlisted many Garhwalis. While Fraser agreed with Young's proposals for a local corps of Paharis, and that highlanders were best for service in the hills, he insisted that Pathans and Mewattis were the best fighters, that Garhwalis were no better than the inhabitants of Jaunsar, Puchad and Jubal, and (probably correctly) that the Nepalese Army had more Kumaoni soldiers than Garhwali.

Fraser agreed with Young's recommendations that until Paharis could be procured and trained, the irregular force should be divided into smaller bodies under European officers. However, Fraser made the important point that 'as many British officers as can be procured properly selected, with reference to the duties they are intended to discharge and their knowledge of the Asiatick character, are obviously desirable. An intemperate, hasty, boisterous person would do more harm than good.' Neither Fraser nor Young made any specific reference to the inclusion of deserters or captives from the Nepalese Army.

Ochterlony's qualification about using the services of Kishen Singh 'if he can be trusted' was justified. Kishen Singh had boasted that if he had 10,000 men he could drive the Nepalese across the Jumna. However, with money provided by the British he raised fewer than 1,000 men for William Fraser's irregular corps, almost half of them unsoldierly plainsmen. In the disastrous action of 21 February 1815, fifty-five of Kishen Singh's plainsmen had been killed and ten wounded; the other 365 had all deserted (see appendix A). Evidence of Kishen Singh's untrustworthiness and indiscipline soon followed. On 28 February 1815, Young felt it necessary to report to Martindell further desertions from the irregular force.[409] As ordered by Colonel Mawby, Young had directed 557 Mewattis and 400 of Kishen Singh's men to march into Syne. Kishen Singh refused to move with his men until all arrears of pay had been made up. Young, who found Kishen Singh's accounts unintelligible, 'had reason to suspect that the sums he mentioned as disbursed were not actually paid to them'. Having no money available, Young ordered Kishen Singh to march immediately for Syne where arrears of pay up to 15 February would be forwarded. Kishen Singh then insisted on all hillmen being placed under his command, and, when this was refused, he and his 400 left for Nahan. Some of them defected.

Despite all this and the fact that Young had said he would never again agree to take Kishen Singh under him as a commander, it was decided to negotiate the return of Kishen Singh and his men. Completely out of character, Fraser requested Stevenson on 2 March 1815 to consult Martindell: 'His wishes on the point will mainly influence my conduct because it is ridiculous to put troops into his service and command of which he may have a poor or bad opinion.'[410] Whereas Fraser felt the British could do just as well without Kishen Singh as with him, he clearly hoped Martindell would find it 'expedient at the present moment to avail himself of the use of his [Kishen Singh's] men'. As to Kishen Singh himself, Fraser felt 'rather inclined to forgive and recall him but if the General is decidedly against his being pardoned I will tell him to make the best of his way to Puteeala'.[411] On the same day Stevenson replied to Fraser that Kishen Singh's men had paraded at his tent and had been given a 'pretty eloquent speech' which they had received with 'plaudits' promising no more 'tumultuous conduct'. In return for promises to make up their pay and to care for the wounded and those incapable of further service, the 400 hillmen agreed to rejoin Young. Stevenson assured Fraser: 'I think you will find them obedient in future.'[412] Martindell's reaction was predictable: 'If Mr. Fraser is of opinion that Kishen Singh should be employed after what has occurred, I have no objection providing he is satisfied it will be for the benefit of all interests.'[413] Fraser wrote a hasty undated note to Stevenson insisting that Young, being the person commanding his corps, must be chiefly consulted. He added: 'to tell the plain truth I have not a much worse opinion than before of Kissen [sic] Singh's conduct. He has been himself a fool, a passionate hasty blockhead.'[414] Evidently Young agreed and the hillmen nucleus of the shattered irregular corps was retained.

Martindell's views on irregular troops seem to have been ambivalent. Prior to the disaster of 21 February 1815, his attitude to them appeared to be softening. In a note to William Fraser dated 7 February 1815, Martindell suggested: 'I have reason to believe the wounded irregulars are in great distress for moneys to afford them the common necessities of life. Would it not be proper to give them a month's pay?'[415] On 25 February 1815 Martindell wrote to Young: 'It was with concern and surprise I found from your note of yesterday evening that a general disquiet prevails amongst the irregulars. It is however indispensably necessary immediate measures are taken to put a stop to it, and the only method of doing so is to ascertain the cause lest it should be something other than you mention.'[416] Martindell was, however, concerned with maintaining a large force of irregulars. In an undated note to William Fraser, written probably in March 1815 when the irregular force was being reconstructed, he stressed: 'I cannot at present say if the number of irregulars, viz. 5,000, will be sufficient but do not believe we have a man too many.'[417]

It must have been with Martindell's knowledge that the irregulars were still further increased, as the following muster roll figures show:

Table 3. *Strength of William Fraser's reconstituted irregular corps*

	Native Officers	Nagies	Sepoys	Non-Combatants	Totals
March 1815	207	710	5,408	297	6,622
April 1815	226	769	5,800	318	7,113
May 1815	216	727	5,432	306	6,681

The instability of the irregular corps remained. The muster rolls show the following desertions or discharges over the same period:[418]

Table 4. *Men who deserted or were discharged*

	Native Officers	Nagies	Sepoys	Non-Combatants	Totals
March 1815	4	20	193	7	224
April 1815	25	94	779	32	930
May 1815	—	—	23	—	23

The figures for April 1815 in table 4 probably relate to what James

Fraser described as 'a brush which took place on the night of the 29th [March 1815] between our irregulars and the Ghorkas. Between 600 and 800 irregulars were routed of whom 10 or 12 were killed and plenty ran away among precipices.'[419] Alexander Fraser, seeking to exonerate William, wrote on 12 March 1815 to his brother James: 'I am sorry to find William's irregulars have behaved so ill, but he could not make soldiers. He could only select and I suppose there was little room for selection.'[420] William's own view of his irregulars was disclosed in a letter of 22 May 1815 to Alexander Fraser: 'You need not be by any means vexed at the behaviour of the irregulars. They have effected as much as was required of them and as much as men raised under similar circumstances have done elsewhere. Getting together 7,000 men in such a way must be an accumulation of rubbish and scum in which a little gold is mined with a great deal of lead.'[421]

It is important to note that none of these irregular troops was from the Nepalese Army. Upwards of 200 Nepalese troops who had been taken prisoner by Martindell's division from isolated outposts were held at Nahan. James Fraser wrote in his diary (28 March 1815): 'Last night my brother's Ghoorka company came in. Such ragamuffins I have seldom seen. They have Chinese faces, sallow complexion, dark shaggy hair cut short by the ears and very bushy. Upon their heads they wear a peculiar turban somewhat like the broad Scottish Bonnet. Their garments are filthy. They carry besides a tulwar a short crooked knife in their cummerbunds.'[422] William Fraser recognised that 'as in Scotland, filth seems necessary to keep out the cold'.[423]

Although the Nepalese prisoners were well treated they were not armed or committed to active service against their former masters. They were however used to instruct the irregular corps in the art of constructing stockades: 'The irregulars make a stockade in the Ghoorka fashion – a Jemmadar and a party of the regular Ghoorka company show them the way.'[424] In addition to the prisoners from captured outposts, a steady trickle of deserters came across to the British. James Fraser recorded in his diary (10 April 1815): 'William was examining a deserter from the garrison [Jaithak]. He proved to be one of Bulbudder's orderlies and had deserted from mere hunger. He says there is great scarcity of grain in the fort . . . 1, 2, 3 or more are deserting every day. He says the Ghoorkas [regard] our sepoys as about equal to their common army but their Gorucka Pultan is equal to our Europeans.'[425] A further entry in James Fraser's diary (30 April 1815) reports '20–30 deserters from the Goruck Pultan. Still the General talks of 2000 fighting men in the stockades and fort. More deserters daily – 10 to 12 - and are said to desert to Nahn.'[426]

The following table summarises details given in pay abstracts and abstracts of muster rolls for 'the Corps of Goorkas under Lieutenant Frederick Young', signed by William Fraser and Young and counter-signed by the Military-Auditor General:[427]

Table 5. *The Corps of Goorkhas under Lieutenant Frederick Young – the first intakes*

	Officers	NCOs	Sepoys	Non-Combatants	Totals
March-April 1815	2	2	48	—	52
May 1815	31	110	1,098	1	1,240

That there was indeed a steady trickle of Nepalese Army deserters in March and April 1815 is born out in the day-by-day intake shown in the muster roll abstracts. The first to arrive seem to have been a subedar and two sepoys on 18 March, a sepoy on 23 March and two sepoys on 3 April. All these deserters were paid on similar rates as the irregular corps, i.e. subedar Rs.30, jemadar Rs.20, havildar Rs.8, and sepoy Rs.6. An extraordinarily large intake on 1 May 1815, of a jemadar, eight havildars, nine naiks, a major (not the equivalent of the British commissioned rank) and 505 sepoys suggests that captured men as well as deserters were then included in the 'Corps of Goorkas'. The eventual surrender of Jaithak to Ochterlony in mid-May doubtless accounts for the further substantial intake. Of this more will be written later. For the present it is necessary to comment on the significance of a note in the pay and muster roll abstracts that one Havildar, one Naik and forty-nine sepoys of the Corps of Goorkas were 'on command with Mr. Fraser'.[428]

On 31 March 1815 William Fraser wrote to Ochterlony enclosing a lengthy paper of 'Notes and Memorandums' concerning a plan for joint action by irregulars raised in Jubal district (northern Sirmur) by Fraser himself and troops of the Raja of Kulu to promote greater military activity and so help to end the war in the west.[429] Fraser sent copies to the Political Secretary on 5 April 1815 explaining that he preferred this form of communication with Ochterlony 'as it comes before him in the shape of a simple information and detail without assuming what might otherwise be unjustly construed in a tone of suggestion and instruction'.[430] Ochterlony may have thought otherwise. Fraser had written to him earlier in March on matters 'upon which I considered you would deem it expedient to give an opinion and decision'. Ochterlony had not replied. Perhaps he saw in the plan a thinly disguised opportunity for Fraser to obtain an independent military command.[431]

At the end of April 1815, when the first campaign of the war was virtually over, William Fraser was appointed Commissioner for the affairs of Garhwal. This called for a tour to familiarise himself with the country prior to making new land settlements. It allowed him to take with him a military escort large enough to cut off the retreat of isolated Nepalese troops from the Cis-Sutlej campaign and to encourage Garhwali leaders to eliminate scattered groups of Nepalese soldiers in their territory. Martindell must have welcomed the prospect of losing not only William Fraser but William's brother James who was hardly less scathing than William in his attitude to Martindell. James wrote in his diary (17 March 1815): 'this old man the General [Martindell] seems gifted with the very soul of procrastination and the marrow of obstinacy'. He added (19 March 1815): 'the despair and vexation of every officer in the army is great but the old mule will listen to nothing, neither his Engineer nor artillery officers nor to those men of experience'.[432] The two brothers set off on 6 May 1815 on a tour of Jubal, Comharsein, Bashahr and Garhwal.[433] They took with them from the corps of irregulars 2 Indian officers, 26 nagies, 307 sepoys and 2 civilian pay clerks.[434] In addition they had the fifty-one soldiers from Lieutenant Young's Corps of Goorkas (referred to above). It may well have been the presence of these Nepalese troops which persuaded the garrison at Chaupal in Jubal, Subedar Subhir Singh Thapa and 126 all ranks,

to surrender and to join the British service.[435] William and James Fraser
were at Mangnee in Comharsein on 25 May 1815 when they heard that
Jaithak had surrendered and that the campaign in the west was over.
Their tour ended on 29 July 1815 and by 19 August 1815 they were back
in Delhi.

The failure of the two eastern divisions led by Marley and John Wood
to achieve their objectives,[436] and the slow progress of Martindell's
division in Garhwal, left open communications between Kathmandu
and the Nepalese Army in the west. Hastings therefore decided to
begin operations in Kumaon [437] in order both to prevent reinforcements being sent to Kaji Amar Singh Thapa, and to cut off his retreat
eastwards. He was aware that 'Kumaon was almost destitute of
enemy'.[438] As he was unable to redeploy regular troops for the purpose,
the Governor-General decided to appoint Lieutenant-Colonel William
Gardner, a cousin of the Hon. Edward Gardner, to command a corps
of 3,000 irregulars to be recruited largely from Afghan immigrants in
Rohilkhand, and a further 1,000 Pathan and Mewatti irregulars already
forming under Captain Hearsey.[439] Hearsey, who had volunteered his
services to the Governor-General, had been given authority to raise
an irregular battalion under his command for service in Kumaon.[440]
This battalion was to be based on Hearsey's plan for a corps of 1,500
men organised in fifteen companies as follows:[441]

Table 6. *Hearsey's planned corps, 1815*

5 Companies Sepoys Muskets	Hindoos	Men	500
5 Do. of Nujeeb Dhamakahs	Mixt [*sic*]		500
2 Do. of Mewatties Matchlock	do.		200
3 Do. of Patans	Mussulmans		300

Hearsey conceived that this plan

> would be most suitable for the service, embracing all the kinds of troops
> that would be required: the Patans for attack; the Mewatties for defend-
> ing posts, for agility, and surprises by night; the Dhamakah corps for

convoys and regular duty; and the sepoys for discipline, for covering a retreat, and forming as a reserve to the rest of the party. The Dhamakah (or crooked-stocked matchlock corps that carries a fusil ball) will be composed of Hindoos and Mussulmans; the Mewatties the same; the Patan corps entirely Mussulmans: so that the Hindoos may predominate. The Mussulmans are inherently slack in discipline, are easily surprised, and when attacked are frequently dismayed, and fly without considering the numbers opposed to them.[442]

Hearsey added that 'by the addition of two subaltern European or country-born officers the whole will form a most compact and useful body of men ready for immediate service'. Events were to prove him disastrously wrong.

Part of Hearsey's original elaborate plan had been to raise two of the five sepoy companies from Kumaoni deserters from the Nepalese Army 'who would be anxious to enter under our banners'.[443] The five Dhamakah companies were to be composed of a mixture of 'Hindoos and Mussulmans, most of the officers being Mussulmans'. Hearsey believed them to be brave, orderly, obedient and trustworthy and to form 'the very best kind of Hindoostanee troops there are'. Of the Mewattis, Hearsey wrote that they 'move quicker in bodies, are good marksmen and hardy, and for defences of small posts, depots or bridgeheads are unequalled by any Hindoostanee troops. They are bold in night attacks and behind any cover will fight to extremity.'

His decision to recruit companies of Pathans is not supported by his own testimony:

Much cannot be said in favour of the Afghans and Pathans in storming forts and towns. Plunder induces them to lead on boldly; if checked, it is very difficult to lead them up again to attack. They abhor discipline. The generality are mutinous, and not even subordinate to their own officers. Being masters of their own arms and equipments, they, if successful in plunder, immediately desert, and their treachery is notorious over all India, changing sides. They are a race hard to keep under control in a body, and their excesses would draw down the ill-will of the inhabitants of the mountains. They besides cannot endure hunger and thirst, with what patience a Hindoo bears them.[444]

Hearsey, who like William Gardner had served as an officer with the Marathas, lacked Gardner's authority and charisma. Gardner took no unnecessary risks in fulfilling his orders while awaiting the arrival of Lieutenant-Colonel Jasper Nicolls and his regular troops before attacking Almora. Hearsey, who had had three months in which to raise and train his force, was determined to make a name for himself in an operation which was small in comparison with the campaign in the west. He had a very low opinion of Nepalese soldiers and their equipment.[445]

William Gardner, committed to recruit itinerant Pathans and 'as many troops in the service of the enemy, exclusive of Goorkas, as may be disposed to join you', led his troops with great skill.[446] He entered Kumaon on 15 February 1815, and taking a circuitous route without serious incident, reached the vicinity of Almora by the end of March. Hearsey ignored the pleading of William Gardner to secure the ghats on the Mahakali river against possible reinforcements from Doti (in Nepal). Unwisely Hearsey distributed his troops in a vain attempt to capture Katalgarh, the strongest fortress in Kumaon[447] while at the same time holding the foot of the Timla Pass and besieging forts at the top of the pass. For guarding the river ghats he assigned a mere 300 men. Nepalese reinforcements under Hasti Dal, one of Nepal's best commanders, crossed the Mahakali and on 2 April 1815 defeated Hearsey, whose troops fled. Hearsey himself was severely wounded and taken prisoner. Others in his scattered force withdrew to the plains in terror. The Nepalese garrison at Almora was reinforced.[448] Regarding the disastrous result of Hearsey's theorising, Prinsep noted: 'In every action between the Goorkha regulars and Rohilla [Pathan] Nujeebs or other levies, the former were always victorious.'[449] Alexander Fraser had another explanation. In a letter dated 30 April 1815 to his father, he wrote: 'Many corps of irregulars have been raised; of these one large body was committed to the charge of Captain Hearsey, formerly in the Mahratta service. Hearsey's detachment consisted entirely of new levies and he is accused of having collected a parcel of ragamuffins who engaged to serve for trifling pay. He converting to his own profit the difference between what Government allowed and what these worthless troops consented to accept.'[450]

Fortunately, a body of about 2,000 regular troops had set out for Almora under the command of Colonel Nicolls. On joining with Gardner's force on 8 April 1815, Nicolls assumed overall command and immediately began a sustained and highly successful attack on Almora which ended in the death of Hasti Dal and the occupation of the town on 1 May 1815.[451] Edward Gardner, whom Hastings had appointed Commissioner for the affairs of Kumaon and Agent to the Governor-General in that Province, conducted with the Nepalese Governor of Kumaon negotiations which led to a Convention whereby Kumaon was annexed by the British (see appendix C).[452]

CHAPTER 6

The first campaign, Ochterlony's success in the far north-west: 1815

While the other divisions of the Bengal field army were meeting with disaster or ignominy, Ochterlony's Third division made steady and methodical progress in the far north-west. In a letter dated 7 March 1815 Alexander Fraser explained to his father that:

> The General Officers commanding divisions having been appointed during peace were chosen by seniority without reference to talent or merit. Now that war is commenced, to remove them without trial was so invidious that they were allowed to retain their commands to the dishonour of the British army and to their own disgrace. For poor Marley is at length superseded . . . General Wood, it is said, is also to be removed and I think that Martindell (with whom Willie is) will also be superseded by some more efficient officer. Ochterlony is the only man of judgment and decision hitherto employed, except Gillespie, who notwithstanding he is accused of rashness, I think was an excellent officer.[453]

Hastings put his faith in Ochterlony's powers as a field commander to achieve his vital objectives in the far north-west. He was not to be disappointed.

Having been given discretionary powers by Hastings, Ochterlony relied on his own judgement that Kaji Amar Singh Thapa 'either at the entrance of the Nalagarh Pass, or in some chosen strong position on the way to Arki, will make his first and principal stand with every man he can collect and with every defensive art of stockade etc., which they have in use'.[454] Ochterlony, who did not agree with Hastings' view that he would be engaged in the pursuit of a mobile Nepalese

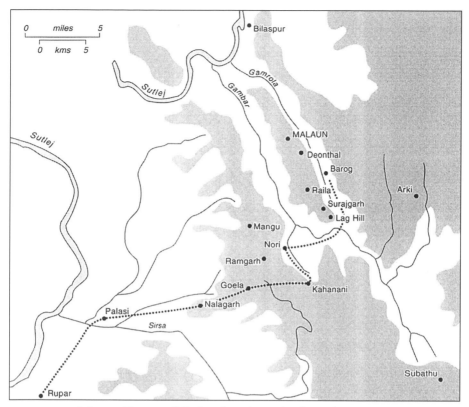

Map 5. Route of Ochterlony's main force in 1814–15.

army, decided to take with him a formidable array of artillery. Ochterlony set out from Rupar and moved via the Hindur capital Palasi towards Nalagarh (see map 5). He was resolved to spend whatever time was necessary surveying the terrain and, with the unstinting support of the Raja of Hindur's labour force, constructing roads and pathways for his guns: two eighteen-pounders, ten six-pounders, two heavy howitzers and two heavy mortars. The eighteen-pounder battering guns and the six-pounder field guns were capable of firing single solid round-shot, and multi-shot canister shot (alias case-shot). The howitzers lobbed explosive shells and carcasses (incendiary projectiles). The mortars also fired shells but had a shorter range.[455]

The Third division was faced with the daunting prospect of crossing the Hindur mountains, which rose sharply out of the Sutlej plains in precipitate parallel ridges buttressed by massive spurs. Covering the primitive tracks across this rugged landscape, Kaji Amar Singh Thapa had carefully spread his defences in a network of forts and stockades. The first of these defences, on a bluff overlooking Palasi, was the fort of Nalagarh.

Ochterlony pitched camp three miles short of the fort and sent his field engineer, Lawtie, with a small party on a wide and circuitous route to reconnoitre the surrounding heights. Lawtie found a suitable site for a battery only 225 yards from the walls of the fort. Two six-pounders and the two eighteen-pounders were hauled into position by elephants. A breach was made by the six-pounders and, under threat from the heavier battering guns, the garrison surrendered. There were few British casualties.

Hastings wrote to the Court of Directors:

> While your Honourable Court will regret the disasters which have attended the operations of the Second division of the Field Army, you will derive sensible gratification from the success of the Third division under the personal command of Colonel Ochterlony to whom the fort of Nalagarh and the dependant fort of Tarragarh surrendered on the 5th of November [1814].[456]

As has already been stated, the ninety-five troops from the garrisons of Nalagarh and nearby Taragarh were handsomely treated as prisoners of war and sent back under escort to Ludhiana. Recognising the effectiveness of the Nepalese kukri in close fighting, Ochterlony took the opportunity 'to purchase from the prisoners their hookeries [*sic*] which I had given to them as private property and had promised should be returned with their swords at Ludhiana. This small number will be served out as directed and others purchased as opportunities occur.'[457]

In the meantime word reached Ochterlony that Kaji Amar Singh Thapa had moved his main force, almost 3,000 men, and 1,000 auxiliaries of the Raja of Bilaspur from his bases in Arki and Subathu to Ramgarh. Anxious to counter this advance, Ochterlony sent Colonel Thompson with his troops immediately towards Goela, a village on the crest of the first ridge of hills. From Goela, the track fell into the valley of a tributary of the river Sirsa before climbing steeply via the

Ramgarh pass onto a second and higher range of hills. At some 4,500 feet on the crest of these hills, and astride the abruptly sloping head of the valley, lay the seemingly impregnable fort of Ramgarh.

Ochterlony, following Thompson, with the rest of his division took with him his ordnance. He was by now more than ever convinced that heavy guns were crucial to success. In a letter to the Adjutant-General he wrote: 'So far from meditating retreat, Ummer Singh has chosen the positions he will defend; and the nature and character of the war in this quarter may be considered as decided.' Ochterlony therefore proposed that 'our force should be concentrated on certain points; and however tardy their progress, that no one should move without a gun or guns sufficient to throw open the bourgs and stockades of the Goorkas'. So long as he was able to surmount the difficulties he would take his battering guns to Ramgarh and 'all that part of the hills which they [the Goorkas] seem determined to defend'.[458] Hastings concurred.[459]

Helped by Hinduri labourers, the pioneers began the difficult task of preparing a road for the guns. With great skill and application, ten artillery pieces were brought forward to Thompson's position at Bari-yan, allowing him to advance to Goela. From the heights he could see Ramgarh where the Nepalese were busily erecting stockades above and below the fort. Ochterlony arrived with the rest of his division at Goela on 12 November 1814 and quickly assessed through his telescope that Ramgarh fort was unassailable from the front. However, he thought it might be possible to attack a fortified position at Kot a mile to the south of Ramgarh and about 200 feet higher.[460]

Ochterlony sent Thompson with an augmented force onto the crest of the second ridge to Kahanani, about two miles from Kot. Lawtie, who had accompanied Thompson, went out nightly for a week making a comprehensive reconnaisance of the Ramgarh ridge with detailed sketches. He confirmed Ochterlony's assessment that Ramgarh fort was inaccessible from the front. However, he drew Ochterlony's attention to Nori, a settlement in the Gambar valley. Lawtie thought that it might be possible to mount an assault from there on the rear of the fort.

Ochterlony, who had great faith in Lawtie's judgement, decided to make his base at Nori.[461] In so doing he took a calculated risk that the Kaji would not attack before Ochterlony's troops could move to cut off the Nepalese supply line from Bilaspur. Nori, which lay on the Kaji's line of communication with Arki, seemed to provide the least difficult approach onto the Ramgarh hills. Ochterlony was in no great hurry to achieve his ultimate objective of driving the Nepalese Army towards Malaun fort where (as he had learned from intercepted letters) Kaji Amar Singh Thapa's relatives and treasure were installed. This was as well, for the development of the road from Goela down to the valley and, more especially, up to and beyond Kahanani presented an enormous challenge to the strength and perseverence of the labourers.

While his main movement was proceeding, Ochterlony left a battalion of native infantry under Lieutenant-Colonel Adams, with the eighteen-pounders and two other guns, to move up the western approaches to Ramgarh as a diversion. The division's baggage and bazar were left for the time being in a stockaded post at Goela. Field guns were taken from their carriages and lashed to the backs of elephants, and 7,000 coolies were employed to drag the empty carriages and carry the ammunition to Kahanani which was reached by 19 November 1814. Stores and baggage followed the next day, and two days later camp was pitched at Nori.[462]

Meanwhile Kaji Amar Singh Thapa, having discerned Ochterlony's intentions, had made an assault on Ramgarh more difficult by building stockades and redoubts on spurs overlooking the Gambar valley. When Ochterlony had a battery for his field guns constructed in front of the nearest stockade, it was found to be out of range. Lawtie, therefore, was sent off by Ochterlony with 100 men towards a hill which seemed to offer a possible site for a new battery. Unfortunately Lawtie's detachment was fired on from the heights of both flanks, and, when his men established themselves on the hill they were attacked by a large party of Nepalese soldiers. Immediately he heard the firing Ochterlony sent reinforcements under Lieutenant Williams. But they arived too late. Lawtie's men, unable to extricate ammunition from ill-fitting boxes carried in their leather pouches, were forced to retire under heavy fire from three sides. Williams and forty-one sepoys were killed and thirty-three injured. Ochterlony blamed himself for sending a weak reconnaisance party instead of mounting a proper attack.[463]

At about the time of this disheartening setback, Ochterlony received the news of the Second division's failure to take the small hill fort of Kalanga. It made him realise that he was probably alone in facing the Nepalese western army. Moreover, the Kaji, although opposed on three sides, still occupied the heights of the Ramgarh range, and his communications with his source of supplies in Bilaspur were still secure. Ochterlony, on the other hand, needed reinforcements, not least because a good many of his soldiers were falling ill.[464]

The arrival of fresh troops commanded by Lieutenant-Colonel Lyons below Ramgarh enabled the eighteen-pounders to be brought over the ridge to Nori by 27 December 1814. At about the same time two field howitzers and four light mortars arrived there from Kanpur.[465] Ochterlony now felt strong enough to attempt to cut off Kaji Amar Singh Thapa's army from Bilaspur by capturing the fort of Mangu which lay about four miles north of Ramgarh. He sent Thompson from Nori by night with fourteen companies of sepoys, 1,000 auxiliaries, two six-pounders and two howitzers. However, before he reached Mangu he was intercepted by the Kaji, who withdrew all his men from the stockades south of Ramgarh and gave them new positions on the ridge to the north. He moved his own headquarters to Mangu and attacked Thompson's camp at dawn on 29 December 1814 with an army estimated at between 2,000 and 2,500 men. Thompson's position allowed enfilade fire to be brought to bear on the attackers who with great courage continued their assault until forced to withdraw with their wounded leaving an estimated 150 dead. Thompson lost nine men killed and forty-four wounded.[466]

In such precipitous, heavily defended terrain, the demands on Lawtie as Ochterlony's field engineer were fearsome, requiring great military skill and phenomenal endurance. Despite this, Lawtie still found time to write to William Fraser. In a letter of 29 January 1815 giving an account of the prolonged operations, he wrote: 'Our men have had too much peace and too much luxury to fight such brave fellows without a few months breaking in.'[467] Some indication of the strain of such mountain warfare can be sensed from Lawtie's letter of 17 February 1815 to William Fraser: 'We left the General's camp on the 11th, had gained a height commanding Ramghar [*sic*] next morning at day-break, had four mortars and a six-pounder on the 13th and two eighteen-pounders in the battery on the 15th on a mound 790 feet above the plain. Got possession of Ramghar yesterday evening and of Joojooroo this morning both by capitulation. Great labour and no loss. I'm knocked up.'[468]

Here, especially in view of the important part he was to play in the events leading up to the recruitment of Gorkhas and other hillmen into the Bengal Army, it is necessary to give a brief background to Lawtie's short but outstanding military career and of his close association with Ochterlony. Peter Lawtie, a highland Scot, was born in Banff on 25 February 1792. His father, George Urquart Lawtie, resigned an infantry commission to become a merchant in Calcutta. Peter, a Woolwich cadet, arrived in India on 16 November 1808. He was commissioned as an ensign fireworker (artillery) on 15 December 1808 and transferred four days later to the Engineers. From 1810 to 1812 he was based at Kanpur and from 1812 to 1814 at Delhi where, as has already been stated, he became a close friend of Alexander and William Fraser and of Charles Metcalfe, the Resident. Having been posted to Ochterlony's division Lawtie quickly won the admiration and affection of Ochterlony who appointed him as his ADC as well as his field engineer. Testimony to Ochterlony's complete trust in Lawtie's judgment is given in his despatches. For example on 4 November 1814 Ochterlony reported to the Adjutant-General from near Nalagarh: 'A very dense jungle, which extends from hence to the very base of the hill on which the fort is situated, has compelled me to encamp at a distance of near three miles from the fort. On the day of our arrival, Lieutenant Lawtie, by a circuitous route, ascended the heights which seemed to have the most command of the fort and was desired to send down instant information of any spot of which he might think it advisable to take immediate possession . . . In the course of the morning, the position for the battery was most judiciously selected by Lieutenant Lawtie, and highly approved by Major McLeod.'[469] On 6 November 1814, Ochterlony wrote again to the

Adjutant-General to report the surrender of Nalagarh, adding: 'But I have feebly expressed my sense of Lieutenant Lawtie's services, whose youthful energy carried him to points which I could not have ascended, and whose active and intelligent mind furnished me with the most useful information.' [470]

While he himself was based at Nori, Ochterlony was content to involve Lawtie in the execution of his plans. Lawtie's close involvement is clear from a letter he wrote to William Fraser on 29 January 1815 about operations on the Ramgarh hills: 'Colonel Arnold moved on the 17th from Dibboo on Bilaspoor with ten days provisions and coolly carriage. Though Bilaspoor is only five easy marches from Dibboo he, Colonel Arnold, is now only at Nund. It is true he has had bad weather but I don't think he can have understood the General's plans, though they were explained in every bearing. We had a large irregular force at Roondriboo just over Bilaspoor and had Colonel Arnold got on at all, the Bilaspoor Raja would 'ere this have been on our side and all the irregular force disposable.' [471]

Despite his achievements in operations at Nalagarh and Ramgarh, Lawtie's greatest contribution was to be on the Malaun range where the hills were yet higher than those of Ramgarh and still more daunting. Here he was privileged to be the first British officer to lead Nepalese soldiers into action.

The importance of this development is such that it is necessary here to digress in order to explain how it came about. As early as 24 January 1815, Ochterlony had signed and sealed a memorandum of four propositions offered by Jeykishen, a Brahmin Subah of Kumaon, and approved by Ochterlony subject to several amendments which are shown on the copy at appendix D. This agreement established that every man who joined the British from the Nepalese Army with his musket would receive ten rupees and be retained in the British service on the Nepalese rates of pay. Subedars, jemadars, and other officers would receive the pay of their ranks for one month as a reward and afterwards be retained and receive their fixed allowances. Ochterlony decided he would judge the rewards to be paid to killadars (garrison or fort commanders) and would refer to the

Governor-General for consideration Jeykishen's request for a jagir in reward for his services.

In addition Jeykishen would receive monetary rewards according to the following scale:

one rupee for every man he brought over;
60 rupees a month for a whole company;
150 rupees a month for 5 companies;
300 rupees a month for a battalion.[472]

Because of his preoccupation with plans to defeat Kaji Amar Singh Thapa and his army at Malaun, it was not until early April 1815 that Ochterlony informed Hastings (as Commander-in-Chief) of these arrangements. By that time he was able to report that, after a slow start, considerable numbers had entered the British service. He now had in his camp a body of about 324 men including 'the Chambah Garrison who most willingly took service after being told that they might if they preferred live at ease till the conclusion of the war'. Ochterlony felt 'the most perfect confidence in the fidelity of these men' who had proved most useful in works of labour 'which they performed from habit with great celerity and with the greatest cheerfulness, appearing always gratified when they can be made in any way useful'.[473]

Ochterlony's proposals to form them into a battalion called the 'Nusseeree Pulteen', to arm them with muskets and to send them into the interior under Lieutenant Ross to bring over Kirthi Rana and his troops,[474] received enthusiastic approval from the Commander-in-Chief who suggested that those taken prisoner at Nalagarh and sent to Ludhiana might also be invited to enter British service.[475] Ochterlony's adoption of the designation Nusseeree (or Nasiri), which Hastings regarded as 'peculiarly appropriate', is interesting. In *The 1st King George's Own Gurkha Rifles* (London, 1925), P.L. Petre wrote: 'the term Nusseeree is used in contemporary correspondence without explanation. Apparently it is based on the Hindustani word Nasir, defender or friend.' Tradition therefore has it that the Nasiris were 'friendlies'. However, of his Nasiri Battalion, Ochterlony wrote: 'I consider myself their Commandant and Patron. These trifles have great weight and I must confess myself sanguine in my hopes of their not discrediting my favour.' [476] The references to 'great weight' and 'favour' suggest some deeper significance in the term Nusseeree than a general sense of friendly. Petre may not have been aware that Ochterlony, who had defended Delhi and the Mogul Court from the Marathas in 1804, had been dignified by Shah Alam with the title Nasir-ud-Daula (Helper or Victory Giver of the State). The title is etymologically connected with 'nasr', a word of Arabic origin meaning help or victory, and it is entirely reasonable to suppose that the name Nusseerees (Nasiris by academic transliteration) was given to those troops to indicate that they were in effect 'Ochterlony's Own'. [477]

Operations in and around Ramgarh were still proceeding when Ochterlony put into effect his brilliant plan to trap Kaji Amar Singh Thapa and his army. On 16 January he moved his headquarters and main force from Nori round Lag hill and up the Gamrola valley to Battoh near the village of Barog (see map 5). Lieutenant Ross with 2,000 Hinduri troops pressed on rapidly to occupy the heights overlooking Bilaspur, thereby causing the Raja of Bilaspur to flee in terror across the Sutlej and then to change his allegiance from the Nepalese to the British to whom he now provided supplies. As soon as Kaji Amar Singh Thapa became aware of Ochterlony's move from Nori, he gathered all but a few of his men from the main defensive positions on the Ramgarh hills and, as Ochterlony had foreseen, withdrew from Mangu to Malaun. Once Arnold's force had relieved Ross at Bilaspur all that remained to be done was to take Ramgarh fort and clear the Ramgarh range of Nepalese troops sending them, in accordance with Ochterlony's orders, to add to the Kaji's supply problems on the Malaun hills. Lawtie set out from Nori with 600 Hinduris on 12 February and cleared the outlying stockades on the Ramgarh ridge without much difficulty. However the capture of Ramgarh fort necessitated dragging the battering guns from the valley onto the heights. At first, despite heavy bombardment and severe damage to the walls of the fort, the garrison refused to capitulate. However further damage from prolonged bombardment, together with the effect of shrapnel shells forced them to surrender the fort on 16 February. They were

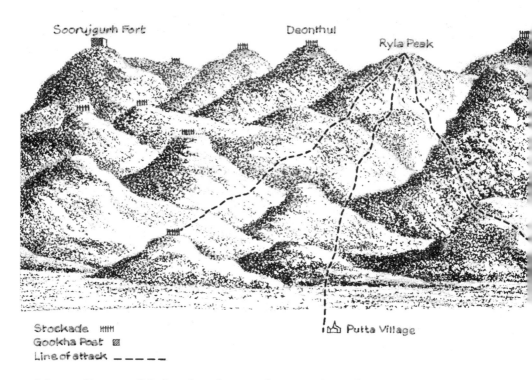

Map 6: Route of Ochterlony's assault on Malaun fort in April 1815 [478]

allowed to march off to Malaun with their arms, colours and belongings. The garrison at Jojoru fort surrendered next day on the same terms. The capture of both forts had been achieved without loss.

While Cooper repaired and strengthened the defence of Ramgarh to form a depot, Lawtie led his Hinduris six miles north to capture Chamba fort on 16 March with the aid of an eighteen-pounder gun. With the Ramgarh ridge cleared and with detachments of auxiliary troops manning captured forts and stockades, Ochterlony and his division were poised to close the trap. An indication of the steep and rugged terrain is given by illustrations 5, 6 and 7 and and by map 6. James Fraser noted in his diary (19 March 1815): 'Auchterlony [*sic*] is proceeding slow and sure but Malaun is a very strong place. He will have a tough job of it.' [479]

Ochterlony's masterly approach onto the Malaun hills was based

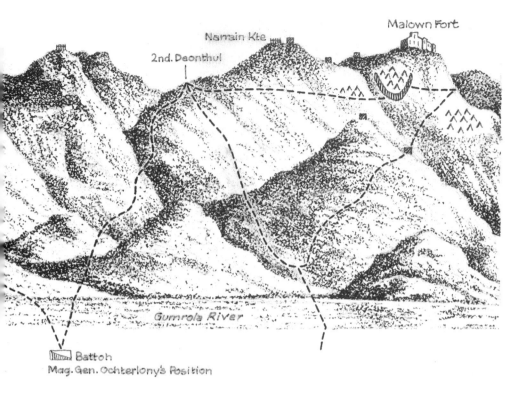

Battoh

Maj. Gen. Ochterlony's Position

on Lawtie's painstaking reconnaissance and his own observation which showed that two strategic hilltops, Ryla (or Raila) and what came to be called second Deonthal (see map 6) were undefended. Operations began on the night of 14 April 1815 when some 300 Nasiris under Lawtie and 800 irregulars under Lieutenant Fleming climbed silently onto Ryla where the Nasiris constructed a strong stockade. On the morning of 15 April the position was reinforced by two columns: a Grenadier battalion under Major Innes with two six-pounder guns; and a force under Captain Hamilton. The securing of Ryla by so strong a force cut off Bhakti Thapa and his troops in Surajgarh. Simultaneously, on the 15 April two columns moved on to second Deonthal: the main force of 1,300 regulars of the Light Battalion and 300 pioneers, with two six-pounder guns; and a force of 400 irregulars under Captain Lawrie. As a distraction, two feint attacks were made on the Nepalese cantonments below Malaun fort, one led by Captain Bowyer, the other by Captain Showers. A copy of a letter dated 20 April 1815 from

Rugged terrain in the Malaun Hills.

5.
Malaun fort from near the summit.

6.
Escarpment near Malaun fort.

7.
View from Malaun fort towards the Sutlej.

8. Distant view of the Sutlej from Malaun fort.

Lieutenant Ross to Captain Birch at Ludhiana, describing the operations, is given at appendix E.[480] At about the same time Lawtie wrote to William Fraser:

> I send you a sketch which will explain the movements of the 14th, 15th, 16th and 17th which have ended up by giving us possession of Soorujghar and the seven stockades between it and [second] Deonthal. My share has been previous enquiry and accompanying the night movement of the 14th, just being too late to have a share in the repulse of the enemy from [second] Deonthal on the morning of the 16th, having arrived from Ryla with 300 Goorkhas only 10 minutes after the affair and a long but unsuccessful pursuit with 150 of our Goorkhas after some of the Soorujghur fugitives. On the morning of the 17th we missed a pair of colours by about 60 yards.[481]

A description of the heroic but unsuccessful attempts led by Bhakti Thapa to capture second Deonthal, and of Bhakti Thapa's death, is in Ross' letter to Birch at appendix E. Lawtie recorded in his letter to William Fraser: 'the poor Goorkhas who came for Bukhtee's body emphatically said that the blade of the Talwar went broke and only the handle remained. I never witnessed a more affecting sight. He appears from every account to have been as mild, kind and good a man as he was a gallant, excellent soldier.' Our concern, however, lies with the Nasiris.

On 18 April 1815, the day after the crucial battle of Malaun and several days before he received the Commander-in-Chief's approval, Ochterlony proudly transmitted to the Adjutant-General an official report on the conduct of his Nasiris, 'a corps in which I feel a great and peculiar interest'.[482] Ochterlony's decision to give Lieutenant Lawtie the honour of being the first to lead his Nasiris into action against the Nepalese Army was both a mark of his great esteem for Lawtie's military skills and at the same time a recognition of Ochterlony's pride and confidence in the discipline and reliability of the Nasiris. Lawtie reported that he had the greatest reason to be satisfied with their exertions, 'the closeness of their files and the perfect silence with which they moved on the night of the 14th instant [April 1815 when they climbed the steep slopes of the Malaun heights] over the most rugged roads proved them to be peculiarly [specially] adapted for operations which require celerity and concealment'.[483]

On 15 April 1815 the Nasiris sustained their first casualties, one man killed and two wounded, while stockading an exposed hilltop position at Ryla. The next day, with Ochterlony's permission, the Nasiris readily agreed to move to second Deonthal to strengthen the position which Colonel Thompson was holding against repeated attacks. Lawtie recorded: 'the rapidity of their march shewed at least their anxiety to share in the dangers of the day'.[484] However, the enemy attacks had ceased by the time the Nasiris arrived. On 17 April the Nasiris were given another opportunity to engage the enemy. While they were taking possession of advanced positions between second Deonthal and Narain Kot, parties of the Nepalese Army fled towards Narain Kot. Lawtie sent 150 Nasiris in rapid pursuit, withdrawing them only when there was no hope of success in order to continue the vital work of stockading the advanced positions. Lawtie noted that everything the Nasiris did 'was done with cheerfulness, good humour and an ac-

9. The approach to Malaun fort from Narain Kot.

knowledgement of gratitude for the kindness of their present employers'. His report was written to enable Ochterlony 'to judge the value of a new and so peculiarly [specially] formed a Corps'.[485] Of this Ochterlony had no doubt.

James Fraser recorded in his diary (20 April 1815): 'today we have full and authentic accounts of Auchterlony's success at Malaun'.[486] On learning that Ochterlony had successfully embodied, armed, and actively employed captured Nepalese soldiers, William Fraser was keen that more than 300 deserters from Ranjor Singh Thapa's forces at Jaithak and 250 others captured from forts elsewhere by Martindell's division should be similarly employed. This would help to make up the numbers of irregular troops for which he had already obtained the Governor-General's approval. However, Martindell had no wish to employ, still less arm, enemy deserters. He had once given his opinion to William Fraser: 'I fancy you will agree with me that a Goorkah for fighting is worth at least double any of our irregulars.'[487] He made clear in a letter dated 16 April [1815] to Fraser that he had no intention of introducing Nepalese soldiers into Fraser's

10. Malaun fort from near where Bhakti Thapa was killed.

irregulars: 'Colonel Kelly has no deserters with him but Ghoorkhahs [*sic*]. I will, however write him to send any inhabitants of Gurhwal and Kumaon that may come in up to you.'[488] Martindell also wrote to William Fraser on 17 April 1815: 'regarding the issue of arms to defectors from the Nepalese Army, I do not consider myself authorised to give them without special orders for so doing.'[489] Stevenson wrote privately to Fraser: 'I am sorry to see the General so damned obstinate in not arming the Goorkahs. Do you know that I have reason to think that he is alarmed at the number of unarmed fellows we have here. The General could easily give you arms by indenting for them.'[490] Not for the first time Fraser chose to ignore Martindell's views. Before setting out for Jubal he wrote to the Political Secretary on 27 April 1815 in his capacity as Political Agent for Garhwal, 'I am satisfied they would be judged valuable and very superior troops. With this connection I have no hesitation in recommending permanent service being offered and promised to bodies deserting or individuals who may be brought away from their pledge.'[491]

Fraser sought the Governor-General's authority to arm and equip the new Corps and to unite it with irregulars already under the command of Lieutenant Young. In his reply of 8 May 1815 the Political Secretary conveyed the Governor-General's approval to Fraser's proposals as 'a Corps of this description formed by Major-General Ochterlony has been found to be of the highest utility, and that Officer's experience has shewn that the utmost reliance may be placed in their fidelity, while regularly paid and well treated. Of their value in all the essential qualities of soldiers there can be no doubt.'[492] When embodied the Corps was to be placed under the command of Lieutenant Young, subject to Fraser's general control and superintendence. There was no suggestion that these Nepalese soldiers should be called Nasiris.

Between 20 April 1815, when Bhakti Thapa was killed at Malaun, and the beginning of May, the Nasiris were employed in strengthening the stockades, redoubts, and outworks captured from the Nepalese. Into these positions close to Malaun fort Ochterlony moved his regular and auxiliary troops. With Lawtie desperately ill from typhus and exhaustion, Ochterlony turned to his other close aide, Lieutenant

11. Ochterlony's 18-pounder guns lying in Malaun fort

12. The same guns relocated in Subathu on 7 Dec. 1995

Robert Ross, whom he had already entrusted with the important task of subverting the Raja of Bilaspur. Ochterlony had been greatly impressed by Ross's leadership and firm control of 2,000 Hinduri troops (see page 117) who had been intent on wreaking vengeance on the Bilaspuris.

Robert Ross, a Scot, was born on 20 January 1789 in Perth, where his father, John Ross, was a merchant. Robert arrived in India as a cadet on 10 September 1805 and was commissioned as an ensign on 26 September 1805. In 1806 he was posted as a lieutenant to the 2nd/6th Bengal Native Infantry, in which Battalion he served as Adjutant before being assigned to the Intelligence Department in 1814. In this latter capacity he joined Ochterlony's Third Field Division for the Anglo-Nepal war.

On 3 May 1815, Ochterlony sent Ross forward with the Nasiris to take up a position close to the enemy at a stockade under Colonel Thompson's advanced post near Malaun fort, and to open a short and safe road by which those of the enemy who might wish to come over from a heavily bombarded redoubt could cross to the British side. Most importantly, Ross was to take stock of the possibility of mounting an attack on the redoubt supported as necessary by up to 300 of Thompson's regular troops. Ochterlony wrote: 'The establishment of the post by the Nusseerees is of importance, without reference to the ulterior designs.' [493] Ross, having ascertained the straitened circumstances of the enemy and the readiness of large numbers of them to cross to the British, climbed the heights with the Nasiris without opposition and took possession of the redoubt and of positions to its left and right. He then beckoned to the enemy who, after some hesitation, passed through the Nasiris unmolested to the rear. Ross then advanced further towards Malaun fort while more and more of Kaji Amar Singh Thapa's troops and their women and property passed them on their way to the British positions. Ross and the Nasiris occupied unopposed a strategic position covering the enemy's principal water supply and within heavy artillery range of the fort and went on to take possession of Narain Kot.[494]

On 5 May 1815, Peter Lawtie died. Grief-stricken, Ochterlony issued orders that the officers of his division were to wear mourning for a month. He also arranged for monuments to Lawtie's memory to be erected in the cathedral church of Calcutta and in the parish church of Banff. Charles Metcalfe's letter to William Fraser dated 10 May 1815 was in the form of a eulogy: 'I am sure you will be grieved beyond measure to learn that our dear and invaluable friend Lawtie has terminated his short but splendid career of glory . . . a more perfect being, one with greater excellencies and fewer faults I think I never knew.' [495] A Governor-General's Order dated 21 May 1815 included a special tribute: 'It is painful to think, in this hour of exultation, that an individual whose skill, whose judgment, and whose animated devotion materially forwarded the proud result, should not have survived to share in the triumph; but the grateful recollection of his fellow soldiers and of Government will associate the memory of Lieutenant Lawtie with all the trophies which he so eminently con-tributed to raise.' [496] One of these trophies would eventually be the Indian Army's Gurkha Brigade.

The draining away of Kaji Amar Singh Thapa's forces, the tight blockade of Malaun fort, the accurate bombardment by Ochterlony's field guns and howitzers and the arrival of heavy artillery near Narain Kot persuaded the Kaji to surrender. [497] Ensuing negotiations culmi-nated in a Convention between Kaji Amar Singh Thapa and Ochterlony on 15 May 1815. A copy is given at appendix F. Full honours were to be accorded to Kaji Amar Singh Thapa in recognition of 'the skill, bravery and fidelity with which he has defended the country committed to his charge', and to his son Ranjor Singh Thapa, in consideration of his gallant conduct. In return, Kaji Amar Singh Thapa was to send immediate orders for the surrender of all forts and fortresses held by Nepalese troops between the Jumna and Sutlej rivers, including Jaithak, and for the evacuation of the territory of Garhwal.

Clause 5 of the Convention was as follows: 'All the troops in the service of Nepaul, with the exception of those granted to the personal honour of the Kajees, Ummer Singh and Runjore Singh, will be at liberty to enter into the service of the British Government, if it is agreeable to themselves and the British choose to accept their services, and those who are not employed will be maintained on a specific allowance by the British Government, till peace is concluded between the two states.'

The Governor-General gave his approval on 21 May 1815 to the agreement with Kaji Amar Singh Thapa by which 'a most important object of the war has been accomplished'.[498]

The Governor-General's approval to the Almora Convention (appendix C), was conveyed in a letter dated 3 May 1815.[499] This Convention, completed on 27 April 1815 between Edward Gardner and Bam Shah, did not contain a clause on the lines of Clause 5 of Ochterlony's Convention with Kaji Amar Singh Thapa.[500]

Under the two Conventions, the three principal Nepalese field commanders duly crossed the Kali river into Nepal. Bam Shah, who had the shortest journey, crossed on 14 May 1815; Kaji Amar Singh Thapa and Runjor Singh Thapa soon after. They took with them their families, private property and the regular troops who had stayed with them in defeat. Kaji Amar Singh Thapa left with about 250 troops together with their arms, accoutrements, colours and two guns. Runjor Singh Thapa was allowed 200 men with their arms, colours and one gun.[501] Bam Shah took with him the regular troops of the Almora garrison and their arms, ammunition and eleven guns.[502] Nepalese troops based in Srinagar, capital of Garhwal, were also released.[503]

About 5,000 men who had joined the British service were left behind.[504] Of these about 300 were at Almora;[505] the remainder were in the far west.

CHAPTER 7

The second campaign
and the treaty of Segauli: 1816

Confident that the war was virtually over, Hastings appointed Ochter-
lony Superintendent of Political Affairs and Agent of the Governor-
General in the territories of the Seikh and Hill chiefs between the
Jumna and the Sutlej. He was to be assisted in his military duties by
Captain Birch for the affairs of Sirmur and neighbouring districts, and
Lieutenant Ross for those of the more western tracts. Lieutenant
Murray was to assist Ochterlony in the discharge of his station duties
in Ludhiana.[506] 'By the reduction which has been effected in the power
and resources of the enemy,' wrote Hastings, 'we shall be enabled
either to command and secure an honourable peace, or if the war be
prolonged by his obstinacy, to prosecute another campaign with the
certainty of success.'[507]

Despite the defeat of its forces west of the Mahakali river, the
Nepalese Government's refusal to capitulate made an eastern campaign inevitable. Hastings, who had expected a single short and
successful campaign, had anticipated overtures for peace being made
by the Nepalese Government as early as October 1814.[508] In November
1814, Major Bradshaw, who was attached to Major-General Marley's
division as Political Agent, was authorised to negotiate and conclude
a peace treaty with the Government of Nepal, subject to the ratification
of the Governor-General in Council.[509] Any such treaty was to be
founded on the principles of a Draft Treaty dated 26 November 1814[510]
comprising twelve Articles which required, inter alia, the surrender of
the disputed territories on the East India Company's northern border,
part of the Terai, and all lands west of the Mahakali river, the payment
of a large sum of money as reparations, the renewal of the commercial

treaty concluded in 1793, and the exchange of accredited Ministers. At a time when the British were suffering defeats and failures it was hardly surprising that the Nepalese Government declined to accept what must have seemed excessively harsh stipulations. They would have been all the more dismayed had they known that Bradshaw had been instructed that 'the first object to be effected is the reduction of the Terai'.[511]

Despite some modifications to the draft treaty early in 1815, the Nepalese would not be drawn.[512] Negotiations, reopened in May 1815, were complicated by the inability of the British to establish who among four potential negotiators was authorised by the Raja of Nepal to agree terms.[513] Moreover, the Nepalese were well aware that the British would not recommence operations in the hot season. Hastings recognised that 'the procrastination of the Goorkas in concluding a treaty is not to be wondered at. The subscribing to the loss of half their Empire is a painful submission for a proud people.'[514]

The British, who had no intention of occupying Nepal,[515] were anxious to conclude a lasting peace which left them 'secure from the consequences which would ensue were Runjeet Sing, or any ambitious and powerful chief, to establish himself in the hills beyond the Sutleje'. In his letter of 2 August 1815, the Governor-General explained to the Secret Committee of the Court of Directors: 'by the possession of Kumaon, the Dhoons of Deyra and Kyarda, of Nahun, Subathoo, and Malown, and the passages of the rivers, your Honourable Committee will observe that we have in our hands a continued and unbroken chain of communications in the hills from the Kali [Mahakali] to the Sutleje, while the whole of the country beyond it, as far back as the Snowy [Himalaya] Mountains, is possessed by feudatory and dependant chiefs enjoying our guarantee and looking to us as the common guardian and protector'. By now fully persuaded by the advice of Metcalfe and Ochterlony, the Governor added: 'we could not, without a commanding influence in the hills on this side of the river [Sutlej], and the possession of a frontier enabling us to penetrate and occupy them at any time, ever be secure against the danger of a chief of that character establishing his own power there, and thus taking in flank one of the most valuable and important positions of our north-western frontier line. From such a danger, which will perhaps not be deemed chimerical, we are now effectually secured.'[516]

As has already been pointed out, Ochterlony and Metcalfe had long regarded Ranjit Singh as a potential threat to the British in the north-west, and had convinced Hastings of the need to hold a line on the Sutlej. Ranjit Singh, who had earlier shown an interest in expanding the Sikh state into the Cis-Sutlej hills, had been developing his army on British lines. Greatly impressed by Lake's army in 1805 (when Lake pursued Holkar into the Punjab) Ranjit Singh admired the disciplined strength of British-trained infantry. In March 1809, when Metcalfe's escort was attacked by between four and five hundred Sikh Akali cavalry, the two companies of Bengal native infantry stood firm and defeated them. Ochterlony estimated the size of the Sikh Army, including regular and irregular troops, to have been 10,400 in 1804 and 12,850 in 1809.[517]

It seems that William Fraser, on his return to Delhi from his tour with his brother James, was intent on a military command. Ochterlony wrote to him on 17 September 1815, when negotiations to conclude a treaty were being pursued with the Nepalese Government: 'By a letter dated the 4th instant from Benares I think there will be no call for your military services, my dear William, in any shape or form. Everything they [the Government] say wears a pacific appearance and I am desired not to send on any people.' Ochterlony added: 'I shall not however be surprised if the Goorkha humility may deceive them and in such an event any arrangement you may make at headquarters will be acceptable to me.'[518] The Nepalese Government still hoped for outside help.[519]

A peace treaty was eventually signed at Segauli on 2 December 1815.[520] However, despite an ultimatum by the Governor-General to the Raja of Nepal,[521] the treaty was not ratified by a stipulated deadline. Alexander Fraser, having informed his father on 16 June 1815: 'the war is I believe virtually at an end',[522] wrote to him eight months later: 'The Nypalese have completely outwitted our Government. Deceived by their pretended anxiety for peace, Lord Moira [Hastings] ordered all preparations for action to be discontinued in December last . . . Under the persuasion that the Treaty would be ratified, the detachments and trains of artillery marching to the several points of rendez-vous were ordered to return to their depots and the stores of grain that had been laid up for the campaign sold. The Nypalese bought the grain for almost nothing and after amusing us a little longer with hopes of ratifying the Treaty have finally rejected it. And now the season for hostilities is past, so they have put us to an enormous expense and gained a whole year's respite by their diplomatic finesse.' [523]

Alexander Fraser's prediction that the war could not be resumed until December 1816 was unduly pessimistic. On 12 January 1816, the Governor-General in Council informed the Secret Committee of the Court of Directors of their decision that operations should be commenced without delay, and that Ochterlony had already been appointed to command the British forces and had been given sole authority for all political arrangements and negotiations connected with the war and for relations with the Nepalese Government.[524] Ochterlony assumed his command on 25 January 1816 [525] charged with virtually the same objectives which Marley had failed to achieve in 1815.[526] These were, always assuming that the Nepalese Government had not in the meantime ratified the peace treaty, to occupy the Makwanpur valley and capture its forts. This was expected to force the Nepalese to conclude peace, failing which Ochterlony was to advance into the Nepal valley and attack the capital, Kathmandu.[527] On 27 January 1816, Ochterlony informed Gujraj Misra, the Nepalese envoy who had returned without the treaty, of his authority for all future negotiations with Nepal. He added: 'It is important that you should inform all the servants and establishments of the Rajah of Nepaul that all negociation [*sic*] has ceased between the two Governments, and also that the Maharaj has himself decided on a renewal of war and contest.' [528] On 21 February 1816, the Governor-General in Council informed the Secret Committee of the Court of Directors that military operations had begun.[529]

On the face of things it was likely to be an unequal contest. The battle-hardened troops of the Nepalese Army in the west were now unavailable to defend the homeland. The formidable Bhakti Thapa was dead. The hero of Nalapani, Balbahadur Thapa, had joined Ranjit Singh's army. Kaji Amar Singh Thapa, though well received on his return to Kathmandu in 1815, had failed to raise support for his implacable opposition to ratifying the Treaty of Segauli.[530] The Kaji's own soldierly belief that 'If we win, we can easily settle the differences on our terms. If we suffer defeat, it is better to die than to accept dishonourable terms,' found no favour with the Nepalese Government.[531] Ranjor Singh Thapa, his son, did serve in the defending army, only to be defeated at Hariharpur.[532]

Hastings was able to put into the field his most successful general and a force of approximately 33,000 men and over 100 pieces of ordnance. Against this the Nepalese were able to muster probably no more than 6,000 regular troops and a few field guns. Brigadier-General S.P. Sharma and his fellow editors, Dr T. Baidya and Dr T. Manandhar, have estimated that at the beginning of the Anglo-Nepal war there were fewer than 12,000 men in the Nepalese Army, most of whom were new, and that they were deployed roughly as follows:

3,000 west of the Mahakali river
2,000 east of the Kosi river
3,000 in the Palpa area
4,000 in the area of Makwanpur[533]

This suggests that at the outset of the war about 7,000 were available for the immediate defence of Kathmandu and the Nepal Valley. In his report dated 2 August 1815 to the Secret Committee, Hastings wrote of the Nepalese Army: 'Their regular force did not exceed an establishment of twelve thousand men probably not kept up to its nominal rate at the time of rupture. Whatever force they possessed beyond this was a rude and hastily collected militia: brave indeed, but ill-trained and without discipline . . . The total numbers could not in any period of the war have amounted to 16,000.' Of the regular troops, Hastings thought 6,000 were distributed east of the Mahakali river.[534] Allowing for the fact that some reinforcements were sent from Nepal to the western theatre during 1815, Sharma's figures seem to accord with those of Hastings. It is therefore not unreasonable to suppose that, in the second campaign, Ochterlony and his division were faced with a trained army of about 6,000 men.

Ochterlony had under his immediate direction 19,400 men

organised in four brigades and including three regular British battalions. This division was charged with the main thrust towards Makwanpur. A further 6,600 under Colonel Nicolls were to move from Oudh into the westernmost provinces of Nepal, with a force under Lieutenant-Colonel Adams invading Doti from Kumaon. Despite his earlier failure, Major-General John Wood, with 4,900, men was assigned a similar diversionary role operating northwards from Gorakhpur. Captain Latter, based at Titalia, was made responsible for the defence of the East India Company's north-eastern frontier with a force of 2,400.[535] However, despite this huge advantage in numbers, not everything favoured Ochterlony. He had first to assemble his division and to gather essential supplies, carriage and ordnance at a time when, on the erroneous assumption of imminent victory, these had been dispersed. Then, to achieve his objectives, he had to cross the dense and inhospitable sal forest of the Terai (a process which had earlier brought disaster to the British) and climb the precipitous and heavily fortified hills of the Churia range. And all this had to be accomplished in little more than two months before adverse climatic conditions and disease brought campaigning to a halt. There was therefore no time for the slow, methodical approach which had ensured him victory in the western campaign by capturing one fort or stockaded position after another through the building of roads and the accurate siting and use of artillery.

Ochterlony wasted no time. On 13 January 1816, his battering train and pioneer companies crossed the Ganges near Dinapur. Next day he followed, heading northwards to a rendezvous with his division near Balwi, some six miles from the edge of the Terai forest (see map 7). In the meantime Ochterlony had sent Colonel Kelly with the 1st Brigade on a right flanking movement from Bhagwanpur to capture Hariharpur and close on Makwanpur. He had also sent Colonel Nicol[536] with the 2nd Brigade on a wide sweep to the left through Mahajogri to approach Makwanpur via the Rapti valley. On 3 February 1816, Ochterlony led the 3rd and 4th Brigades up to the sal forest where he constructed a fortified stockade for his heavy ordnance at Simra Basa. On 9 February 1816 the 3rd Brigade, followed next day by the 4th Brigade, marched unchallenged through the forest to Bichakori.[537]

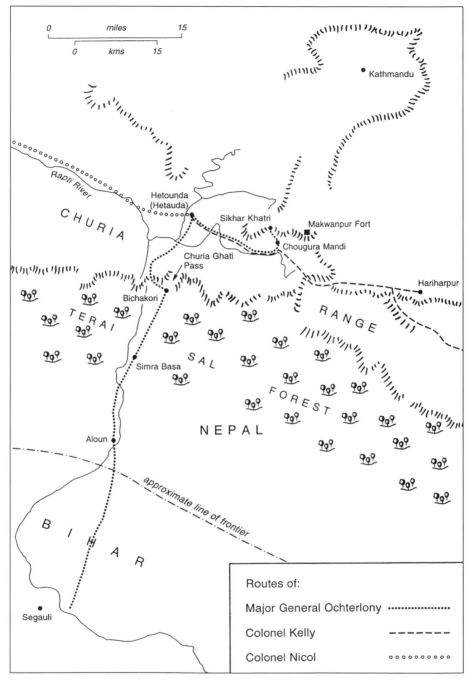

Map 7. Ochterlony's approach to Makwanpur in 1816.

There, in the words of Lieutenant Shipp of the 87th of Foot, they were confronted by 'hills rising like stairs, summit above summit'. A further fortified depot having been established, reconnaissance revealed 'ahead nothing but stockade upon stockade and fort upon fort. But,' wrote Shipp, 'we had at our head a commander [Ochterlony] with just the right gift for such a campaign, and he began to seek a more practicable route.'[538] On 14 February 1816, Lieutenant Pickersgill, who was in charge of the Guide and Intelligence department, informed Ochterlony of an alternative pass 'unguarded and practicable, though difficult'[539] (see map 8). The use of the term 'difficult' was a gross understatement. Nevertheless, Ochterlony achieved the seemingly impossible by leading the 3rd Brigade up a very steep and narrow ravine, leaving the 4th Brigade to create a deception by occupying the 3rd Brigade's tents. He wrote: 'That it has been effected is to be ascribed to great good fortune, as well as to the most persevering labour, the greatest exertion and most persevering fortitude.'[540] The move of the troops, travelling light, from the Bichakori camp to a point five miles beyond the pass lasted twenty-five hours. It took the pioneers a further two days to construct a passage for the (unladen) elephants and for the manhandling of the guns.

The sudden and totally unexpected appearance of the 3rd Brigade beyond the Bichakori defences threw the outposted Nepalese troops into confusion and forced them to withdraw from their stockades to join the main Nepalese position at Makwanpur. On 19 February 1816 Ochterlony arrived with the 3rd Brigade at Hetounda where he posted troops and six-pounder guns in a strongly fortified base depot. On 27 February 1816 he marched the rest of the 3rd Brigade and its field train to set up his headquarters at a camp near Chougura Mandi below the Makwanpur hills (see map 7). They were joined next day by the 4th Brigade and the heavy battering train from Simra Basa. In circumstances not unlike his arrival before Malaun, Ochterlony discovered that an important hill position at Sikhar Khatri had been abandoned by the Nepalese troops. Ochterlony sent a strong force including men of the 87th of Foot to occupy it.[541] Further reconnaissance along the Makwanpur ridge drew determined counter-attacks from the Nepalese which Ochterlony resisted with reinforcements and artillery. The battle

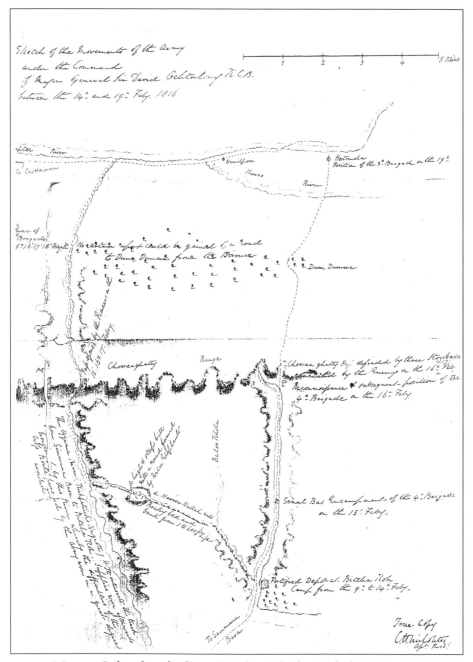

Map 8. Ochterlony's diversion through the Bichakori Pass in
February 1816. Archive ref: Gurkha Museum OPS/008 map 1816.

grew in intensity until almost 3,000 Nepalese troops were committed in waves of brave but unsuccessful attacks reminiscent of Bhakti Thapa's gallant attempts to capture the second Deonthal position at Malaun. British casualties numbered 222,[542] while the Nepalese killed and wounded were estimated to be at least 800.[543] The arrival of Colonel Nicol with the 2nd Brigade enabled Ochterlony to move his heavy ordnance into position within 500 yards of Makwanpur fort by 5 March 1816. The fall of Hariharpur to Kelly and the 1st Brigade on 2 March 1816,[544] together with the immediate threat to the Kathmandu Valley finally persuaded the Nepalese Government to ratify the Treaty of Segauli without further delay and brought hostilities to an end.[545] The 'exchange of ratification' of the Treaty of Segauli (see appendix G) took place very early on 5 March 1816.[546]

None of the four battalions raised in 1815 played an active part in the second campaign. The two Nasiri Battalions were stationed in the west at Subathu and Jaithak, and the Kumaon Battalion was still forming in Almora. A detachment of 610 all ranks of the Sirmoor Battalion, which was based at Dehra Dun, was allocated to Nicolls,[547] but the war was over before Nicolls (like Wood and Adams) could move his troops into action.[548]

There seems to have been little or no increase to the numbers of Gorkhas and other hillmen recruited by the British during the first campaign. Attempts by Captain Latter to recruit eastern Nepalese (the Kiranti hill tribes, also referred to in the *Papers Respecting the Nepaul War* as Kirata or Kerauts) to the British cause had been unsuccessful.[549] In supporting a request by Captain C.P. Hay for permission to recruit 'natives of Nepaul' to fill up vacancies in the Champaran Light Infantry Local Battalion (which Hay commanded), Ochterlony reported to the Adjutant-General that a Havildar and four regular soldiers of the Nepalese Army had come to his camp to join the British having 'long suffered from privations and scarcity of pay'. This had reminded him of the great success he had had during the first campaign of 'drawing over' a large proportion of the Nepalese troops. He had therefore sent for Subah Lal Sahi and 'a small party of intelligent Goorkas' from his own 1st Nasiris 'to extend this defection among the enemy's troops very considerably' so that those who came over might be embodied separately under 'intelligent European officers' or 'made over to form part of the fixed establishment of the local battalions'.[550] The Commander-in-Chief had regarded it as 'highly expedient' for Ochterlony to proceed with his plan and for sufficient defectors to be enrolled to fill vacancies in an existing mountaineer company attached to the Champaran Light Infantry corps and to raise a second mountaineer company should Ochterlony deem this expedient.[551] Any further defectors were to be embodied into the Nasiri, Sirmoor and Kumaon battalions, it being made clear to them that they would be bound to serve 'on any frontier of the Company's possessions' should the interests of the service require. The Commander-in-Chief had thought it best that, pending disposal, all defectors should be embodied as a distinct corps under 'an intelligent officer' selected by Ochterlony for the purpose.[552] In the event, Ochterlony's advance was so swift, the withdrawal of the Nepalese troops defending Bichakori, Hariharpur, and Hetounda so comprehensive, and the Nepalese capitulation so unhesitating that Ochterlony had no time in which to put his plan into effect. Any expectation of a further large-scale enrolment of Gorkhas was therefore unfulfilled.

Ochterlony's strategy in the second campaign was related more to his anxiety to achieve a rapid and total victory than to any immediate need to increase the number of the Bengal Army's Gorkhas. Ochterlony made no attempt to include in the Treaty of Segauli a clause allowing the recruitment of Gorkhas by the British. Yet at one time he evidently had contemplated the need to amend the Treaty. He wrote to Adam: 'I feared the displeasure of the Right Honourable the Governor General, who was much and justly incensed at their [the Nepalese Government's] conduct, and who must naturally wish to inflict severe punishment on their delay and duplicity, which had occasioned us a considerable expense and the loss of some valuable lives, though he might not, and I was certain did not attach the slightest value to their mountainous territory'.[553] Ochterlony decided instead to exact from the Nepalese plenipotentiaries a written declaration of 'a related engagement' (see the end of appendix G) to the effect that 'they had nothing to hope or expect from the British Government but a strict adherence to the very letter of the treaty signed at

Seegowli'.[554] Ochterlony gave Adam his reasons for seeking to ratify the treaty immediately: 'The advanced state of the season, the diminished state of our Commissariat to what they were intended to be, the unhealthiness of the country, the impossibility of getting our supplies through these pestilential regions, and a recollection of what men are capable of doing when driven to desperation'. He began to withdraw his troops on 7 March 1816:[555] Ochterlony need not have worried. The Governor-General approved absolutely the course of action he had taken.[556] Indeed the Governor-General in Council wrote to the Secret Committee of the Court of Directors on 30 March 1816, 'the decision of Sir David Ochterlony was, in every respect, judicious, and deserving of our unqualified approbation, which it has accordingly received'. They added: 'The treaty, as it now stands, appears to us to provide for every object of desirable attainment in any settlement with the Goorka power, leaving it in the condition of a substantive State.'[557]

General Bhim Sen Thapa who, as Prime Minister and Commander-in-Chief, had been strongly in favour of the war with the British, had to deploy all his political skills in the bitterness of defeat. Wisely, he did not support Kaji Amar Singh Thapa's attempt to involve the Chinese.[558] He was content to keep quiet while the Governor-General reassured the Chinese that the British had no intention of dominating Nepal.[559] However, Kaji Amar Singh Thapa's death on 16 August 1816 was followed three months later by the death of King Girbana Yuddha Bikram Shah. This caused a further upsurge of factional intrigue and a plot to depose Bhim Sen Thapa.[560] Again wisely, Bhim Sen Thapa turned to the Army for support. He not only gave the Army his patronage but revitalised it, giving influential army officers the crucial function of defending Nepal against possible invasion by the British. This restored the Army's self-esteem and sense of purpose, and gave its Commander-in Chief the aura of Champion of the State. Bhim Sen Thapa's control was thereby strengthened both at the Court and in the country. He was well aware that the British posed no threat to Nepalese independence.[561]

Two aspects of the Treaty of Segauli were painful to the Nepalese Government: the loss of territory in the Terai, and the appointment of a Resident in Kathmandu. Article 3 of the Treaty meant that Nepal was to lose about 6,300 square miles of its most fertile land. This was a crippling blow. Not only was the Terai a major source of government revenue, it enabled prestigious rewards to be made to senior state officials: jagirs to those still serving; tax-free birtas to distinguished military commanders in retirement.[562] Article 4, which provided for an annual indemnity of 200,000 rupees as compensation to jagirdars during their lifetime, added to Nepal's internal problems. It appeared to put the jagirdars concerned 'on the payroll of the Company', and it interfered with Nepal's Pajani system under which serving officials might be posted elsewhere or dismissed. The continuing grant of a jagir helped to ensure loyalty. In Stiller's words, the Terai was 'the glue that held the Nepalese state together'. To yield it was to surrender national unity.[563]

Articles 3 and 4 of the Treaty of Segauli were not really advantageous to the British. The Company was not only committed to an indefinite and sizeable annual outlay in compensation but was faced with the difficult and costly management of large stretches of what, to the British, was very unhealthy territory.[564] The paramount British aim of a secure border with Nepal had not been attained. Upon reflection, the Governor-General decided to give up about 4,500 square miles of the Terai in return for an agreed and demarcated border between Nepal and India. The other approximately 1,800 square miles of Terai, adjoining Oudh, was ceded to the Nawab Vizier in settlement of a second loan of ten million rupees obtained during the war.[565]

Having learned of the activities of British Residents at the courts of Indian States, and having observed their intrusion into politics and military affairs, the Nepalese Government had long resisted the appointment of a British representative in their capital. Article 8 of the treaty, which read: 'In order to secure and improve the relations of amity and peace hereby established between the two states, it is agreed that accredited ministers shall reside at the court of the other', must have rankled. Kaji Amar Singh Thapa had written a long letter to the King of Nepal on 2 March 1815 insisting that the war should be continued and that a Residency in Kathmandu should not be entertained. He pointed out: 'If we decline receiving their mission they will insist; and if we are unable to oppose force, and desire them to come unaccompanied with troops, they will not comply. They will soon begin by introducing a company; a battalion will soon follow, and at length an army will be assembled for the subjection of Nepal.' [566]

If the appointment of Edward Gardner as Resident in Kathmandu displeased the Nepalese Government, it evidently disappointed William Fraser. In what seems to have been his last letter to his father, Alexander Fraser wrote from Delhi: 'We hear on good authority that Gardner, our second assistant, who is at present Commissioner for the conquered provinces of Cumaoon, goes to Khatmandoo as Resident. See the result of the Lord's [Hastings'] fine promises. William superseded by his Junior Assistant! Patience!' [567]

The speed with which the British moved to set up their Residency may have added to Nepalese suspicions. [568] At the Governor-General's request, Ochterlony sent Lieutenant Boileau to act as Resident, with specific duties until the arrival of Edward Gardner, and thereafter to remain as commander of the Resident's escort and Postmaster to the Residency. [569] Boileau presented his credentials to the King of Nepal on 17 April 1816.

The British were not unaware of Nepalese sensitivities regarding the Residency. They had hopes of cultivating the friendship of Bhim Sen Thapa and that, 'By judicious and conciliatory conduct on the part of the Resident, and the careful avoidance, in the early stages of our intercourse, of every measure calculated to excite jealousy or apprehension, we may hope, in due time, to improve the existing relations into a connexion of reciprocal cordiality, friendship, and goodwill.' [570] Gardner was instructed, if Ochterlony judged it advisable, to apply for permission to take the direct route through the hills from Almora to Kathmandu, or, if the Nepalese Government objected, to proceed by some other convenient route. [571] As to his escort, he was not to risk offending the feelings of the Nepalese Government. Should he decide to take an escort of hill troops, he might select some from the Kumaon Provincial Battalion, excluding 'any men who came over to us under such circumstances as would make their appearance at Catmandoo essentially an insult to their former masters'. [572] Gardner arrived, without incident, in Kathmandu on 8 July 1816. One of his first tasks was the delicate negotiation of the boundary line with Nepal. Terai land was released on 8 December 1816 and the boundary was duly surveyed and agreed. Work on marking the borderline with pillars of masonry was completed in February 1818.[573] However Hunter points out that Bhim Sen Thapa ensured that unsurveyed gaps were left for possible future encroachments and 'for endless annoyance to the British officers'.[574] It was not until 1830 that the final demarcation of the boundary of the western Terai was completed; and 1833 the boundary of the eastern Terai.[575]

Part III

*The Bengal Army
and its Gorkha Battalions*

CHAPTER 8

The formation of the first British Gorkha battalions

In 1815, at the conclusion of the first campaign of the Anglo-Nepal War, about 4,700 men of the Nepalese western army[576] surrendered to the British in the far west. Under the terms of Clause 5 of a Convention between Major-General Ochterlony and Kaji Amar Singh Thapa, those who volunteered to serve with the British and who were considered suitable were enlisted into the Bengal Army. There are several reasons why Ochterlony decided to recruit them.[577]

After early misgivings, probably founded on the opinions of others, Ochterlony was completely convinced of the discipline, fighting qualities, and mountain warfare skills of Nepalese troops. Indeed he was so convinced that he bestowed on his Nasiris, who had been tested and proven on active service with the British, his patronage and his own Mogul title. He was well aware that the Bengal Army had no troops trained in mountain warfare and that there was a need to protect the hills of the North-West Quarter of the Company's territory against potential invasion by Ranjit Singh or some other 'ambitious chief'. He was also aware that Hastings needed to end the war with Nepal decisively before embarking on a major campaign to subdue the Marathas and to eliminate the roving predatory bands of Pindaris. Ochterlony perceived that if the British did not employ the Gorkha captives and deserters they would become a serious liability rather than a potential asset; so, too, would unemployed Kumaoni and Garhwali soldiers. Impoverished communities of Gorkhas and their families who had settled in the Cis-Sutlej hills might pose a further threat.

Ochterlony would have known of the existence of the Bhagalpur

Hill Rangers for localised defence and that such irregular units were less costly than Bengal Native Infantry.[578] This factor was bound to appeal to the authorities in Calcutta and London.

However, as a good general, Ochterlony would surely have given his foremost consideration to fulfilling his orders from Hastings. This he did to the letter. For what better way could there be of destroying Nepal's Army of the west than by absorbing it into the Bengal Army? And what better way of removing Kaji Amar Singh Thapa's influence and authority in the west than by allowing him to return to Nepal with honour as a gallant adversary? With the support of his friend Metcalfe, Ochterlony had long found favour with Hastings. Now, as the only successful general in the first campaign, and a man whose knowledge and experience of the North-West Quarter and of the Gorkhas was unsurpassed, he must have known that Hastings would support his views.

Hastings decided that in restoring the 'ancient Chiefs' to their former territories he would 'render them feudatory to the British Government' so that they surrendered the command of their military force when required, and the right of investigating and arbitrating disputes among themselves. To make this policy effective, he proposed to 'retain some strong places in the hills' and to establish a British officer to control affairs on the spot under the orders of Major-General Ochterlony.[579] Bearing in mind the cost of maintaining a substantial frontier force, Hastings gave orders for the withdrawal of almost all the regular troops who had been engaged at Malaun and Jaithak, and for the discharge of all irregular troops except 'those composed of Goorkas who have entered our service in considerable numbers, and other hill tribes'.[580] The wording is significant in considering the ethnic composition of the intake. Part of this irregular force was to be used to garrison the forts which were being retained in the hills; the remainder was to be transferred to the restored Hill Chiefs, who would bear the cost of maintaining them. William Fraser wrote to his brother Alexander on 19 July 1815: 'All our irregulars are disbanded. Young's Goorkha corps alone amount to 2,000, and Ross's, under Ochterlony, to as many – equal to 4 battalions.'[581]

Hastings had been convinced of the military qualities and reliability of Gorkha troops by reports and despatches on the 'Nusseeree Goorkha Companies' from Ochterlony and Lawtie.[582] When it came to organising the irregular force of Gorkhas and other hillmen, it was natural that he should turn for advice to Ochterlony, for whose military judgment and political skill he had the highest regard.[583] Ochterlony thought that for a long time it would not be prudent to leave less than 1,500 'firelocks' on the north-west of the Tonse. He recommended that this requirement should be met by forming the Nasiris into two battalions, each battalion comprising either eight companies of 100 sepoys or ten companies of eighty-four sepoys, and each company including native commissioned officers and non-commissioned officers. The battalions, each with a European commandant and a European adjutant, should be stationed one at Jaithak and the other at Subathu.[584]

As yet no records have been traced in India or Britain which would help to identify the Nepalese Army units from which came the 4,700 men who joined the Bengal Army in the far west, nor of the 450 who returned to Nepal with Kaji Amar Singh Thapa and Ranjor Singh Thapa. If such records exist in Nepal, they are not readily available.[585] The Royal Nepalese Army Headquarters' publication, *Royal Nepalese Army Colours: a short history* (Kathmandu, 1991), makes no reference to the colours brought back to Nepal by Kaji Amar Singh Thapa and Ranjor Singh Thapa under the terms of Clauses 1 and 2 of the Convention with Ochterlony. Although it gives some evidence of the Nepalese units which fought in the west, the 'short history' is confined to 'major achievements'. The heroic defence of Nalapani (Kalanga) and the tenacious hold on Jaithak certainly come within this category. The Nepalese Army's heroism at Malaun seems not to be regarded by the Nepalese as a major achievement.[586] Nothing about the battle of Malaun is included in *Royal Nepalese Army Colours: a short history*. S.P. Sharma (et al.) includes an account of the 'Battle of Deuthal' (Deonthal, close to Malaun fort) in *The Military History of Nepal*.[587] Another reference to Malaun is made in a letter dated 27 November 1814 written in Hindoor by Kaji Amar Singh Thapa and intercepted by the British.[588] In this letter the Kaji wrote that he had directed his son Ranjor Singh Thapa to remain at Nahan and had ordered Jaspu Thapa to join him (the Kaji) with the Old Gorakh company, 'said to be 1,200 strong', under his command. However, before he received the order, Ranjor Singh Thapa had sent Jaspu Thapa and two other commanders, Nansur Thapa and Ran Bhim Karki, from Nahan to 'Raj Gurh' (Malaun) with four other companies. It is quite likely that these units remained there; and they may have been joined by another company which 'was stationed in the far west'. The crucial importance of Malaun to the Nepalese cause is demonstrated by the fact that Bhakti Thapa, who commanded a unit at Jaithak, joined Kaji Amar Singh Thapa at Malaun and played a distinguished part in its defence.[589] The Kaji had already sent another son, Ram Dass, 'with our families to Raj Gurh, considering that fort the key of our western frontier, in which we shall be able to stop the progress of the enemy and overawe the Zemindars'. He added: 'By remaining in command of Raj Gurh, our authority will be maintained and our subjects prevented from forming conspiracies.'[590] It was from Malaun fort that Kaji Amar Singh Thapa emerged with his family and possessions, and the remainder of his troops, to return to Nepal. It seems highly probable that, as army commander, the Kaji had with him a strong force of his finest troops when he made his last stand at Malaun. Indeed the determination, discipline and unflinching courage of the 2,000 men led by Bhakti Thapa in repeated attempts to capture second Deonthal confirm this.

The question remains, who were the 4,700 troops of the Nepalese western army taken by the British? There is no precise answer as to their ethnic origins. There are, however, several indications. In August 1814 Hyder Hearsey gave his opinion that 'the army in the field under Ummer Sing Thappa does not exceed six thousand fighting men. Their army is composed of about eighteen hundred or two thousand real Goorkas; on these all their dependence rests. The remainder are Palpese, Jumlees, Kumaonees and Gurhwallis.'[591] In a memorandum, dated 3 November 1814, Hearsey estimated that 'The Goorkas have near eight hundred Kumaonees in their employ'.[592] Kaji Amar Singh Thapa himself gives some credence to this composition. In a letter dated 2 March 1815 to the King of Nepal, he wrote that at Nalapani (Kalanga) the Nepalese commander had 'a nominal force of six hundred men, but scarcely amounting to five hundred', which 'consisted of the Old Gorukh and Burukh (which were only partly composed of the inhabitants of our ancient kingdom) and of the countries from Bheri [in western Nepal, where the people resembled those of Kumaon] to Gurhwall'. He added: 'my army is similarly composed'.[593] Ochterlony was 'persuaded that Bakti Thappa's corps was more than half from Kumaon'.[594] Moorcroft considered that two-thirds of Bakti Thapa's troops consisted of the natives of the subjugated countries.[595] The Political Secretary to Government wrote to the Adjutant-General on 9 July 1815: 'A large proportion of the western army of the Ghoorkahs was understood to be composed of Kumaonees.'[596] Hodgson, in a memorandum dated 10 February 1825, recorded that 'the greater part of the troops which they [the Government of Nepal] formerly had in their extensive subject provinces were . . . raised on the spot as Kumaonies in Kumaon and so forth, and this class (of locals) [*sic*] were those which principally fell into our hands at the termination of the [first campaign of the] war'.[597]

It therefore seems not unreasonable to assume that upwards of half – perhaps as much as two-thirds – of the Nepalese western army comprised Himalayan hillmen other than Gorkhalis. This, however, also suggests that of the Nepalese troops retained by the British as many as 1,500 were Gorkhalis, that is to say Chhetris, Magars and Gurungs from western Nepal whom Prithvi Narayan Shah would have recognised as Gorkhalis in the tradition of his army and his edicts. This figure excludes the 450 men who were allowed to accompany Kaji Amar Singh Thapa and his son Ranjor Singh Thapa on their return to Nepal. These die-hards were almost certainly Gorkhalis of regular companies, some of 'the flower of the Goorka troops'.[598] Ochterlony would certainly have been able to distinguish between Gorkhalis and others under his command. The three original commanders of his Nasiri companies were Jeykishen (a Kumaoni Brahman) and Lal Sahi and Mani Raj Rana (both Gorkhali sirdars). Lal Sahi was a Chhetri from Piuthan in south-west Nepal. Mani Raj Rana was a Magar-Chhetri from the southern foothills of central

Nepal.[599] Ochterlony had a special admiration for the Gorkhalis and it is likely that there was a strong nucleus of Gorkhali soldiers in the Nasiri companies led by Lal Sahi and Mani Raj Rana.

Conscious of the need to reduce and reorganise his forces, Ochterlony perceived a particular role for the Kumaonis. Following correspondence with Colonel Nicolls, he wrote on 5 June 1815 to inform the Adjutant-General of 'a measure he trusted would meet with the approbation of the Commander-in-Chief'. Considering the great number of men who had come over from the enemy and 'the monthly expense they would occasion in a quarter where they made no collections and where all our funds were supplied from the Delhi Treasury', he had come to the conclusion that a detachment of Kumaonis should be sent to Colonel Nicolls at Almora. He felt that a body of such troops might be beneficial there 'in a political point of view and their services eminently useful as soldiers as well as from their local knowledge and peculiar habit'. Ochterlony had therefore instructed Lieutenant Ross, who was to escort Kaji Amar Singh Thapa and his party to Naraingarh en route for Nepal, to propose to Subah Jeykishen that he proceed 'with all the Kumaonees and as many others more eastern as would consent to go with him', to join Colonel Nicolls. With his letter to the Adjutant-General, Ochterlony appended a return,[600] a copy of which is given at appendix H, of the number of Kumaoni and Garhwali troops who had marched on 29 May 1815 with Subah Jeykishen to Almora. All had been paid up to 14 July 1815 and had 'marched with their swords and kookries only'. The return, signed by Lieutenant Ross, Commanding Nusseeree Battalion, shows that nine junior officers (jemadars) and 670 fighting men (muskets) had been accompanied by eight colour-bearers ('nishaunchees') and sixty-two non-combatants, making a total of 749.

Ochterlony's view that these would 'prove a very useful body of men in that quarter under proper European officers', was confirmed by Nicolls in a letter dated 21 June 1815 to the Adjutant-General: 'It is with a very great satisfaction that I observe a very striking similarity of opinion in Major-General Ochterlony's despatch of 5th instant with that which I ventured privately to offer through you to His Excellency the Commander-in-Chief the same day.' Following Ochterlony's example, Nicolls recommended the appointment of a commanding officer and an adjutant to this 'Provincial Corps'.[601] He also recommended the enlistment of about 200 Kumaonis and others who had claims to be retained 'from their early accession to our cause'.[602] Combined, these detachments were to form a Kumaon Provincial Battalion for the internal security of Kumaon.

Lieutenant Ross's return of 26 May 1815 (appendix H) shows that, after Jeykishen had left, Ochterlony had eight sirdars of whom at least six were Gorkhalis: Lal Sahi, Bahadur Sahi, Mani Raj Rana, Chumasu Rana, Reharsing Thapa and Pursram Gurung. Although the ethnic origins of 'Bagburn Soobah' are indeterminate, 'Subber Sing' might well have been a Gorkhali.[603] No similar list of sirdars seems to exist for Young's 'Goorka corps'. However, one of the two original Subedars, 'Loobeer Ghurtee', was a Gorkhali Chhetri. The other was a native of Kumaon.[604]

Ochterlony's proposal for two Nasiri battalions took no account of more than 1,700 'Goorka' troops from the Nepalese western army who had gathered at Nahan in Sirmur under Lieutenant Young. Although Major-General Martindell had been authorised to embody them on the lines of the Nasiris,[605] they were still not formed into a corps by the end of June 1815; and neither the strength of the corps nor the rates of pay of the various ranks had been fixed.[606] Nevertheless, on joining the British, the troops under Young had been promised permanent service. Ochterlony's faith in the Nasiris was such that he seems, at least initially, to have considered it unnecessary to retain regular troops in the western hills. He may have been aware of the view expressed by the Governor-General: 'I do not calculate on the necessity of retaining any regular troops in the hills west of the Jumna, and but a few in Gurhwall.'[607] However Ochterlony seems to have been persuaded to change his mind. The Adjutant-General records: 'It would not be prudent in the opinion of the Commander-in-Chief to trust the security and tranquillity of these territories [the land between the Tonse and the Sutlej] entirely to the fidelity of the Goorka troops in our pay whatever grounds their character as soldiers and their conduct since they have been in our employ may afford for reliance on them, and this seems to be also the opinion of Major-General Ochterlony.'[608]

The ambivalent tone of the Adjutant-General's letter of 28 June 1815 to the Political Secretary suggests that the Commander-in-Chief's advisers were in something of a quandary in framing advice for the Commander-in-Chief to give to the Governor-General concerning Ochterlony's plan. On the one hand they saw no place for Young's men in the proposed irregular force; on the other they were aware that Young's men had been promised permanent service with the British on the authority of the Governor-General. Moreover, neither Ochterlony's plan nor the need to limit costs allowed for more than two battalions of irregulars in the western hills. They came to the conclusion that a detachment of regular native troops from Ochterlony's division, 'which did not suffer from desertion during its arduous campaign', should be stationed in the key hill forts. With such a detachment, two 'Goorka' battalions each of the strength of 800 firelocks would be amply sufficient for all purposes of control and security north-west of the Tonse. However the Commander-in-Chief's advisers were also persuaded that the promises made to Young's men could not be ignored. Their advice to the Commander-in-Chief had therefore been that one of the two 'Goorka' battalions should be formed from Young's men on the same strength and rates of pay as those fixed for the Nasiris. They further recommended that the remaining 1,600 or 1,700 men could usefully be formed into 'puttees' (reinforcement groups) each comprising a jemadar, two havildars, two naiks, and 25 sepoys, to replace casualties and fill vacancies in the complement.[609]

That the Governor-General had no wish to offend Ochterlony was made clear by the Political Secretary: 'The formation suggested by Major-General Ochterlony with certain modifications appears to the Governor General to be on the whole the most expedient arrangement.'[610] The most important of these modifications was that, in addition to the two Nasiri battalions proposed by Ochterlony, a Sirmoor battalion was to be raised in order to honour the promises made to Young's men in the name of the Governor-General. The corps to be composed of 'Goorkahs and other Hill troops who have entered our service' was therefore to comprise not two but three battalions for service north-west of the Jumna. Each battalion was to have eight companies of 100 firelocks and the number of native officers judged to be expedient, those surplus to complement being carried supernumerary pending vacancies. Ochterlony was to be allowed to retain, so long as was necessary, the superior native commissioned rank of subah in the two Nasiri battalions.[611] Young's battalion, which had no subahs, was to use the normal most senior native rank of subedar. The first call on those supernumerary to the requirements of the three battalions was the completion of the 'proposed Provincial Corps in Kemaon'. Ochterlony's plan of transferring troops to Nicolls was to be extended as necessary but not restricted to natives of Kumaon, there being 'no objection to an intermediate line, in smaller proportions, of other classes'. In addition, a tenth company of Pioneers was to be formed.[612] The remaining unallocated troops were to be organised in puttees, as proposed by Ochterlony, and attached to the battalions, including, if necessary, the Kumaon Provincial Corps. Alternatively, those who did not object to being based in the plains might be formed into provincial corps for service in Rohilkhand and Saharanpur. Finally the Governor-General concurred with the use of some regular troops in the Cis-Sutlej territory, thereby furthering their experience of hill service.[613]

General Orders by the Commander-in-Chief issued on 27 July 1815 began: 'Major-General Ochterlony will be pleased to form the whole of the Goorkhas who came over during the late campaign to the westward, both Nusserees and those under Lieutenant F. Young, into three battalions . . .' Among other things, the Orders included instructions regarding uniform[614] and that 'the Nusseree and Sirmoor Battalions are to be armed with musquets until a sufficient number of fusils can be obtained. Each man to retain and wear his kookrey in a leather waistbelt . . .'

In framing a detailed draft General Order for the approval of the Governor-General, the Adjutant-General noted that the latest returns received from Ochterlony and Young showed that as at 1 July 1815 the Nasiris had a fighting strength of 2,102 and Young's troops 1,553, making a total of 3,655 all ranks. In addition there were 'establishments' of non-combatants: 367 with the Nasiris and 111 with Young's men, 478 in all. Further details are given in the following tables:

Table 7. *Fighting men of the Nasiris and Young's Goorkhas*

	Soobahs	Subedars	Jema-dars	Adjts	Hav-ildars	Naiks	Sepoys	Totals
Maj-Gen Ochterlony's Nusseeree Goorkahs 1 July 1815	2	14	97	18	248	186	1,537	2,102
Lt. Young's Goorkahs	—	9	49	3	99	82	1,311	1,553
Totals	2	23	146	21	347	268	2,848	3,655

Table 8. *Establishments of the Nasiris and Young's Goorkhas*

	Major-General Ochterlony's Nusseeree Goorkahs	Lt. Young's	Total
Subedars	19	4	23
Jemadars	38	2	40
Havildars	105	82	187
Naicks	2	—	2
Sepoys	100	—	100
	264	88	352
Nesanchies	1	—	1
Bhisties	32	—	32
Blacksmiths	24	10	34
Bellowsmen	16	—	16
	73	10	83
Details	20	—	20
not	10	—	10
disclosed	—	10	10
	—	3	3
	30	13	43
Totals	367	111	478

On this basis the Commander-in-Chief recommended that the three battalions (two Nasiri and the Sirmoor) should each comprise eight companies of a subedar, four jemadars, eight havildars, eight naiks, and 120 sepoys, i.e. in total 3,384 fighting men of all ranks. The number of sepoys in each company was increased from 100 to 120 to absorb more fighting men who would otherwise be supernumerary. Each battalion should also have an 'establishment' of 199 non-combatants: 597 in all. In arithmetical terms, these complements left only 271 fighting men for disposal in puttees and vacancies for 119 in 'establishments'. However, there was a disproportionate number of native commissioned and non-commissioned officers in post, more especially in the Nasiris.[615] Ostensibly the retention of the two subahs in the Nasiri battalions (subject to their own wishes) was on the grounds that 'the active services of the officers and the influence they must be supposed to possess over the Gorkahs may under present circumstances be beneficially exercised, and that some inconvenience is to be apprehended from their retiring at this moment to a state of inactivity; the very proposal might seem to argue mistrust'.[616]

The formation of a Kumaon Local Battalion was to be on the same terms as those of the Nasiri and Sirmoor Battalions, based on the large detachment sent with Subah Jeykishen from the Nasiri Gorkhas and about 200 Kumaonis and others in Almora whom Colonel Nicolls believed to have justified claims to be retained in the British service. The proposed arrangements were approved in their entirety by the Governor-General, who further suggested, as Ochterlony had before, that only two of the Gurkha battalions be stationed west of the Jumna, the third being stationed 'with advantage to the public interest in the Deyra Doon and in the Province of Gurhwal'.[617] Ochterlony did not accept the need for a battalion in Garhwal. He wrote to William Fraser on 28 October 1815: 'The Goorkhas have not overtaken me and I hope you have released me from them by taking them into your Gurwaul corps tho' with all deference what you want with a corps in that central region is not exactly within the comprehension of D.O. [David Ochterlony]. I am the more surprised at their giving it as Young's corps. Being in Sirmoor or west of the Jumna was not in my contemplation tho' as matters now are it can be turned to advantage.'[618] Ochterlony had seen no military need for a battalion to be stationed between his two Nasiri battalions and the battalion in Kumaon. However, his original plan was probably based on economic as well as military considerations. He was unlikely to object to Hastings' decision to employ all those Gorkhas and other hillmen found suitable for service with the Bengal Army. It also seems that Ochterlony did not equate Young's corps with his Nasiris. He wrote to the Adjutant-General on 5 June 1815: 'Lieutenant Young's corps and the Nusseerees must be in a very degree different from the different circumstances in which they were raised. Lieutenant Young's came over uninstigated from the highest to the lowest.'[619] By this Ochterlony seems to have implied that Young's men were deserters whereas his Nasiris (having been embodied as the result of capture or enforced capitulation) were not. Ochterlony's professed surprise at the title 'Young's corps' is interesting. It may have reflected his belief that, as Young came under William Fraser's superintendence, the corps should be known as 'Fraser's corps'. Or he may have wished to please his friend William with such a notion.

In accordance with the Governor-General's wishes, the General Order was published by the Vice-President in Council, on 26 August 1815. It began: 'The Right Honourable the Governor-General having determined to embody and form into battalions for the service of the conquered territories in the hills the Goorkah troops who came over to the British arms during the course of the western campaign, and having issued the necessary orders to that effect to His Excellency the Commander-in-Chief, resolved that the following establishments of these corps as approved by the Governor-General be published in General Orders together with the regulations for their formation and organisation. His Excellency the Governor-General also determined and ordered that a Local Corps should be raised and formed for the service of the Province of Kemaon, resolved that the establishment of that Corps as approved by His Excellency, be published in General Orders.'[620]

The Nasiri Gorkhas were denominated the 1st and 2nd Nasiri Battalions, under the command respectively of Lieutenants Ross and MacHarg; the men under Lieutenant Young were denominated the

Sirmoor Battalion; and the Kumaon Battalion was established under Sir Robert Colquhoun. Each commanding officer was given a European adjutant and each battalion was to have an overall complement of 1,330 all ranks including 1,088 firelocks.

While these arrangements were being made, the Governor-General was writing his lengthy account of the war in a report to the Secret Committee of the Court of Directors.[621] He went into great detail on the history of British relationships with Nepal and the causes of the war. Although Nepalese encroachments and aggression were given as the reason, the underlying cause was revealed in the following statement: 'It is, perhaps, under all the circumstances of the case, fortunate that the rupture has occurred. The passion of the Goorkas for war and conquest had been inflamed, but not satisfied with the success of their arms over the Rajahs of the Hills, in the course of which they had met with no check, till the result of their attack on Kote Kangra, and the successful opposition of Runjeet Sing restrained their advance in that direction.' Hastings pointed out that the Nepalese had been 'consolidating their strength and improving their military resources', 'encouraged by the easiness with which their encroachments were submitted to'. It was therefore not unreasonable to presume 'that they would have chosen for a more formidable attack on us, a time when the occupation of our arms in another quarter would have left our Northern Provinces at their mercy'.[622]

This was the military argument which Ochterlony had put forward to Hastings through Charles Metcalfe. The Nepalese had to be dealt with first before crucial military measures could be taken elsewhere in India. Among the British in Calcutta not everyone agreed that the war with Nepal was justified. Alexander Fraser recorded: 'I believe in this war we had justice on our side. It was provoked by insolence and defiance but on this head much difference of opinion prevails.'[623] Hastings reminded the Secret Committee that the Court of Directors had 'lately declared its conviction that we should be compelled to resort to arms for the maintenance of our rights against the systematic encroachments of the Nepalese'.[624]

Having described the course of the war and the surrender of Kaji

Amar Singh Thapa, Hastings was anxious to reassure the Court of Directors that no time had been lost in 'breaking up the divisions employed before Malown and Jyetuck, and sending the corps to their allotted stations, for discharging extra establishments, and reducing all extraordinary staff; and generally, for putting an end to all expenses of a nature to be only requisite in the prosecution of active operations'. The whole of the irregular troops in Martindell's division had been disbanded – except the 'Goorkas'.[625]

Hastings was satisfied that 'the Goorka troops, in whose fidelity perfect reliance may, I think, be placed, with the addition of a very few regulars, will be found fully adequate to garrison these countries' [the newly acquired territories between the Sutlej and the Mahakali rivers]. He added: 'My persuasion of their fidelity to us is founded on the fact of the active, zealous and meritorious services performed by those who were embodied by Major-General Ochterlony in the progress of the campaign. Major-General Ochterlony's despatches, especially one enclosing a report from the late Lieutenant Lawtie, will show your Honourable Committee the sense entertained of their value by these officers.' Hastings sanctioned the embodiment of all the 'Goorkas' taken into British service in three battalions (two Nasiri and one Sirmoor) and a Kumaon Local Battalion on the grounds that 'It would neither have been prudent nor consistent with good faith, to discharge from the service of the British Government any portion of the troops who came over from the enemy. Severed from their own country, they could not be practised upon to any purpose by their former commanders, therefore they are for the moment efficient for us. But were they cast adrift, they having not either habits or means of industry, must through necessity repair to their old standards, and range themselves in arms against us, or must betake themselves to predatory associations for sustenance.' The Secret Committee of the Court of Directors were reassured that the arrangements were for a temporary establishment and that the numbers would be reduced through normal wastage until an appropriate permanent establishment was reached. 'What this will be I am not prepared to state,' wrote Hastings, 'but certainly it will be very considerably within the number actually in our pay.'[626]

Thus far the progress and constitution of the Nepalese Army have been traced from its beginnings in Gorkha under Prithvi Narayan Shah in the mid-eighteenth century to the defeat of Kaji Amar Singh Thapa's western army by Major-General Ochterlony in the Cis-Sutlej hills in 1815 and, so far as this is possible, the ethnic origins of those of the Kaji's soldiers who took service with the British in that same year have been considered.

Of the 4,700 soldiers of Kaji Amar Singh Thapa's western army who joined the British service in May 1815, perhaps two-thirds were Kumaonis and Garhwalis. It is reasonable to deduce that the rest, as many as 1,500, were Gorkhalis. In accordance with tradition nearly all the officers and probably a good many of the non-commissioned officers were Gorkhalis.

Seema Alavi's conclusion, that the East India Company invented its own model of a Gurkha soldier,[627] is not supported by the evidence. The hillmen of Kumaon, Garhwal, and Sirmur did not 'flock' to the British. Some deserted, but by far the greater number were among the Nepalese troops forced into capitulation at Malaun and Jaithak. A solid core of these troops, perhaps 1,500, were Gorkhalis. Far from inventing a model Gurkha, the British took over a highly efficient force and maintained its skills under the immediate command of its own Gorkhali officers.

CHAPTER 9

Gorkhas and the changing role of the Bengal Army

Under Hastings, the primary role of the two Nasiri Battalions and the Sirmoor Battalion was to defend the Cis-Sutlej hills and Garhwal from possible invasion by Ranjit Singh or some other 'ambitious chief'; that of the Kumaon Battalion was to secure Kumaon from potential incursion from Nepal across the Mahakali river. All four battalions had the further task of stabilising the hill regions in which they were stationed.

By August 1823, when Amherst became Governor-General, the loyalty and efficiency of these irregular battalions had been recognised by their designation as potential front-line troops, with a wider role.

By 1828, when Bentinck succeeded Amherst, doubts about the reliability of Indian troops in the Bengal Army were already well established, and there were calls for more Gorkhas to be recruited. Owing to retrenchment, and for other reasons, this additional recruitment had not been achieved by 1835 when Bentinck left India.

In his long report of 2 August 1815, Hastings reassured the Secret Committee of the Court of Directors that the arrangements whereby some 5,000 Gorkhas and other hillmen from the Nepalese western army had been embodied into the Bengal Army, were for a temporary establishment. This was eventually to be reduced 'very considerably' to an 'appropriate' permanent establishment. In reply the Court of Directors wrote: 'we are willing to admit the propriety of establishing some local corps in the Hilly Districts lately acquired from Nepaul, but with these exceptions [the three Gorkha corps, the Kumaon Provincial corps, and two Pioneer Companies] we cannot consent to authorise any further Extra Establishments'.[628]

The need to maintain a strong force of mountain troops in the Cis-Sutlej hills had been acknowledged.

Ranjit Singh not only posed a potential threat to the British with his growing Sikh Army, but through competition in the recruitment of Gorkhas. William Fraser pointed out, in a letter dated 27 April 1815 to the Political Secretary, that 'the Rajah of Lahore who obtained, at the period that Umr Sing [*sic*] besieged Kangarh [1806–9], a considerable number, found them to be excellent'.[629] Kohli's research into payrolls in the Khalsa Darbar Records shows that Ranjit Singh's regular infantry did indeed include 'Gurkhas'.[630] These 'Gurkhas', the original so-called 'lahuris', had settled with their families in and around Bilaspur. They were attracted to Ranjit Singh's service by his promise to pay his sepoys between seven and eight and a half rupees a month.[631] At that time, these were more than British rates of pay, but payments were not always made on a regular basis. Impressed by the fighting qualities of the 'Gurkhas' and by early Nepalese successes against the British in the western campaign of the Anglo-Nepal War, Ranjit Singh sent his agents across the Sutlej to entice more to join his Gurkha Battalion.[632]

In a letter dated 17 April 1816 to Metcalfe, the Resident at Delhi, Lieutenant Ross wrote: 'I have the honour to acquaint you that I have this day received from Lt. MacHarg [Commanding the 2nd Nasiri Battalion at Kotgarh, a small hill station north of Simla] a report of his having apprehended and despatched under guard to Subhuttoo, an emissary of Raja Ranjit Singh who had entered the cantonment at Kotgurh under instructions to make known to the 2nd Nusseeree Battalion that men of all ranks would readily [be] admitted in Ranjit Singh's service where the pay for a Subedar would be 80 rupees, of a Jemadar 25, Havildar 16, Naick 13, and Sipahee 8, per mensem. Such as might embrace the offer were recommended to proceed through Coolloo.'[633] Ross reported that an attempt had been made on 3 March 1816 to entice men from his 1st Nasiri Battalion by means of three letters delivered by a Brahman. The Gorkha officer recipients had brought and read out the letters to Ross, and the Brahman had swiftly disappeared. Ross added: 'No impression was made on the officers but such as was disadvantageous to the writer. I derived much gratification from witnessing their ingenuous and honest feelings on the occasion.'[634]

Doubtless word went back to Ranjit Singh not only of the Nasiri Battalions' loyalty to the British but of their smartness and discipline. Elsewhere Ranjit Singh's agents met with some success. Balbahadur Thapa, the heroic defender of Kalanga fort against Gillespie's Second division, joined Ranjit Singh and commanded his Gurkha battalion. In 1823, Balbahadur and his men died gallantly fighting against the Afghans in the Yusufzai hills. Ranjit Singh wrote of them: 'Among all my trained soldiers, only the Gurkhas stood their own against the Muslim attack.'[635]

Between 1811 and 1823 there had been a rapid growth in the numbers of regulars in the Sikh Army:[636]

Table 9. *Sikh Army strengths 1811–23*

	Infantry	Cavalry	Artillery	Total
1811	2,852	1,209	—	4,061
1819	7,748	750	834	9,332
1823	11,681	1,656	1,688	15,025

Recognising that by long tradition Sikhs regarded infantry as inferior to cavalry, Ranjit Singh took special care to enhance the status of his infantry. He personally inspected every infantry recruit, attended drill parades, and gave rewards and encouragement by distributing gifts.[637]

Ranjit Singh also sought to emulate the British in artillery. By 1811–12, he had collected thirty-nine field guns, six mortars, and eighty-six camel swivel-guns. He was fascinated by the appearance of a galloper gun in Ochterlony's escort on the occasion of the wedding in 1812 of Ranjit Singh's son. By 1814, seven Sikh gun-batteries were horse-drawn.[638] Training was carried out by European and Indian deserters from the Bengal Army, the first European artilleryman joining Ranjit Singh in 1809. The French mercenary commanders Ventura and Allard arrived in 1822.[639] By 1823 Ranjit Singh had transformed his Sikh Army from loose associations of ill-disciplined light cavalry into a trained, well-equipped and integrated force comprising infantry, artillery and cavalry. The recruitment of 'Gurkhas' continued, and by 1842 the Sikh Army had two Gurkha battalions.[640]

With recruitment in Nepal strictly forbidden[641] Ranjit Singh's competition for Gorkha recruits was, in the long term, to prove a disadvantage to the British. However neither this nor the failure of the British to recruit more Gorkhas into the Bengal Army in 1816 was a serious handicap initially. As the following table shows, the need for recruits for the Nasiri and Sirmoor battalions between 1816 and 1823 was small.[642]

Table 10. *Recruitment to the Nasiri and Sirmoor battalions 1816–23*

	Nasiris	Sirmoor
1816	20	61
1817	23	23
1818	21	32
1819	45	56
1820	26	44
1821	5	9
1822	3	2
1823	1	2

Despite the Nepalese Government's ban on recruitment in Nepal by the British, a certain amount of illicit recruiting was probably done in the western hills. Relatives and friends of serving soldiers were no doubt induced to join them, and the benefits of a secure livelihood under British protection must have drawn some hill farmers westwards in their quest for land.[643] However, recruits from Nepal were probably few in comparison with the intake from communities which, under the Nepalese regime in the Cis-Sutlej hills, had settled in cantonments and villages near military garrisons for example at Malaun and Jaithak. See illustrations 13 and 14.

In his detailed report dated 29 December 1829 to the Adjutant-General, Young (who had commanded the Sirmoor Battalion since its formation) referred to a school which had been established in 1815 in

13. Gorkha cantonments below Malaun fort in 1815.

Dehra 'for the sons of Native officers and men'. Here they were taught to read and write, and were drilled and trained to march. Young wrote that such children 'possess all the military ideas of their predecessors, tho' not accustomed to the same rigour of spartan discipline and bodily labour. Thus did the Lines at Deyrah furnish a more than sufficient Depot for keeping up the Sirmoor corps with the best possible materials for recruits.' [644] Many such recruits were the sons of soldiers who had married local women of other ethnic origins. Young explained: 'in strength of limb, the old Nepalese [Gorkhali] soldier outdoes the cross which springs from the women of Kumaon and Garhwal, but for upright and soldier-like carriage the rising generation (of which there is a fine display in the cantonments at Deyrah) bears the bill'. [645]

This evidence together with the evidence presented in chapters 6, 7, and 8 of this book does not support Caplan's view that 'at first the

14. Gorkha cantonments below Jaithak fort in 1815.

Gurkha regiments were apparently not too discriminating in their recruitment policies'.[646]

The task of stabilising the hill regions in which the Gorkha battalions were stationed was made easier by the empathy which, in marked distinction from Indian battalions, existed between the British officers and their men (see also below pp. 197–8). As a soldier himself, Hastings would have been well aware of the value of such a relationship to military discipline and morale, and hence of its beneficial influence on a local civil community. British officers of the Nasiri and Sirmoor battalions were constantly in close association with their Gorkha officers and men, and were sympathetic not only to their needs but to the needs of their families living close by in the battalion lines. This bond engendered a corporate, family spirit which in turn brought a sense of security and belonging. The bearing and disciplined behaviour of the Gorkha battalions had a stabilising influence on the region in which they were stationed. Their presence also helped to stimulate local agriculture and trade and to bring money into the hill country.

Political stability in north India, which followed the agreement of frontiers with Nepal and the victory over the Marathas and Pindaris in 1818, gave the Gorkha battalions time to establish themselves and to train in their hill stations under the command of dedicated and experienced British officers. The effectiveness of this is well illustrated by the following Division Order issued at Subathu on 8 April 1823:

1 Major-General Reynall [Reynell] having concluded the first regular Inspection that the 1st Nusseeree Battn. has undergone since it was formed, congratulates Captain Kennedy upon the result which has been most creditable to him and the other officers of the Bn. Every circumstance that has come under his view in the Drill, Discipline, Books and interior economy, bears the stamp of good management on one part, and of great good will on the other.

2 The character of this Discription [*sic*] of Troops is too well known to doubt the soldierlike feeling by which the sepoys are animated, and there is a something in the whole appearance of this Corps so peculiar [i.e. special] and so decidedly indicative of efficiency and Military Spirit, as at once to ensure the existance of this feeling in its fullest force.

3 The Major-General in making his Report to the Commander-in-Chief, will not fail to bear in mind the very favourable terms in which Captain Kennedy has acknowledged the useful and indefatigable exertions of the Adjutant Lieutt. Nicolson [James Nicholson] in promoting the discipline of the Battalion, and the kind manner in which his Drill Instruction is conducted. He will also have much satisfaction in bringing

to the notice of His Excellency, the high character and respectable demeanour of the Native officers, as well as the general good conduct of the Non-Commissioned [officers] and Sepoys.

By order of the Major-General
F Meade ADC [647]

Hastings' tenure of the Governor-Generalship came to an end in January 1823, by which time both Ochterlony and William Fraser were no longer directly associated with the Bengal Army's Gorkha battalions. John Adam, the senior member of Council, acted as Governor-General from 13 January 1823 until the arrival of Lord Amherst from England. From the same date Lieutenant-General Sir Edward Paget assumed the appointment of Commander-in-Chief which Hastings had also vacated. During Adam's tenure of the Governor-Generalship, a General Order in Council dated 2 May 1823 (but probably initiated by Hastings) was issued to regularise the pay and establishments of all the irregular troops serving under the Bengal Presidency.

Fourteen Local battalions (see table 11), including the three Gorkha battalions and the Kumaon battalion, were raised not only 'for the service and defence of the Provinces and districts in which they were formed' but 'elsewhere on emergency'. They were liable to active service in the field and were to have rank and precedence next after the troops of the line. [648]

In contrast, thirteen Provincial battalions were solely for civil duties in Bengal, ranking next after the Local Corps. [649]

In chapter 4 of her thesis 'North Indian Culture in Transition *c.* 1770–1860', [650] Seema Alavi gives a detailed account of 'The Military Experiment with the Hill People'. This experiment, which began in 1780 with the raising of a corps of Hill Rangers at Bhagalpur, was later discontinued, 'only to be revived again', so Alavi asserts, 'in the form of the Gurkha military tradition'. [651] There seems to be no evidence in the official records to show that the establishment of the Nasiri, Sirmoor and Kumaon battalions was on an experimental basis. It is, nevertheless, almost certainly true that Captain Richards' suggestion to Ochterlony in 1813 that 'a great many of the Nepalese on pay of 6 rupees a month

Table 11. *Bengal Local battalions, 1 June 1813*

Number	Date of formation	Title
2	29 June 1795	Ramghur Local Battalion
3	24 April 1792	Bhaugulpore Hill Rangers
4	4 Sept. 1813	Dinagepore Local Battalion
5	4 Sept. 1813	Chumparun Light Infantry
6	24 April 1815	1st Nusseri (Gorkha) Bn.
7	24 April 1815	2nd Nusseri (Gorkha) Bn.
8	24 April 1815	Sirmoor (Gorkha) Bn.
10	16 May 1817	Rungpore Light Infantry
11	20 Jan. 1818	Gorukpore Light Infantry
12	1 May 1818	Rampoorah Local Battalion
1	29 June 1795	Calcutta Native Militia
9	24 April 1815	Kemaon Battalion
13	28 Jan. 1822	Bencoolen Local Battalion
14	1 Jan. 1820	Mhairwara Local Battalion

would take service and form a corps of excellent Hill Rangers'[652] owed something to the existence of the Bhagalpur Hill Rangers.

The Bhagalpur Hill Rangers did not, however, set the pattern for the Gorkha battalions. Their roles were quite different. From 1782 the Bhagalpur Hill Rangers had come under the supervision of the Revenue Board. Raised by Augustus Cleveland (1754–84), Collector of the district of Bhagalpur and Rajmahal, they were for 'the subjection of the lawless and savage inhabitants of the jungle-terry [terai] of Rajmahal, who long infested the neighbouring lands by their predatory incursions'. Cleveland's methods were 'without bloodshed or terrors of authority, employing only the means of conciliation, confidence and benevolence'.[653] In the words of Lady Nugent, a visitor to Bhagalpur, Cleveland died 'having civilised the savage inhabitants of the neighbouring hills'.[654] Although, under the reorganisation of 1823, the Bhagalpur Hill Rangers became liable to service 'elsewhere on emergency', it seems they were not called away from their original location.[655]

Men of the Gorkha battalions were, however, destined for active service away from their hill stations. Indeed men of the Sirmoor Battalion had already been made available for service on the plains. In 1816, a detachment joined Colonel Nicolls at Sitapur as part of a force intended to invade western Nepal.[656] In 1817–18, men of the Sirmoor Battalion served under Ochterlony during the war against the Marathas and Pindaris.[657] Although on these occasions they did not see action, in 1824 a detachment of 350 men of the Sirmoor Battalion was sent against 'a gang of rebels and outlaws who had plundered the Treasury Party, and possessed themselves of the Mud Fort of Koorja [Kunja]; the fort was stormed by means of a Battering Ram applied to the gate'. For this action near Saharanpur, the first occasion on which men of a British Gorkha battalion were engaged in actual combat,[658] Young and his battalion were 'thanked in terms of the highest approbation' by the Divisional Commander, the Commander-in-Chief, the Governor-General and the Court of Directors.[659]

These operations demonstrated not only the readiness of Gorkha hillmen to serve on the plains but their capacity to do so efficiently. Young reminded the Adjutant-General in 1829 'with regard to serving in the Plains wherever their presence is required, my corps has not the slightest objection, on the contrary, on every occasion they to a man volunteered their services'.

Lord Amherst, who became Governor-General on 1 August 1823, was quite unlike Hastings. Without political or military standing, he did not command the respect given to his predecessor. He had had little experience of public office, and was largely unknown outside his own immediate circle. His appointment was, to say the least, inauspicious. He was grudgingly accepted by several of the Court of Directors after other more acceptable candidates had declined. In addition to lacking support in both Britain and India, Amherst had doubts about his own competence. He wrote to Morley on 23 August 1825: 'I would not have you suppose that I deem myself a man of sufficient calibre to govern India in difficult times.'[660]

The Court of Directors, anxious to restore their finances, looked to Amherst for an era of peace. It was through no fault of his that India became committed to two years of very costly war with Burma in

1824–6. And it was also unfortunate that two of the three members of his Council were away from Calcutta when he needed their advice. Paget, who abhorred India in general and the Calcutta bureaucracy in particular, went on tour until two months after the war began. Adam became seriously ill and went to Bombay to recuperate. As had been recommended to him before he left London, Amherst turned for guidance to Thomas Munro, the Governor of Madras Presidency, whom he had met in Madras on his journey to Calcutta. Amherst was able to maintain a regular correspondence not only with Munro but with Adam, despite the latter's deteriorating health.[661] Adam impressed upon Amherst the crucial importance of vigorous action not only to win the war with Burma but to preserve the image of British invincibility. Munro supported this view.

The following infantry figures, given to a Select Committee of the House of Commons in 1832, show that the reorganisation of the Bengal Army in 1823 brought no significant increase in size compared with 1816. The proportion of irregular troops remained the same at approximately 28 per cent.

Table 12. *Bengal Army Infantry, regular and irregular troops*

	Regular troops (King's)	Regular troops (Company's)	Regular troops Totals	Irregulars	Totals[662]
1816	5,995	66,887	72,882	28,551	101,433
1823	5,241	69,377	74,618	30,380	104,998
1824	5,720	74,103	79,823	31,285	111,108
1825	6,392	90,300	96,692	32,128	128,820
1826	6,075	86,192	92,267	33,376	125,643
1827	6,684	79,567	86,251	29,173	115,424

However, the military demands for fighting the Burma War (1824–6) caused an increase of almost 24,000, of whom all but about 2,000 were native infantry. The cost in time and money of bringing out King's regiments ruled out any prospect of substantial reinforcements from

England. Regular troops, normally based strategically near the main centres of north India were sent to fight in Burma. 'Local' irregular battalions, who in 1823 became liable for service 'elsewhere on emergency', were either not thought suitable for the exigencies of warfare in the steamy heat of Burma, or could not be taken away from their normal roles. 'Provincial' irregular battalions were restricted to civil duties in the major towns. There was therefore something of a military vacuum in the plains of north India, and in consequence a fear of insurrection.

Evidently Bishop Heber sensed this. During his visit to Bhagalpur in August 1824, he wrote: 'in the possible event of any general insurrection in India, it might be of great political importance to have a force of native troops who prefer (as these do) [the Bhagalpur Hill Rangers] the English to the Hindoos'. He qualified this by pointing out that 200 of the 700 Bhagalpur Hill Rangers were 'not genuine mountaineers but Hindoos from the plain, a mixture not found advantageous to the former, and which must from their superstitions, materially impede the efficiency of the unfettered and unprejudiced Puharee' (hillman).[663] These 'superstitions' raised another serious problem for the British.

The British had for long recruited their Bengal Native Infantry from the wheat-growing plains of north India and had encouraged a high-caste identity for its sepoys.[664] By the early nineteenth century the Bengal Native Infantry sepoy ate his food according to a complex set of strict dietary rules associated with extreme ritual purity. These rules concerned the kind of food, the methods of its preparation, and rituals before, during and after meals. To safeguard them against caste pollution, the sepoys were allowed to have their own cooking pots so that each man could cook his own food and eat alone. This entailed the hiring of carriage cattle (for which the sepoy paid) to carry for each man several cooking pots and sufficient uncooked food for two or three days, as well as his arms, some linen, a carpet and a quilt.[665] Inevitably there were problems in supplying food, and an inordinate amount of time was spent in taking meals. Transport arrangements were cumbersome and delays ensued on the march. By the 1820s the Government began to realise that 'military Hinduism'

had disadvantages.⁶⁶⁶ One of these disadvantages was the strong religious objection of Hindu troops to seaborne travel.

Rumours among Hindu troops that they were to participate in a
seaborne landing at Rangoon, added to previous complaints concerning the unavailability of bullocks to convey their cooking utensils,
food, bedding, arms and equipment, led to a mutiny by the 47th Native
Infantry stationed at Barrackpur. This increased a growing sense of
unreliability on the Bengal Army.

Peers has drawn attention to another problem in the Bengal Native
Infantry which arose at about the same time. There was a growing
'social distancing' between British officers and their sepoys. Some
officers tended to emulate the 'disdain for all things Indian, including
the language' affected by officers of the King's regiments.⁶⁶⁷

Although Gorkhas, like almost all Bengal Native Infantrymen, were
Hindus, they did not practise the same high-caste rituals and dietary
standards. Gorkhas were not fastidious. They were accustomed to
travelling light and carrying their own rations, and were willing to
cook and eat together. As Young explained:

> In disposition they [the Gorkhas] are loyally attached to the British
> service to which they look for protection. They are at the same time
> proud of the name of Goorkahs, which carries with it recollections of
> martial deeds. They look down on the regular Native sepoys, to whom
> they consider themselves superior, but they have the highest opinion
> of the Europeans as soldiers, and respect their courage and discipline
> and wherever they have been associated with European troops a mutual
> good understanding and the best feeling has existed. ⁶⁶⁸

Young also referred to another important asset, Gorkha willingness
to serve:

> This Corps [the Sirmoor] is differently constituted from most others.
> The families of [Gorkha] officers and men are with them in the Can-
> tonement [*sic*] of Deyrah which they look upon as their only Home.
> This tie would prevent them being brought upon the Roll of General
> Relief, as it would be impossible for them to carry their families along
> with them. But if permitted to consider Deyrah their Headquarters and

thus be certain of the families being taken care of, and provision made for their subsistence during their absence, they are ready to undertake any service however distant.[669]

And, in another letter he wrote: 'In Cantonements they are orderly and well behaved and on service active, vigilant and bold.'[670]

From the beginning of the Anglo-Nepal War, Ochterlony had set an example for his officers by his sympathetic treatment of captured Nepalese soldiers.[671] This attitude, which permeated the relationship between British officers and Gorkha officers and men of the Gorkha Corps, had been recognised by General Reynell during his first inspection of the 1st Nasiri Battalion at Subathu in 1823.[672] No doubt Ochterlony's influence ensured the appointment of Ross, MacHarg, and Young as the first Commanding Officers respectively of the 1st and 2nd Nasiri and the Sirmoor Battalions, officers on whom he knew he could rely to maintain and pass on the high standards he had introduced. In reforming Young's irregular hillmen in 1815, Fraser had stipulated British officers should be 'properly selected with reference to the duties they are intended to discharge and their knowledge of the Asiatick character – An intemperate, hasty, boisterous person would do more harm than good'.[673] In 1816, Ochterlony stressed the need for 'intelligent European Officers'.[674]

Although Paget had a low regard for Indian troops, he evidently recognised the value of Gorkhas. In a letter dated 8 January 1825[675] to the Political Secretary (Swinton), the Adjutant-General made it clear that, subject to the Governor-General's views on the political implications, a proposition to establish a recruiting depot at Lohughat in eastern Kumaon in order to enlist Gorkha recruits from Nepal would receive the Commander-in-Chief's 'most earnest recommendation'. Paget believed that 'the advantages which would accrue from an accession of Goorkah sepoys into our Hill Corps would be of the utmost consequence to their efficiency'. The proposition had come originally from Captain Lawrence, Adjutant of the 2nd Nasiri Battalion, who had noticed in the Governor-General's Orders that 'an augmentation of the two Nusseera [*sic*] and the Sirmoor battalions is directed and that Goorkahs are specified as the class to be entertained'.[676] On the assumption that political considerations ruled out the possibility of sending recruiting parties into Dhoti in western Nepal, Lawrence saw two major advantages in setting up a recruiting depot at Lohughat, a day's march from the Nepalese border. The first was that this would prove an inducement to soldiers discharged from the Nepalese Army under the Nepalese system of annual engagements.[677] The second was that this would overcome the difficulty of enlisting sufficient Gorkhas in competition with Ranjit Singh. Lawrence pointed out that, latterly, potential recruits had shown a preference for the less rigorous discipline of the Sikh Army despite drawing less pay than under the British.[678]

Paget, although an admirer of the Gorkhas, thought it 'improbable that men accustomed to the pure air and temperate climate of the hilly countries in which this people are accustomed to serve, would be able to preserve their health and continue efficient for a length of time in low and marshy situations'. They were therefore not employed in the Burma War.

On 14 January 1825, Swinton wrote to Edward Gardner, the Resident at Kathmandu, enclosing the correspondence with the Adjutant-General concerning the 'enlistment of an additional number of Goorkha soldiers'. Swinton sought Gardner's views on 'the special point of forming the [recruitment] Depot at Lohooghaut on the very verge of Nepalese Territory, as well as on the general questions of the feasibility of augmenting our Goorkha Battalions for general service, and their willingness and fitness or otherwise to serve on the frontier and on expeditions beyond seas'. 'The enquiry which you may find it necessary to institute on these several points', Swinton added, 'will, of course, be conducted with your usual prudence and without any reference to the Nepalese authorities.' [679] In the same letter, Swinton asked Gardner for his considered opinion on the doubts held in Calcutta as to which side the Bengal Army's Gorkha troops might take in the event of any further rupture between the British and Nepalese governments. Gardner, whose primary concern was not to antagonise the Nepalese Government and who had recently warned Swinton of the troubled state of Nepal,[680] nevertheless suggested that a body of Nepalese Army reservists be recruited. Nothing came of this suggestion.

In the meantime a serious confrontation arose between Ochterlony, Resident at Delhi, and Amherst. This was to present the Gorkhas with another opportunity to demonstrate their prowess. Early in 1824, Ochterlony had complied with an earnest request by Baldeo Singh, Raja of Bharatpur, ceremoniously to invest his infant son (aged five) as his heir apparent. The Raja's purpose was to thwart his nephew, Durjan Singh, whom he suspected of seeking to supplant his son. A year later, when Baldeo Singh died, Bulwant Singh succeeded as Raja with his maternal uncle as Regent. Durjan Singh, having won the support of the Army, killed the Regent and assumed power himself. Ochterlony immediately issued a proclamation denouncing Durjan Singh and calling on the people to support their legitimate ruler. When Durjan Singh refused to hand over Bulwant Singh into British care, Ochterlony lost no time in preparing to march on Bharatpur. This caused Amherst, who was already under criticism in London, great anxiety. With many troops away from northern India, he feared that any repetition of Lake's disastrous failures to take Bharatpur in 1805 would gravely undermine British authority. Ochterlony was peremptorily ordered to cancel his proclamation and to halt the march of his troops. He resigned and, following a rapid decline in health and spirits, died in Meerut on 14 July 1825. The curtness of Amherst's orders from Calcutta is reminiscent of the letter of dismissal Ochterlony received from Adam in 1806, when he was Resident at Delhi for the first time. It seems that despite his long and outstanding services in India, Ochterlony was to be allowed no opportunity to retire with dignity.

The undeserved censure of a great servant of the Government was brought home to Amherst by Metcalfe, who having been summoned to return to his old post as Resident at Delhi, gave Amherst firm advice that the British were bound to uphold the right of Bulwant Singh to be Raja of Bharatpur. By then Durjan Singh had gathered his troops and prepared his defences. Lord Combermere,[681] who had succeeded Paget as Commander-in-Chief, took to the field with 21,000 troops and more than 100 pieces of ordnance. Metcalfe went with him. This time cavalry prevented the flooding of the ditch around Bharatpur, and mines were used to tear breaches in the city walls. As though to do justice to Ochterlony's memory, men from the 1st Nasiri and

Sirmoor Battalions were in the forefront of those who stormed the breaches. The following extract from Division Orders (Headquarters Meerut) 14 March 1826 records their success:

> The moment when the detachment of the Sirmoor and 1st Nusseeree Battns. are ordered to rejoin their corps, appears to the Major-General Commanding the Division [Reynell] to be most appropriate for recording his sense of gallantry and devotion to the service so uniformly displayed by those troops during the late seige [sic] and conquest of Bhurtpore. He has the authority of Major-General Nicolls as well as information through other channels for knowing how fully the Sirmoor detachment under Lieutt. Fisher's command upheld the character which that corps acquired at Koonjah in 1824.[see p. 171]
>
> The 1st Nusseeree detachment having attached to His M's 14th Foot and thus constantly near the Major-General impowers him from his own observation to assert that the conduct of the two Companies forming the detachment was calculated from first to last to reflect the highest credit on the Regiment to which it belongs, and the Major-General has much satisfaction in assuring the two Commanding Officers, Major Young and Captain Kennedy, that the spirited behaviour of the men of both detachments whenever called upon for any particular enterprize or service not only attracted the notice of the Right Hon'ble the Commander-in-Chief but left in His Excellency's mind a most favourable impression of the Goorkha Sepoys.[682]

In paragraph 6 of his report to the Adjutant-General dated 4 September 1830, Captain Kennedy, Commanding Officer of the Nusseeree Battalion wrote: 'The absence of all fastidiousness in regard to nature or preparation of their food adds greatly to the efficiency of the individuals composing the bulk of this corps, and enhances their value as soldiers, as was proved at Bhurtpore by the circumstances of their remaining without relief in the advanced trench during the whole seige [sic].'[683]

There was a yet further advantage in employing the Gorkha battalions. At a time when the Government in India was obliged to cut costs, these units were comparatively inexpensive. As originally raised, each Gorkha corps had an establishment of only three European officers, a Commanding Officer (Captain), an Adjutant (Lieutenant), and an Assistant Surgeon. Out of a total complement of 1,327 all ranks per battalion this represented a ratio of one officer to approximately 440. The following table gives comparable figures for King's regiments, Native Infantry, and Irregular Infantry in the Division commanded by Ochterlony at the outset of the second campaign of the Anglo-Nepal War in 1816.[684]

It will be seen from table 13 below that the ratios of European officers to all other ranks in these categories are approximately:

King's regiment	1:30
Native Infantry	1:90
Irregular Infantry	1:180

Under the reorganisation of 1823, the complement of British officers in the Nasiri and Sirmoor Battalions remained at three while the total for all other ranks was reduced to 769, giving a ratio of approximately 1: 260. In 1830, by which time a Second-in-Command had been added, the ratio was 1: 190. Bearing in mind that the Commanding Officers of the 1st Nasiri and Sirmoor battalions were also Political Agents of the Governor-General in their respective territories, the Bengal Government had not only a highly efficient but an economical asset in the Gorkha battalions.

Further evidence of this may be deduced from figures presented to a Select Committee of the House of Commons in 1832, and set out in tables 14 and 15 below.

Table 13. *Comparison of European Commissioned Officers in Major-General Sir David Ochterlony's Division by Battalion of King's Regiments; Native Infantry; Irregular Light Infantry (January 1816)*

	European Commissioned Officers				European Commissioned Staff				Totals European Officers	Totals all Other Ranks
	Col-onel or Lt. Col	Major	Capt or Capt. Lt.	Lieut	Surgeon	Asst Surgeon	Adjt.	QM/ Interpt.		
King's Regiments										
24th Foot	1*	2	4	21	1	1	1	—	31	931
87th Foot			7	9	—	2	1	1	20	785
66th Foot	2#	2	8	19	1	1	1	1	35	853
Total:	3	4	19	49	2	4	3	2	86	2,569
*Colonel – acting Brigadier					Includes a Colonel acting Brigadier					
Native Infantry										
1st Bn 18th N.I.	1	—	2	10	—	1	1	1	16	847
2nd Bn 4th N.I.	—	1	—	5	—	1	1	1	9	894
2nd Bn 8th N.I.	1	1	—	3	—	—	1	1	7	916
2nd Bn 9th N.I.	—	1	—	4	—	1	1	1	8	919
2nd Bn 12th N.I.	—	1	1	5	—	1	1	1	10	991
2nd Bn 15th N.I.	1	1	1	3	—	1	1	1	9	886
2nd Bn 22nd N.I.	1	1	1	7	1	—	1	1	13	909
2nd Bn 25th N.I.	—	—	1	7	—	—	1	1	10	955
1st Bn 8th N.I.	—	1	1	9	1	—	1	1	14	874
2nd Bn 18th N.I.	—	1	1	3	1	—	1	1	8	916
Total:	4	8	8	56	3	5	10	10	104	9,107
Irregular Light Infan-try										
Champaran L.I.	—	—	1	5	—	1	1	—	8	1,387

Table 14. *Comparative monthly costs (actual costs of numbers present of European and Indian troops)* [685]

Regiment	Number of all ranks	Total monthly cost (rupees)	
		Net	Gross
H M Infantry (10 Companies)	844	20,066	51,745
E I Company's European Infantry (8 Companies)	783	20,039	46,500
Indian Infantry (8 Companies)	792	14,385	24,492

No similar figures were made available for irregular Gorkha units. However, Holt Mackenzie (Secretary to the Territorial Department in Bengal), who gave evidence before the Select Committee on 19 April 1832, to the question put to him, 'Would the Goorkha force you have referred to be as cheap as the present force?' replied as follows: 'I should think certainly as cheap. I imagine indeed they might be cheaper, though I cannot say what terms they might make to induce them to take general service; but those employed in the hills, I think, are got at a lower rate than the sepoys in the plains.' [686]

The following figures taken from statements presented to the same Select Committee suggest that the cost of an (irregular) Gorkha battalion may have been half that of a Bengal Native line regiment. [687]

Table 15. *Comparative costs of Bengal Regular and Irregular Infantry, 1823 and 1830*

	Numbers	Total costs (£)	Approx cost per man (£)
1823			
Bengal Native Infantry	68,023	1,414,247	21
Bengal Irregular Infy.	30,380	315,952	10
1830			
Bengal Native Infantry	58,425	1,434,366	24
Bengal Irregular Infy.	22,057	245,204	11

Lord William Bentinck took up appointment as Governor-General on 4 July 1828.[688] Like Amherst, he was not the first choice. Although he held the rank of General, he was not given the dual appointment as Commander-in-Chief until 16 May 1833, following the recall of Sir Edward Barnes. Having himself been recalled from the Governorship of Madras in 1806, after the mutiny at Vellore, Bentinck was conscious of his need not to antagonise the Court of Directors or Lord Ellenborough, the autocratic and newly appointed[689] President of the Board of Control. The Court's demands for financial recovery following the war in Burma were all the more pressing, with the Company's charter due to be considered for renewal in 1833. No doubt Bentinck had Ellenborough's threat in mind that if he was not capable of achieving the necessary economies then 'one will be found who is'.[690]

Bentinck inherited from Amherst major financial problems. Amherst had, however, already begun the process of reviewing and reducing the cost of Government expenditure on both civil and military establishments. The greatest drain on government finances was the Army, especially the Bengal Army.

Figures presented to the Select Committee of the House of Commons in 1832 show that between 1803 and 1826 the overall number for all ranks of the Indian Army (all three Presidencies) doubled. Over the same period the size of the Bengal Army almost trebled. From 1813 the Bengal Army formed more than half that of the Indian Army. Following the end of the Burmese War the numbers began to decrease:[691]

Table 16. *Comparative size (totals all ranks)*
of the Indian Army and the Bengal Army

	Indian Army	Bengal Army
1803	140,141	52,853
1804	178,713	78,743
1813	200,071	101,765
1815	227,183	129,542
1816	230,883	130,935
1818	243,240	136,128
1823	237,732	129,834

	Indian Army	Bengal Army
1824	243,427	136,096
1825	276,548	158,612
1826	291,145	157,561
1827	273,615	144,301
1828	259,028	135,810
1829	243,448	126,542
1830	223,476	112,598

The following table shows, however, that despite the reduction in numbers, both in the Bengal Army and in the Indian Army as a whole, by 1830 the costs had not yet been reduced to pre-Burma War levels:

Table 17. *Comparative costs of the Indian Army and the Bengal Army*

	Indian Army Cost (£)	Bengal Army Cost (£)
1823	9,233,174	4,226,636
1824	9,490,589	4,613,104
1825	11,308,185	6,175,912
1826	12,919,258	7,113,114
1827	12,022,754	6,439,617
1828	10,773,966	5,123,364
1829	9,751,155	4,602,913
1830	9,461,953	4,329,537

One reason for this[692] was the overall increase in the numbers of (costly) British troops.[693] Another was the decision to make quick initial savings among the (least costly) irregular units. In 1826, three of the Local battalions, the Champaran Light Infantry, the Rangpur Light Infantry and the Dinajpur Battalion were disbanded.

On 1 February 1830, the 2nd Nasiri Battalion was also disbanded. Men with less than six years service were discharged. Those with six years service or more and who were 'residents of the Nypal territory' were drafted to the (1st) Nasiri and the Sirmoor Battalions. The remainder were offered transfer to the Kumaon Battalion or to line regiments of Indian infantry.[694] Returns from the Military Auditor General to the Vice-President in Council, show that as at 1 May 1829 the 1st and 2nd Nasiri Battalions and the Sirmoor Battalion (each of which had a complement of 776 all ranks) were over strength to the following extent:

Table 18. *Supernumeraries in the 1st and 2nd Nasiri Battalions and the Sirmoor Battalion as at 1 May 1829*

Rank	1st Nasiri	2nd Nasiri	Sirmoor
Subedar	3	—	1
Jemadar	3	14	10
Havildar	3	6	5
Naick	—	1	3
Drummer	2	—	3
Sepoy	11	—	68
Totals	22	21	90

After[695] the disbandment of the 2nd Nasiri Battalion and the redeployment of its troops, the Nasiri and Sirmoor Battalions were over strength, as at 1 May 1830, by:[696]

Table 19. *Supernumeraries in the Sirmoor and Nasiri battalions, as at 1 May 1830*

Rank	Nasiri	Sirmoor
Subedar	5	3
Jemadar	9	12
Havildar	14	12
Naick	10	10
Drummer	8	8
Sepoy	60	71
Totals	106	116

By 1 May 1835 the number of supernumeraries had been reduced to two, a subedar and a native doctor, both in the Sirmoor Battalion.[697] During Bentinck's term of office as Governor-General, therefore, a reduction was made of more than a third of the overall strength of the Gorkha component of the Bengal Army.[698]

Russia's advance in Turkestan and success against the Persians in 1826 caused the Home Government considerable concern. Ellenborough recorded in his diary: 'I feel confident we shall have to fight the Russians on the Indus, and I have long had a presentiment that I should meet them there, and gain a great battle.'[699] And later he wrote that he had resolved 'to go quietly to work... to substitute the King's government for that of the Company'.[700] Bentinck was instructed to turn his attention to the Indus and the North-West Frontier.

In addition to problems of achieving financial economies, Bentinck was now faced with a political dilemma. The Board of Control was concerned with external threats to the Indian empire. The Court of Directors, on the other hand, was alarmed about the dangers of insurrection in the Company's northern territories.

In his minute of 13 March 1835 entitled 'Composition of the Army of India', Bentinck surveyed the potential dangers to India. He saw the greatest of these as internal disturbances,[701] for there was always danger from within a population of 100 million, especially in time of peace.[702] Nevertheless, Ellenborough's fear of Russia and enthusiasm for navigating the Indus meant military commitments to the North-West Frontier, and changes in the role of the Indian Army.

In 1820, Hastings had defined the first duty of government as 'to fix the amount of military force necessary for the maintenance of India' and to ensure that 'adequate provisions are made for its support'.[703] Charles Metcalfe commended 'every increase of the army that our finances will bear', adding 'all my notions of Indian politics begin and end in a powerful army'.[704] Jasper Nicolls, on the other hand, maintained that 'We are in the position of Champion of England; we must fight whenever neighbouring nations throw down the gauntlet.'[705]

The Army in India, including, as it was obliged to do, up to 20,000 King's troops, had within it the nucleus of an imperial task force. Indeed in 1824 the King's regiments in India, greatly expanded above their home complements, amounted to almost a quarter of the entire British Army.[706] Although the Government in India met the cost of this force, doubt remained as to whether the Governor-General in Council had absolute control over its deployment.[707] In London the Government's view was that British regiments stationed in India were readily available to defend all Britain's interests in the East. In contrast, the Court of Directors looked to the British forces in India to provide a stiffening for the Company's Indian troops.

Against this political background it is now necessary to consider what was required of the Bengal Army, and its competence to meet these requirements. With a vast area to cover and a dual role of internal security and frontier defence, the fundamental needs were for reliability and efficiency. These two attributes were vital to maintain the image of invincibility essential to impress potential allies and to suppress possible insurrection. The prospect of involvement on any large scale in the distant hills beyond the Indus called for great improvements in several aspects of military organisation, for example mobility and tactics, supplies and storage, communications and intelligence, armament and equipment, and – by no means least – morale. The plain fact was that the Bengal Army, although apparently strong in numbers, was weak in other respects.

Mention has already been made of the Barrackpur mutiny and the growing sense of unreliability on the Bengal sepoys. However it was not only the sepoys who were the cause of concern. In London there were fears that 'every rank of the Bengal service [is] inattentive to its duties and discontented'.[708] Captain Walter Badenach of the Bengal Army addressed a paper to the President of the Board of Control (Wynn) on the state of the Indian Army.[709]

Most of Badenach's suggestions related to the inadequate rewards for British officers in the Company's service. He insisted that rank not pay was the central problem, and that 'rank, honours and liberal retirement are the real rewards for military men'.[710] He pointed out that in 1796 fourteen general officers were allowed for an Indian Army of 55,000. In 1826, when the Indian Army was more than five times that size, the number of generals had been increased to eighteen, most of whom were of the King's not Company's service. Consequently prospects of promotion for junior officers were bleak. Badenach stressed that the greatest defect in keeping officers so long in junior ranks – not less than twenty-five years to attain the rank of major in the Company's service compared with twelve to seventeen years in the King's regiments – was that when they were promoted they were often unfit.[711] He added that there were very few efficient officers above the rank of lieutenant-colonel and 'a great many worn out even below it'.[712]

To remedy this, Badenach recommended that 'the army should be more numerically officered in its higher ranks'; that, as in the King's regiments, promotion should be by regimental seniority up to lieu-tenant-colonel rank, and that there should be inducements for officers to retire early. Promotion up to captain should be in seven years instead of the current average of seventeen years. Distinguished service should be recognised by the award of brevet rank, and local rank should be allowed for officers of very long standing.[713] Among Badenach's more general proposals, were the abolition of corporal punishment for Indian troops of the Bengal Army, and the creation of Veteran Corps for Indian officers, non-commissioned officers and sepoys of good character who were too old for active service. In the final sentence of his address, he wrote: 'The instrument by which we govern India should not be neglected or mismanaged for a mo-ment.'[714]

Set against this exposition of weaknesses in the Bengal Army, the Gorkha battalions had much to commend them. Since 1815, when Ochterlony had informed the Governor-General that the Company's sepoys could not be brought to match the Gorkhas, and Jasper Nicolls had reported the Gorkhas to be 'the only corps properly equipped for hill service';[715] they had proved themselves to be reliable and efficient. They were not only loyal to the British but were highly regarded by the authorities in India; they were economical in cost and they were mobile mountain troops with a proven capability of fighting on the plains.

In his evidence to the Select Committee of the House of Commons in 1832, Holt Mackenzie mentioned a proposition made by Hodgson, when he was Assistant to the Resident at Kathmandu (Gardner), for enlisting Gorkhas. This had been based on Hodgson's belief that, despite the Nepalese Government's firm opposition, it would be possible to recruit from among the 10,000 reservists of the Nepalese Army. These reservists were unemployed and envious of 'the superior and constant pay received by the [Bengal Army] sepoys'.[716]

Hodgson had, in fact, written about the Nepalese Army in a long memorandum dated 10 February 1825 which Gardner had forwarded to Calcutta. This referred to the Gorkha reservist system whereby, simultaneously, the Nepalese had a peace establishment of 10,000 men 'most of them eminently effective' and a war establishment of 20,000 men 'hardly less so'. The 10,000 in reserve, by annual rotation, had little to do but 'hunt game or amuse themselves at home'. Part of the attractiveness of recruiting them into the Bengal Army was that they were disciplined and trained under British methods with Light Infantry tactics, bugle calls and drills. Hodgson observed that their 'musquets are excellent and their accoutrements respectable, and the six best battalions at Cathmandoo are subjected to the rigours of the British system'.[717] Hodgson did, however, refer to an occasion on which a Gorkha soldier had explained that he could not leave Nepal without permission, obtainable only once a year under pretence of pilgrimage. The soldier had said: 'Some of our fellows go in this way and visit your stations, and here and there one of us gets service. If we ran away, our families would answer for the offence.'[718]

Hodgson proposed that, if the indirect system of recruitment hitherto practised along the border did not fulfil the purpose, a solution might be considered, namely the occasional engagement of a body of troops from Nepal on the lines of 'Swiss battalions'.[719] He added: 'It may perhaps be objected that by an occasional resort to this weapon we should be liable to instruct the Gorkhas in that science in which alone they are deficient, and so raise them into a really formidable enemy, and also that by such occasional resort to them we should only fan the military ardour which is already too glowing.'[720]

From 1832, when Queen Tripura Sundari died, Bhim Sen Thapa's authority weakened. King Rajendra Bikram Shah, having attained his majority, began asserting his independence – encouraged by Bhim Sen Thapa's enemies including a vengeful Pande family. Bhim Sen Thapa tried to strike up relations with the British Resident and the East India Company. Hodgson saw through this ploy and countered it by insisting (to no avail) on the removal of restrictions on the Residency. In desperation Bhim Sen Thapa offered to send his nephew as an ambassador to London. This was declined.[721]

By 1832, when he wrote his paper, 'On the Origin and Classification of the Military Tribes of Nepal', Hodgson calculated that there were 30,000 Gorkha reservists. He wrote: 'I am not sure that there exists any insuperable obstacle to our obtaining, in one form or other, the services of a large body of these men.'[722] Hodgson stressed the advantages of recruiting Gorkhas:

> These highland soldiers who despatch their meals in half an hour and satisfy the [Hindu] ceremonial law by merely washing their hands and face, and taking off their turbans before cooking, laugh at the pharisaical rigour of our [Indian] sipahis who must bathe from head to foot and make puja [religious ritual] ere they begin to dress their dinner, must eat nearly naked in the coldest weather, and cannot be in marching trim again in less than three hours. In war, the former [the Gorkhalis] carry several days' provisions on their backs; the latter would deem such an act intolerably degrading.[723]

'In my humble opinion,' Hodgson added 'they are by far the best soldiers in India, and, if they are made participators of our renown in arms, I conceive that their gallant spirit and unadulterated military habits might be relied upon for fidelity; and that our good and regular pay, and noble pension establishment would serve to counterpoise the influence of nationality.' Hodgson clearly believed that the recruitment of surplus trained fighting men into the Bengal Army would not only provide an outlet for the military tribes of Nepal but would greatly strengthen the reliability of the Company's forces. In this respect he seemed to have advocated the establishment of regular Gorkha units. His advice received the thanks of the Government in India, but no immediate action was taken.

15. Brian Houghton Hodgson – by Louisa Starr-Canziani.

Here it should be noted that by 1832 Hodgson had acquired a good deal of experience in Kathmandu. For almost all the period from 1820 to 1829 he had served as Assistant to Gardner and, on Gardner's retirement, had officiated as Resident from 1829 to 1831. Despite the fact that the Residency continued to be kept in isolation, and pleas for an audience with the King were refused,[724] by one means or another

Hodgson managed to acquire a working knowledge of Nepal and its affairs. He was alarmed at the size of the Nepalese Army and at the possibility that it might one day be sent into British India. Bentinck did not share this anxiety. He wrote: 'An attack from the Gurkhas might partially succeed as a diversion against our hill provinces, but without cavalry or artillery their efforts on the plains could only terminate in disgrace and defeat.'[725]

In his assessment of military policy, Bentinck seems to have had a low regard for Indian sepoys, and no particular interest in Gorkha troops beyond noting the opinion of Ochterlony and Nicolls that the sepoys of the Bengal Army were unequal to contend with the Gorkhas in the hills.[726] However, in a minute dated 27 July 1830 concerning the Nasiri and Sirmoor battalions, he wrote: 'Each Commanding Officer may be asked to state Casts [*sic*], Districts, Provinces and length of service of the members of his corps, particulars which may be exhibited with sufficient accuracy in abstract, without running into details of a Description Roll.'[727]

An analysis of the responses from Captain Kennedy (Commanding the Nasiri Battalion) and Major Young (Commanding the Sirmoor Battalion) provides the following details:[728]

Table 20. *Nasiri and Sirmoor battalions;*
numbers in post by country/district of origin

Country/District of origin	Nasiri Bn	Sirmoor Bn
Nepal	687	418
Kumaon	8	38
Garhwal	119	272
Sirmoor	28	17
Elsewhere	1	8
Totals	843	753

Other returns from Kennedy and Young in response to Bentinck's enquiries reveal that no less than 875 of their men who had joined the British service in 1815 were still serving in 1830:[729]

Table 21. *Men of the Nasiri and Sirmoor battalions recruited in 1815 and still serving in 1830*

	Nasiri Bn	Sirmoor Bn
Subah	—	1
Subedar	13	8
Jemadar	16	8
Havildar	54	40
Naik	50	36
Bugler	—	10
Drummer	19	—
Sepoy	387	233
Totals	539	336

Of these 875 men, a number equivalent in each rank to those held supernumerary were transferred to the Pension Establishment:[730]

Table 22. *Men in table 21 specially retired*

	Nasiri Bn	Sirmoor Bn
Subedar	5	2
Jemadar	9	12
Havildar	14	12
Naik	10	10
Totals	38	36

These seventy-four men were specially exempted from the normal minimum twenty-year service requirement for invalid pensions. The pension of the subedars was fixed at thirty rupees a month, instead of the normal pension of fifteen rupees, in order that they should not suffer too severe a reduction from their erstwhile pay of sixty rupees. Following the retirement of all seventy-four, the remaining 801 (501 in the Nasiri Battalion and 300 in the Sirmoor Battalion) were retained on active service.

As a result of the retirements, promotion was improved and the

Garrison companies, in which those no longer fit for active service had hitherto been held, were abolished. Not least important, perhaps, those allowed to retire on pension were content to settle with their families away from the battalion lines to cultivate land, thereby furthering the social stability of the neighbourhood.

Kennedy and Young replied as follows to Bentinck's request for a classification of their men according to the Hindu hierarchy:

Table 23. *Class composition of the Nasiri and Sirmoor battalions, 1830*[731]

	Nasiri Bn	Sirmoor Bn
Brahmans	69	65
Rajputs	86	651
Khas Gorkhas (Chhetris) Magars, Gurungs, Garhwalis	633	—
Sarkis, Damais, Hindus of inferior class	54	37
Mussulman	1	—
Totals	843	753

It was explained to the Court of Directors that 'no material difference really exists in the caste of the men of the two corps, the apparent difference being caused by a capricious system of classification without any actual discordancy. The men are almost entirely drawn from among the mountain tribes, and in moral and physical power, though short in stature, they possess every requisite of a soldier.'[732]

Dor Bahadur Bista has pointed out that ' "Rajputs" are Kshatriyas, the traditional warriors of Hindu society. Because of Rajput glory in Indian history, all Rajput Kshatriyas prefer to distinguish themselves as just Rajput, omitting Kshatriya or Chhetri as the hill Kshatriyas call themselves.'[733] Kennedy seems deliberately to have separated the high-caste Rajputs, whom he regarded as the 'most troublesome' and 'least efficient' part of his corps, from the less fastidious hillmen who comprised the great bulk of his fighting men.[734] Young, on the other hand, appears to have taken the simpler and perhaps socially more acceptable course of classifying all of them as Rajputs.[735] In this respect it is interesting to note that in 1825, 80 per cent of the Bengal Army was composed of Brahmans and Rajputs.[736]

Despite Bentinck's interest in Gorkhas, and the many attributes in their favour, a reduction in their numbers was inevitable. Bentinck was committed to overall retrenchment and irregular troops were the easiest to disband. What is more, evidence presented to the Select Committee of the House of Commons in 1832 shows that the establishment in Calcutta did not recognise the need to reconstitute the Bengal Army.

The Government in London were not well informed about Gorkhas. Indeed, to some extent they may have been misled. For example, the Select Committee of the House of Commons seems to have been misinformed about the numbers of Gorkhas available for active service. The Minutes of Evidence taken before it include, under the curious heading 'Acquisitions from Nepaul' as at 1 July 1830, a regiment of Native Infantry numbering 862 all ranks who were not Gorkhas. Also included is the Kumaon Battalion, 786 all ranks (largely Kumaonis), which came under the Civil Department and was restricted to duties in Kumaon. No such qualifications were given in evidence.

In presenting his evidence before the Select Committee, Holt Mackenzie made no case for increasing the number of Gorkhas. In their favour, he described Gorkhas as 'very superior in point of physical strength and moral courage to any troops with whom we have had to do. They have a strong feeling of patriotism, with a great deal of personal pride, and are described, indeed, as equalling any troops in the world in the moral qualities of a soldier.' However, in replying to the question 'What difficulty is there in having a greater number of Goorkhas in our service?', Mackenzie said: 'The chief difficulty that immediately occurs to me is this, that they are hardly fit for general service in the plains.'[738]

Holt Mackenzie seems to have taken little account of the current sense of unreliability on Indian troops. When asked, 'Do you consider

Table 24. *'Acquisitions from Nepaul'* as at 1 July 1830[737]

	Numbers		
	Corps	Europeans	Natives
Almorah:			
Company of Pioneers	1	2	103
Regt. of Native Infy.	½	9	421
Kumaun Local Bn	1	5	781
Lohooghaut:			
Regt. of Native Infy.	½	10	422
Dehra Doon:			
Sirmoor Bn	1	6	868
Subathoo:			
Company of Pioneers	1	2	103
Nusseree Bn	1	7	854
Totals		41	3,552

that there is any danger to our rule from the native army?', he answered: 'I am not aware of any circumstance causing immediate danger, but I think, on general principles, that there is much prospective danger.'[739] Indeed, he considered that 'a large native army is quite essential for maintaining the tranquillity of the country' and 'the vast extent of the country seems to render a large native army indispensable'. He added that he would be very sorry to see its defence and obedience trusted to them (Indian troops) without also a large European force. And in reply to the question 'Would they [the Gorkhas] not form a cheap substitution for European forces?', he said: 'I should not consider it safe to rest upon them as a substitute for Europeans.'[740] Holt Mackenzie failed to point out the lack of fastidiousness of the Gurkhas regarding religious ritual. When it was put to him that 'the Hindoos especially appear to suffer from their prejudices as to food, and was asked, 'Are the Gurkhas Hindoos?' he said simply: 'Yes, they are all Hindoos.'[741]

In presenting their evidence before the Select Committee, neither General Sir Edward Paget nor Major-General Jasper Nicolls, both of whom had a high regard for Gorkha soldiers, took the opportunity to speak up on their behalf. Major-General Sir Thomas Reynell, who had so highly praised the 1st Nasiri Battalion on his first inspection of them as their Divisional Commander, made no specific mention of their distinguished part in the battle of Bharatpur. He said only that he had seen 'native soldiers' there 'in the trenches, working at very laborious employments and, I believe, contrary to their own religious feelings'.[742] All three Generals spoke well of the efficiency of the Bengal Army.[743] They may well have thought it politically wise to do so.

There were lingering doubts in the minds of the Indian Government about the loyalty of Gorkhas in all circumstances. In 1825 Swinton had consulted Gardner about the possibility of recruiting more Gorkhas from Nepal and about 'the doubts held in Calcutta as to which side the Bengal Army's Gorkha troops might take in the event of any further rupture between the British and Nepalese Governments'.[744] Gardner's advice was that 'even on entering our service, the Goorkhas would not separate themselves entirely from their native country as they could not remove their families from Nepal, and that, however faithfully they might conduct themselves on general occasions, in the event of any future rupture with Nepal, they possessed that feeling of patriotism which would induce the greater part of them to adhere decidedly to their national allegiance'.[745]

A further indication of the Indian Government's misgivings was given by Holt Mackenzie. In presenting his evidence before the Select Committee of the House of Commons in 1832, he said: 'I imagine the only hill country that would suit [Gorkha soldiers] is that which we conquered from the Goorkhas, and of that there is little frontier requiring defence excepting that which touches upon their reserved territories . . . Upon the frontier which we have to defend against the Goorkhas themselves, we could not propose to station troops levied from among them.'[746]

Long established attitudes may have been weakened by lingering doubts about the reliability of Indian troops. Old prejudices were, however, not to be broken until 1857. In that same year Hodgson added a revealing footnote to his paper, 'On the Origin and Classification of the Military Tribes of Nepal':

> Since this paper was written (twenty five years back) the value and availability to us of the Gorkhali soldier tribes have been well tested, and it is infinitely to be regretted that the opinions of Sir H. Fane, Sir C. Napier and of Sir H. Lawrence, as to the high expediency of recruiting largely from this source were not acted on long ago. So long as my voice carried any weight, I often pressed the subject on the attention of those in authority. But the then prejudice in favour of Brahman and Kshatri sipahis neutralised all my efforts, though the danger of so homogeneous an army of foreign mercenaries was, among other arguments, earnestly dwelt on.[747]

The concept of a mercenary as a soldier hired into foreign service and who was therefore unreliable, had long been established in India. In the eighteenth and early nineteenth centuries, a veritable tide of unemployed soldiers had washed around northern India seeking to hire themselves to the highest bidder. A change of fortune to such men was a signal to change masters. As someone wrote of India in 1832 'the common mercenary passes without remorse and without discredit to alternate sides; today he fights on one side, tomorrow he is found conspicuous on the other'.[748] Such a simplistic definition does not befit the Gorkha soldiers who took service with the British in 1815. These men were not casually hired but were enlisted into the Bengal Army and became full members of a permanent force. Some 800 of the original recruits were still serving, loyally, in the 1830s.

Just as the loyalty of Gorkhas to the British endured, so too did the loyalty of British officers to their Gorkha soldiers. Indeed, there was from the start an empathy, a special relationship between them. Lieutenant Lawtie, who first led the Nasiris into action in April 1815 at the battle of Malaun, felt this empathy and reported to General Ochterlony on the skills and attributes of the men of 'so peculiarly formed a corps'. It seems very likely that Ochterlony had sensed this empathy before giving Lawtie the honour of leading the Nasiris on so important a mission. With his confidence confirmed, Ochterlony wrote proudly to the Adjutant-General, in April 1815, on the conduct of 'a corps in which I feel a great and peculiar interest'.[749] Eight years later, General Reynell used the same word 'peculiar' (meaning special) in a Division Order following his first inspection of the 1st Nasiri Battalion at Subathu: 'There is something in the whole appearance of this corps so peculiar and so decidedly indicative of efficiency and military spirit as at once to ensure the existance of this feeling in its fullest force.'[750] This strong impression was due in large measure to the care and mutual understanding of dedicated British and Gorkha officers. Such a manifestation in Subathu and Dehra was both striking and new. It was striking in that it contrasted starkly with the general state of affairs in Indian regiments. It was new in that not only the Gorkhas but their families were embraced in a corporate enterprise, and that, in their cantonments and battalion lines, they shared in a growing sense of regimental pride.

CHAPTER 10

Continuing problems in the recruitment of Gorkhas

Problems in the recruitment of Gorkhas were to frustrate the British long after Bentinck's failing health forced him to leave India in March 1835. Metcalfe, who was hurriedly recalled from Agra to officiate as Governor-General pending the arrival of Bentinck's successor, had long held the highest opinion of Gorkhas. Some of his enthusiasm may have influenced the newly appointed Commander-in-Chief, Sir Henry Fane, who arrived in Calcutta on 4 September 1835 to be met, and doubtless briefed, by Metcalfe. Indeed it was at Fane's request in December 1835 that the Governor-General in Council gave approval that 'men of the three Goorkah or Hill Corps [Nasiri, Sirmoor and Kumaon battalions] who came over to the British Army from the Nepaul Government during the campaign of 1815, were entitled to transfer to the Pension Establishment for Local Service'.[751] Metcalfe and Fane were to maintain a correspondence and to meet after Metcalfe had resumed in Agra his appointment as Governor of the North-West Provinces.[752]

Lord Auckland took office as Governor-General in March 1836. Ostensibly, he shared the views of Metcalfe, with whom he had been at Eton, that the British should not interfere in the affairs of Afghanistan and the Punjab. No doubt Metcalfe warned him, as earlier he had warned Bentinck, of the perilous wars and ruinous expenditure which would result from any venture beyond the Indus. However, unlike Metcalfe, Auckland dreaded responsibility and lacked the self-confidence to make prompt and independent decisions. Moreover, he was urged by Hobhouse, President of the Board of Control, and by Palmerston, then Foreign Secretary, to raise 'a timely barrier against the encroachment of Russian influence'.

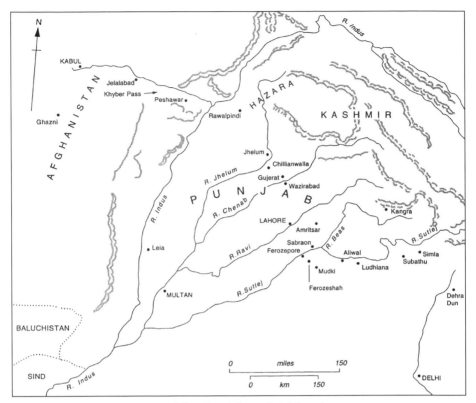

Map 9. The Punjab and Afghanistan.

To the benefit of the Gorkha battalions, Auckland struck up an early rapport with Sir Henry Fane.[753] A General Order of the Commander-in-Chief dated 8 April 1836 records the Governor-General's sanction for 'the established allowance of five rupees per mensem, for the provision of a school room, being passed to the Goorkah battalions stationed at Dehra, Subathoo and Hawaul-haugh, from the 1st proximo'. The reason for this action is clear from a Minute by Sir Henry Fane dated 24 March 1836:

> I learn from the Inspection reports which are made to me, that the Nusseree Battalion and the other Goorkha Corps in the North west Hills have not any allowance made to them for the maintenance of regimental schools. As the Geographical position of these Corps and other circumstances must, I imagine, render their permanent employ-

ment a matter of almost certainty, I deem it desirable that the advantage of such an establishment should be extended to them. A number of children of the original soldiers of these Corps are at this time entering the service and replacing their fathers, and no doubt such will be the continued practice so that, should the Government see fit to extend the proposed advantage to them, the benefit will be reaped hereafter. Sixty Rupees a year is the sum which is granted to Regiments of Native Infantry of the line.[754]

Sir Henry Fane foresaw that sooner or later the Gorkha battalions would be taken into regular service, and he recognised the value of local recruitment from Gorkha families in the Indian hill stations.

His tour of the north-western territories, begun in February 1837, soon confirmed that recruitment from Nepal was difficult. Lieutenant Henry Fane, aide-de-camp to Sir Henry, recorded on a visit to the Nasiri Battalion at Subathu in the Simla hills on 19 and 20 April 1837: 'The men of this corps are Goorkahs, or mountaineers, from the Nepaul hills. They are very short, yet strong and active fellows, brave to a proverb, and eminently formed for the work they have to do. Recruiting is now grown difficult from obstructions thrown in their way by the Nepaul government; and some of a different caste have of late been permitted to enter the corps.'[755] On return to Simla on 26 October 1837, the Commander-in-Chief was again entertained by the Commanding Officer of the Nasiri Battalion in Subathu, who must surely have taken the opportunity further to extol the value of Gorkha soldiers.[756]

However, Sir Henry Fane's tour, which lasted almost the whole of 1837 and much of 1838, had wider purposes. The first of these was to review the East India Company's frontiers and military resources. In a letter dated 30 May 1837 to Lord Auckland, he gave his appreciation that the north-west was the weakest frontier, that the Indus was not a material obstacle to armies from the west, and that the greatest danger to Delhi and Agra was through the Punjab and across the Sutlej. Defence of the Cis-Sutlej hills was therefore vital and 'our forces ought to be placed near the Sutlej, [where] an excellent line parallel to the river exists'. With one modification – that Ferozepur, to the west of Ludhiana, 'ought to be strongly occupied by our troops' – Sir Henry Fane's strategy was that held by Ochterlony almost thirty-three years earlier and adopted by Hastings in 1813.[757] In a further letter, dated 17 June 1837, to Lord Auckland, the Commander-in-Chief wrote 'Having finished an extensive inspection of the Bengal army . . . I have found the troops in a very satisfactory state as respects their general equipment and discipline.'[758] It is hardly surprising that the Nasiri and Sirmoor battalions of Gorkhas were assigned a continuing responsibility for guarding the Cis-Sutlej hills from their respective stations in Subathu and Dehra Dun.

The other purpose of the Commander-in Chief's tour was to take advantage of visits to Ranjit Singh in Lahore to assess the military strengths and weaknesses of the major Punjab cities and to survey the Cis-Sutlej defences. In his Journal he described his impressions of Amritsar as strongly contained within great walls and towers in the manner of Bharatpur, while the fort of Govindgarh, 'half a gunshot' to the north-west was defended by more modern works with walls, towers, and a good ditch surmounted by an escarpment and glacis. Lahore, on the other hand, where Sir Henry Fane was much impressed by units of Ranjit Singh's French-trained army, had weak defences and 'could be easily overcome'. Ludhiana, a British fort on flat country south of the Sutlej, Sir Henry judged to be 'a bad post only capable of defence against a body of horse'.[759] Like Ochterlony, William Fraser and Metcalfe before him, Sir Henry Fane anticipated an eventual war with the Sikhs. When, at the invitation of Ranjit Singh, Sir Henry attended the marriage of Ranjit's grandson at Lahore in early March 1837, he assessed that 67,000 men would be required for the British to conquer the Punjab in two years.[760]

In his letter dated 30 May 1837 to the Governor-General, Sir Henry Fane drew attention to the potential threat of the Nepalese Army:

There is the one mountain tribe, the Nepaulese, whose position is dangerous to the neighbouring province of Bengal because it has been the policy of former Governments (a most unwise policy in my opinion) to permit the state to organise, equip and arm a large body of their Goorkah subjects (45,000). These people have no cavalry and little

16. Sir Henry Fane (mezzotint) engraved by R. M. Hodgetts

efficient field artillery and therefore would not be formidible to contend with in the plains. But the necessity of watching such a force as they have armed, and being prepared to repel any eruption from their mountainous country will be found very troublesome in case of war and very costly also on account of the troops which must be retained to wait upon them in the Benares Division.[761]

Fane's total figure of 45,000 trained men available to the Nepalese Army seems to have been taken from Hodgson's estimates in 1832 of 15,000 enrolled men and 30,000 reservists.[762] Sir Henry Fane's concern was such that in his journal he recorded the return set out in Appendix I. Such details must surely have emanated from the Residency in Kathmandu.[763]

In a report submitted to the Government in Calcutta in 1837, Hodgson warned of chronic unrest in Nepal:

By depriving her [Nepal] of a third of her territory and girding her on all sides by our own Provinces, we imagined that of necessity she would gradually abandon her thirst for arms and conquest, turn her thoughts to the peaceful arts of commerce and agriculture, and ere long be changed from a hostile power which skirted our dominions for about eight hundred miles, to a less powerful, quiet and peaceable neighbour and ally. The reverse is the case, and at this moment Nepal holds a station of offensive power to the full as great as she did in 1814.[764]

Hodgson's answer to the threat from a powerful Nepalese Army was to recruit trained surplus Nepalese soldiery into the Bengal Army. Fane seems to have shared Hodgson's fears. In a letter to Auckland dated 3 August 1839, he wrote: 'Do not forget also that Nepaul is tributary to China and that Chinese money, if they are willing to disbourse it, may put the troops of Nepaul in motion.'[765]

The year 1839 was in several respects a crucial one. The death of Maharaja Ranjit Singh on 27 June 1839 brought disintegration within the Sikh empire and the assumption of power by the Khalsa or Commonwealth Army under the control of local Sikh elders. Bhim Sen Thapa's death by suicide on 20 July 1839 was followed by a further period of ruthless political intrigue, murder and instability in Nepal.

To add to Auckland's worries, an ill-advised venture which reinstated Shah Shuja to the throne at Kabul on 7 August 1839, committed a British army of 10,000 men to remain in Afghanistan in a vain attempt to secure the Shah against the threat of widespread insurrection. As a further blow, the ill-health which had dogged Sir Henry Fane throughout his tour of duty as Commander-in-Chief forced him to resign his appointment and leave India as soon as his successor, Sir Jasper Nicolls, arrived from England.[766]

On 12 May 1839 Fane had written to Auckland: 'I am heartily sorry that I am not at hand to help to relieve you from part of the "sickness at heart and gloom" of which you complain.' It cannot have lifted Auckland's despondency to receive a further letter, dated 20 September 1839, from Fane recommending that 'the Punjab should be the field of our military operations against an invading European army'.[767]

Towards the end of his tour in India Sir Henry Fane made two significant changes which affected the Kumaon Battalion. In 1838 he authorised its relocation from Almora to Lohughat near the Mahakali river (the western border of Nepal) and transferred the administration of the battalion from the civil to the military department in February 1839. By so doing he probably intended to give official notice that the Kumaon Battalion had a dual active role in defending the province of Kumaon from possible attack while encouraging the recruitment of Gorkhas through a border recruiting depot.

Auckland, who had left on a tour of the upper Provinces in October 1837, was away from his Council for two and a half years. During this time he was all too ready to be guided on matters of policy by his junior officials, Burnes, Macnaghton, Torrens and Colvin, all of whom were prone to offer inconsistent and unsound advice, and – like Hobhouse and Palmerston – feared the steady advance of Russian influence in Central Asia. Fateful decisions taken in Simla, where Auckland avoided the heat of summer, committed the British to a war in Afghanistan which they could not win. Auckland disregarded the advice of his Council and his Commander-in-Chief, Sir Jasper Nicolls, that such a war would entail great dangers, vast expense, and enormous problems of supply.

Meanwhile, following the death of Bhim Sen Thapa, a militant party came to power in Nepal. Encouraged by British commitment to a war in Afghanistan, they threatened to invade Company territory. Despite immense difficulties in Kathmandu, Hodgson used all his diplomatic skills to preserve peace. In July 1839 he wrote to his father that the Nepalese were 'ready to break forth or at least to break the treaty and expel the envoy i.e. myself'.[768] Indeed, on 12 April 1840, about fifty Nepalese soldiers crossed the border and seized temporary control of 200 square miles of British territory.[769] Against all odds, Hodgson's diplomacy succeeded in crisis after crisis until a new and less militant government came to power in Nepal. Hodgson so impressed the King of Nepal that in late December 1841 he offered to provide Nepalese troops to help the British in Afghanistan.[770] In politely declining the offer, Auckland took the opportunity, albeit obliquely, to support Hodgson's views:

> Under these circumstances I should have no immediate means of availing myself of the services of the Gorkha army. But I duly appreciate their value as brave and well-disciplined soldiers, and if any future occasion should arise when they might co-operate with the British forces it would afford me the greatest satisfaction to see the Gorkha and the British soldier marching side by side as friends and allies to the attack of a common enemy.[771]

Although the Bengal Army's Gorkha battalions were not involved in the Afghan War, a General Order of the Commander-in-Chief dated 28 April 1840 called for volunteers from the Nasiri and Sirmoor battalions to serve in the 4th (Gorkha) Regiment of Infantry specially raised by the British in India as part of Shah Shuja's force (the aim of which was to secure the reinstatement of the Shah on the throne in Kabul). From each of these two battalions three havildars, four naiks and six sepoys were selected for promotion to the next higher rank. It was made clear in the General Order that such volunteers would be given 'the same scale of pay and marching batta as is allowed for similar grades in the Bengal infantry of the line', i.e. the pay of regular troops.[772] Early in November 1841, insurrection and massacre in Kabul deposed Shah Shuja, and the British garrison there was annihilated. The 4th (Gorkha) Regiment, stationed about three miles away in Charikar, was overwhelmed on 14 November 1841 and its Commandant, Captain Codrington of the Bengal Army was killed. About 150 men escaped into the hills. Some of these, who were rescued six months later when Kabul was recaptured, were enlisted into the Bengal Army's three Gorkha battalions.[773]

The fall of the Whig Government in 1841 had already signalled the end of Auckland's Governor-Generalship. However, pending the arrival of his successor, one of the greatest and most horrifying military disasters befell the British in Afghanistan in January 1842, adding a final humiliation to Auckland's departure and destroying the image of British invincibility.

Lord Ellenborough, appointed as Auckland's successor, arrived in Calcutta on 28 February 1842, having learned of the disaster in Afghanistan while en route in Madras. Sir Robert Peel had approved Ellenborough's appointment as Governor-General despite doubts about his 'precipitation and over-activity'. Wellington, in whose Government Ellenborough had served, had reservations about his 'active habits and disposition'. Unlike Auckland, Ellenborough delighted in power. He found it difficult to shed the ministerial mantle of President of the Board of Control which he had held immediately before leaving England for India. Self-assured and impulsive, he was yet prone to vacillation and sometimes was more willing to accept credit than responsibility. It suited his vanity to be the bearer of retribution in Afghanistan and the restorer of British reputation in the East.

Ellenborough took a root-and-branch approach to his task. All that Auckland had done was to be undone – save, of course, the commitment of enormous expenditure. He would have no truck with 'politicals'. All his Agents in Afghanistan and Baluchistan were subordinated to military command. Hodgson, whose courage, determination and diplomacy had been praised by Auckland and by a grateful Court of Directors in London, was to be replaced as Resident at Kathmandu. This was to be done despite the dismay of the King of Nepal and without consultation with the Council in Calcutta and the Court of Directors. As a small concession Hodgson was allowed to remain in Kathmandu until 1843 in order to complete a treatise on Nepal. He was then succeeded by Henry Lawrence.

Henry Lawrence came from a military family and himself served in the Bengal Artillery from his arrival in India in February 1823 until 1833 when, for five years he was seconded to the Revenue Survey in Allahabad and Gorakhpur. Commenting in 1837 on rumours of war with Nepal, he wrote: 'With regard to Nepaul, I have been long enough on its frontier to feel convinced that we need have no fears of invasion. I surveyed much of the northern boundary of Goruckpoor.'[774] From January 1839 until November 1843, Lawrence held a political appointment as Assistant to George Clerk the Governor-General's Agent in Ferozepur.[775] He assumed his duties as Resident at Kathmandu on 1 December 1843 with no enthusiasm, having expressed a preference for Simla.[776] His instructions from Thomason, the Lieutenant-Governor of the North-West Provinces, were summarised thus: 'Your duties at Nepaul will be twofold, viz. to watch any movements on their part which may be injurious to us, and to offer counsel to them in all state matters in which we may not be concerned, whenever such counsel is sought, or is likely to be acceptable and useful.' In his long rambling letter, Thomason warned Lawrence of Nepalese intrigue. No mention was made of Hodgson's aims to recruit Gorkhas.[777] Perhaps unknown to Thomason, clandestine recruitment had been stepped up. Banskota refers to the establishment in 1843 of an 'undisguised and large' recruitment depot across the Nepal border, and the arrest of a recruiting agent who had been sent into Nepal.[778]

As a military man, Lawrence was conscious that the true basis of British power in India was 'a well-paid and well-disciplined army, relying from experience, on the good faith, wisdom and energy of its leaders'. He also recognised that 'at Cabul we lost an army and we lost some character with the surrounding states. But I hold that by far our worst loss was in the confidence of our Native soldiery'.[779] Fortunately Ellenborough was blessed with careful, firm, and efficient field commanders in Pollock, Nott and Sale. Nott held out in Kandahar and Sale in Jelalabad, while Pollock bided his time to marshal his forces and restore morale before marching through the Khyber in April 1842 to meet up with Sale's 'Illustrious Garrison' in Jelalabad.

With the murder of Shah Shuja in Kabul on 4 April 1842 the original reason for the British presence in Afghanistan disappeared. However, concern in Britain for the recovery of prisoners held by the Afghans caused Ellenborough to take military action. Without even informing Nicolls, the Commander-in-Chief (who was near Ferozepur with a large army in Reserve), he allowed Pollock and Nott, 'if they so decided', to take a circuitous route of withdrawal via Ghazni and Kabul. The army of about 14,000 men set out in two columns in August 1842 wreaking havoc on punitive raids and inflicting heavy defeats on Afghan forces. Ghazni was devastated, Kabul captured on 16 September 1842 and the prisoners released. On 1 October 1842, Ellenborough signed a Proclamation repudiating Auckland's policy and assuring India of the invincibility of British arms. To impress the Indian troops and overawe the Sikhs, he held a Grand Reception for the victorious Army of Retribution at a spot on the bank of the Sutlej where four years earlier Auckland had launched the Army of the Indus. The cost of this Afghan war, about fifteen million pounds, crippled Indian finances for many years. Moreover, stories of incompetence and cowardice circulated in the bazaars of India and helped to germinate seeds of dissension and unrest.

In the meantime, Outram was appointed as special Envoy to the Lower Indus to conclude a treaty with the Amirs of Sind. And in August 1842 Major-General Sir Charles Napier, although new to India, was made supreme commander in Sind and Baluchistan with authority over political and civilians affairs. Encouraged by Ellenborough, he provoked a war with the Amirs, defeated them in battle, and annexed Sind. Napier, a distinguished soldier well liked by his troops, was Governor of Sind from 1843 to 1847, when the Province was taken over by the Bombay Government. Although the Bengal Army's three irregular Gorkha battalions were not involved in the Afghan War or in the fighting in Sind, Napier was to become a great admirer of their soldierly qualities.

Ellenborough's zest for military action was further satisfied by a small contretemps with Gwalior in 1843 to support a nine-year-old heir on the death of the Maharaja. The new Commander-in-Chief, Sir Hugh Gough, was instructed by Ellenborough to assemble a large force near Agra for operations in November 1843. In December 1843, two armies, one approaching from the north under Gough, the other from the south under Sir John Grey, crossed into Gwalior and fought two successful battles near Maharajpur. Although under a subsequent treaty Gwalior was not annexed, a Council of Regency set up by Ellenborough exercised close control of government. The Gwalior army was reduced in number to 9,000 and a British subsidiary force was put into Gwalior fort.

Soon after the Gwalior affair had been settled, mutiny arose at Ferozepur among the 34th Native Infantry, the 7th Light Cavalry, and a company of artillery, with a demand for special pay for service in Sind. There had already been evidence of Sikh emissaries stirring up trouble at Ludhiana in the 64th Native Infantry, on the grounds that the Sikh Army pay was greater at twelve rupees a month. The mutiny was handled badly but ultimately the 34th Native Infantry were disbanded, and when the 64th Native Infantry mutinied, the ringleader was executed and many were discharged.

Three months after the Gwalior episode, Ellenborough was recalled by the Court of Directors who by now were anxious to put an end to military adventures and to restore their fortunes. Characteristically, Ellenborough wrote to the Resident at Kathmandu regarding his successor as Governor-General: 'You may tell the Court [in Nepal] that he has been selected, among other reasons, because he is my brother-in-law and most confidential friend.'[780] When Hodgson was cordially received by the Court of Directors in London in the spring of 1844, the Chairman greeted him with: 'Why, we will carry you back on our shoulders; Lord Ellenborough has been dismissed.' Hodgson explained that he had retired from their service.[781]

In 1842, at Ellenborough's instigation, General Sir Henry Hardinge, Ellenborough's brother-in law, had been offered the appointment as Commander-in-Chief, India. He declined 'for private reasons'. However, on Ellenborough's recall to England, and at the Duke of Wellington's suggestion, Hardinge was invited to become Governor-General. At a farewell banquet held in his honour, the Chairman of the Court of Directors explained what was expected of him:

By our latest intelligence we are indeed to hope that peace will be preserved in India. I need not say that it is our anxious wish that it should be so. You, Sir, know how great are the evils of war. And we feel confident that, while ever ready to maintain unimpaired the honour of the country and the supremacy of our arms, your policy will be essentially pacific.

The Chairman added: 'It has always been the desire of the Court that the government of the East India Company should be eminently just, moderate and conciliatory; but the supremacy of our power must be maintained when necessary by the force of arms.'[782]

Hardinge, who had served in the Peninsular War, was highly regarded by Wellington. When Hardinge was forced to miss the battle of Waterloo through the loss of a hand, Wellington gave him Napoleon's sword in recompense. Hardinge had other things to commend him. His care for his troops had earned him the soubriquet of the 'soldier's friend'. Moreover his twenty years as a member of parliament had included a spell in the Cabinet in 1828 as Secretary at War.

Hardinge arrived in Calcutta on 23 July 1844 and was received at Government House by Ellenborough and the Council. He made known his intention to maintain the Sikh Government in Lahore and to hold to the Treaty of 1809. However, he was conscious of the instability in the Punjab following the death of Ranjit Singh in 1839. He therefore quietly moved troops to the North-West Frontier on the Sutlej, strengthening the defences at Ludhiana and Ferozepur and gathering boats and pontoons against potential operational needs. He also moved quickly to suppress an insurrection in Kolharpur, dismantling the fort, disbanding the militia, and vesting the state in British Agents during the Raja's minority. By 1845, with the Sikh Khalsa army exercising supreme power, and rival factions engaged in widespread political assassination, Hardinge reluctantly accepted that British control of the Punjab was inescapable. In the spring and summer of 1845 he moved more troops and stores to Ferozepur, Ludhiana, and the military bases at Ambala and Meerut.

In the meantime, Henry Lawrence, an active man forbidden to interfere in the internal affairs of the Nepalese Government, had found life in Kathmandu dull. After Ellenborough's departure he did, however, write to give Auckland his observations on Nepal: 'The country

The R.t Hon. Henry Viscount Hardinge. G.C.B.

17. Henry Viscount Hardinge.

is a magnificent one. Thirty thousand men could take it in two months without fear of failure. A much less number and less time might do; but acting on its fastnesses as against a fortress, the matter might be made one of mathematical certainty.' As to the Nepalese Army, 'the soldiery are quiet and orderly, but otherwise I have been much disappointed in them, and I much doubt if the next war will find them the heroes they were in the last'. It is doubtful whether Hodgson would have agreed. He would certainly have approved of Henry Lawrence's suggestion for 'allowing 6,000 or 8,000 Goorkhas to enter our regiments of the line'; but not for the purpose of occupying Nepal.[783]

In late November 1845, the Sikhs began to move large forces to the Sutlej, which they crossed on 11 December 1845 to threaten Ferozepur (see map 9). Hardinge did not hesitate to involve himself in operational moves. On 12 December he withdrew the garrison from Ludhiana to guard the great grain depot and stores at Basayan. On the next day he issued a Proclamation declaring that a state of war existed with the Sikhs, and annexing Sikh territory south of the Sutlej. On 19 December an indecisive battle took place in misty conditions at Mudki, twenty miles to the south-east of Ferozepur. Both sides sustained heavy casualties. Perhaps appreciating the discipline, fervour and armament of the Sikh forces, and knowing the dash and determination of Sir Hugh Gough, the Commander-in-Chief, Hardinge made the extraordinary offer to act as Gough's second-in-command.[784] Gough, who readily accepted, was no doubt surprised at the battle of Ferozeshah on 21 December 1845 to be forbidden to launch an attack until reinforcements had arrived from Ferozepur. When Gough did attack later that day it was in extended line across open plain and through dense jungle, to suffer heavy losses from accurate Sikh guns firing grape and canister shot. The British troops lay low overnight and next morning forced the Sikhs to retreat. Hardinge described the Sikh artillery as 'most formidable' and declared that 'another such victory and we are undone'. He wrote to ask the Prime Minister for Gough to be replaced by Sir Charles Napier.[785]

On 24 December 1845, Henry Lawrence was recalled urgently to Ferozepur to replace the Agent to the Governor-General, Major Broadfoot, who had been killed at Ferozeshah. He left his Assistant Resident in charge at Kathmandu at a time of great instability and political intrigue culminating in the Kot Massacre in September 1846.

This wholesale slaughter of the Nepalese nobles swept Jang Bahadur Rana into power as Prime Minister of Nepal, thereby instituting more than a century of supreme hereditary power for the Rana family.[786] The British had no option but to accept a fait accompli. Cordial relations were established with Jang Bahadur Rana, but no progress was made regarding the recruitment of Gorkhas into the Bengal Army. Jang Bahadur did not openly oppose such recruitment, but he made sure behind the scenes that no worthwhile recruits became available.[787]

Meanwhile, among further reinforcements brought by Hardinge into the war with the Sikhs were the Nasiri Battalion from Jatogh (near Simla) and the Sirmoor Battalion from Dehra Dun. They arrived in Ludhiana in time to take part in the battles of Aliwal (17 January 1846) and Sobraon (10 February 1846). Major-General Sir Harry Smith, the Commander of the Division in which they served, recorded in his despatch on the battle of Aliwal: 'The intrepid little Goorkhas of the Nusseree and Sirmoor battalions in bravery and obedience can be exceeded by none.'[788]

In a despatch of 30 January 1846 to the Governor-General, the Commander-in-Chief wrote:

> I must pause in this narrative especially to notice the determined hardihood and bravery with which our two battalions of Goorkahs, the Sirmoor and Nusseree, met the Sikhs wherever they were opposed to them. Soldiers of small stature but indomitable spirit, they vied in ardent courage in the charge with the Grenadiers of our own nation, and armed with the short weapon of their mountains [the kukri] were a terror to the Sikhs through-out this great combat.[789]

The Governor-General wrote of his own admiration for the Gorkhas in a General Order dated 2 February:

> Great praise is also due to Brigadiers Godby and Hicks who with the 36th Native Infantry and Nasiri battalion, HM 31st, and 24th and 47th Native Infantry, stormed the village of Aliwal, drove the enemy from it, and seized the guns by which it was defended. The Governor-General has much satisfaction in observing the warm terms of admiration in

which the Major-General speaks of the Nusseree and Sirmoor battalions . . . These corps nobly emulated the example of the regular regiments of infantry.[790]

The story is much the same for the battle of Sobraon in which the British forces drove the Sikh army back across the Sutlej and then marched on to camp near the Sikh capital, Lahore. In a General Order of 14 February 1846, the Governor-General expressed his gratitude:

> Her Majesty's 31st and 50th regiments greatly distinguished themselves, as well as the 42nd and 47th Native Infantry and the Nusseree battalion . . . Her Majesty's 29th and the 1st European regiments and the 16th, 48th and 61st Native Infantry, and the Sirmoor battalion, have entitled themselves, by their gallant conduct, to the thanks of the Government.[791]

Hardinge's son noted that Hardinge often repeated that 'he was more than surprised at seeing with his own eyes the steady support the Native regiments afforded their European comrades' and that 'the Ghurka (*sic*) battalions behaved admirably'.[792]

The reliability and value of the Gorkha soldiers had been further recognised and they were now equated with those of regular troops.

In a letter dated 11 March 1846, Hardinge gave instructions to his Agent for the North-West Frontier (the Punjab), Sir Henry Lawrence, 'In all your proceedings you will enforce by your advice, and protests, if necessary, the earliest reorganisation of the Sikh army on the safest system for the permanence of the Sikh Government.' In the same month Lawrence informed Hardinge of a project 'to induce a number of disbanded Sikh soldiers to enlist' in the Bengal Army. He hoped to be able in the course of a month to raise two very fine regiments; and he suggested that 'fifteen or twenty men per company be Mussulmans or Hindoos of our own provinces'. No mention was made of Gorkhas.[793]

From his researches, Bajwa has established that, in 1845, fifty-two of the sixty-two infantry battalions in the Lahore army (45,000 out of 54,000 men) were Sikhs. Of the other ten battalions two (about 1,500 men) were 'Gurkhas'. Ranjit Singh who had recruited 'Gurkhas' before the British recruited them in 1815, still regarded them as 'a great people' in July 1837, and he declared that if 2,000 would come he would employ them and form them into two battalions. Ranjit Singh's successors shared his enthusiasm.[794] J.D. Cunningham in *A History of the Sikhs* (London, 1849, p. 425, Appendix XXIII), lists 'one Goorkha Infantry Regiment in the Army of Lahore as recorded in 1844'. However there seems to be no evidence to suggest that any Gurkhas of the Sikh Army fought against the British in the Sikh War. Perhaps they were deployed in the Punjab hills where their mountain skills and prowess were recognised to be superior to those of the Sikh infantry. It is not clear what happened to the 1,500 Gurkha soldiers of the former Sikh Army. Cunningham makes no direct mention of this in his *History of the Sikhs*. However he records that late in 1846, while the Governor-General and Commander-in-Chief were in Lahore with 20,000 British troops, parties of the Sikh Army came there to be paid and disbanded.[795] There is evidence to suggest that 'Gurkha' troops were still part of the Lahore State force on 20 April 1849, but good reason to believe they would have been disbanded thereafter. (See below, chapter 11 p. 221) There is no record of these or any other 'Gurkhas' of the former Sikh Army being recruited by the British. At the end of the Sikh War, the Nasiri and Sirmoor battalions had returned to their respective hill stations in Subathu and Dehra Dun and had resumed their former duties.

The main provisions of the treaty of Lahore dated 9 March 1846 renounced Sikh claims to Cis-Sutlej territory, transferred to the British land between the Beas and the Sutlej, and imposed an immediate payment of £500,000. Under a separate treaty dated 16 March 1846 'the hill country east of the Indus and west of the Ravi' (Kashmir and Hazara) was transferred to Golab Singh; and the Sikh Army was limited to twenty-five battalions of infantry (20,000 men) and 12,000 cavalry. In return the British agreed not to interfere in the internal administration of the State of Lahore. Hardinge, who had been unwilling to annex the Punjab, was most anxious to establish a stable Durbar in Lahore. He therefore agreed to the Durbar's request for a British force to remain in Lahore for a year – at Lahore's expense.

In October 1846 an insurrection in Kashmir was swiftly put down by the approach of a combined force of eight regiments of Bengal Native Infantry with twelve field guns, and 17,000 Sikhs of the Durbar army who had recently fought against the British. The episode illustrated a discipline and reliability among these Sikhs reminiscent of those shown three decades earlier by Gorkhas under Ochterlony. It also led to a further treaty of Lahore dated 22 December 1846. Under the terms of this latter treaty, Hardinge, who was still unwilling to annex the Punjab, appointed Sir Henry Lawrence as the first British Resident at Lahore with responsibility for supervising the administration of the State of Lahore. In effect these new arrangements gave the Resident controlling authority. It also enabled Hardinge to keep British troops in and near the Punjab while at the same time reducing the army by 50,000 men and saving more than a million pounds in costs. With Native Infantry regiments reduced in strength from 1,000 to 800, economic prospects for recruiting more Gorkhas into the Bengal Army were slim. Financial considerations had always weighed heavily with the Court of Directors of the East India Company, perhaps never more so than after the vast expenditure incurred by Auckland and Ellenborough.

In other respects the arguments for recruiting more Gorkha soldiers into the Bengal Army had been strengthened. Doubts about using Gorkhas in operations on the plains had been dispelled. Admiration for Gorkha discipline and bravery had been warmly expressed by Sir Henry Fane, Sir Hugh Gough, Sir Henry Hardinge and Sir Henry Lawrence. Like Hodgson, they had perceived that, at a time of growing unrest in the Bengal Army's Native Infantry, the recruitment of Gorkhas offered 'a counterpoise to the pampered sepoys of the Gangetic valley' and a new element of strength and safety.[796]

The fundamental problem in recruiting Gorkhas was the Nepalese Government's firm opposition. British commitment to non-interference in Nepalese affairs in the hope of winning favour had failed. And even Hodgson's persistent pressure for British recruitment of Gorkhas had been resolutely resisted. Under Jang Bahadur Rana matters became even more difficult. In order to maintain the strength of their three Gorkha battalions, the British were driven to clandestine recruitment from Nepal, hoping thereby to supplement the potential intake from Gorkha families living in the hill cantonments of Subathu, Dehra Dun and Almora. This hand-to-mouth existence had always to be set against the threat of financial retrenchment and the fact that, as irregular troops, the Gorkha units still faced an uncertain future.

CHAPTER 11

Final Recognition

Despite British success in the Punjab, the underlying threat of mutiny in the Bengal Army and the ever-present danger of insurrection in North India remained. There was an urgent need for a stabilising force in the regular Bengal Army. Hodgson in Kathmandu and successive Commanders-in-Chief in Calcutta had recognised that Gorkhas, with their proven loyalty to the British and disdain for the fighting qualities of Indian sepoys, could provide such a force. However the Court of Directors, and the Government in India and London, failed to appreciate this, and fixed their minds instead on financial retrenchment. Transfer of the irregular Gorkha Battalions into the regular Bengal Army seems not to have been contemplated. In 1850, an extraordinary set of circumstances brought a dramatic change. This occurred so suddenly and was so sharply defined that a record of events leading up to the change requires no more than a short final chapter.

Hardinge, who had wished to retire in 1846, was asked to stay on as Governor-General for another year to consolidate victory over the Sikhs. He eventually sailed for England on 18 January 1848, six days after his successor, Lord Dalhousie, arrived at Calcutta. Aged thirty-five, Dalhousie, who had had experience as President of the Board of Trade, was autocratic and strongly assertive of his authority. His father, a general in the Peninsular War, had been Commander-in-Chief, India from 1829 to 1832. The Duke of Wellington, Commander-in-Chief of the British Army from 1842 to 1852, was a family friend and Dalhousie's patron to whom he wrote on military as well as political matters.

Dalhousie had expected to find perfect tranquillity in India, for Hardinge was reported to have claimed that he had 'drawn the teeth of the Sikhs'.[797] Instead, he found himself faced with a second Sikh

18. James Ramsay, 1st Marquess of Dalhousie by Sir John Watson-Gordon.

War. Mulraj, the Diwan (Tax Collector) of Multan, a Province of the State of Lahore, resigned his appointment in March 1848, having been found guilty of misappropriating revenue on a massive scale. Sirdar Khan Singh Man, who was appointed by the Lahore Government to succeed him, set out for Multan with an escort of 500 Lahore State troops. He was joined there by Mr Agnew, British Political Agent, and Lieutenant Anderson of the Bombay European Regiment, Assistant Political Agent. On 19 April 1848, they rode into Multan fort with the Sirdar to take formal charge. On coming out, the two British officers were attacked and wounded. On the following day they were murdered and their murderers rewarded by Mulraj in return for the officers' heads.[798] Dalhousie gave the following account in a letter dated 10 May 1848 to Couper:

> They had an escort of a regiment of infantry (Ghoorkhas too, famous for their fidelity), some cavalry and 80 artillerymen with guns. Their reception was most friendly. He [Mulraj] gave over charge to the Government but on their coming out of the fort the Diwan's [Mulraj's] sepoys attacked and wounded the officers. Next day they attacked the camp. The Lahore escort troops went over in a body, and the two officers were butchered, not a man being scratched even except themselves. The Diwan [Mulraj] is now in open revolt; troops, the disbanded Khalsa soldiers in particular, are flocking to him; the [Lahore] Durbar has told the Resident that they cannot rely on their troops, particularly on their regular army, to act against the Diwan, and they cannot punish him or give reparation for the insult and injury to the British power.[799]

It is important to note here that the 'Ghoorkha' battalion involved was of the Lahore State force and had no connection whatever with the three Gorkha battalions of the Bengal Army.

Public indignation in India, and the danger of insurrection, demanded an urgent and powerful response. However, operations were delayed until November 1848 because of the need to strengthen the Army after Hardinge's large-scale reductions.[800] Delay was also due to adverse climatic conditions and to the lack of transport for military equipment.

When operations did begin, the battle of Chillianwalla (a village fortified by the Sikhs) on 13 January 1849 caused heavy British losses, and was at best 'a dearly bought victory'.[801] Gough, the Commander-in-Chief, explained: 'Indeed I had not intended to attack today, but the impudent rascals fired on me. They put my Irish blood up, and I attacked them.'[802] In a long letter dated 22 January 1849 to the Duke of Wellington, Dalhousie reported that Gough's order to advance sent 'a line of three miles, without support, against one of more than six miles, through jungle, against an enemy they could not see'.[803] Two days earlier Dalhousie had written to Couper: 'I grieve to say much gloom prevails in the army. One and all, Generals of Division, officers, soldiers, sepoys, publicly attribute this great loss [about 650 killed and 1,725 wounded at Chillianwalla] and small results [twelve guns captured and three lost] to the total incompetence of the Commander-in-Chief, and justly so. They have totally lost confidence in him. In the hands of Lord Gough I feel no confidence against disaster. If Napier had been here it would have been closed 'ere now.'[804]

The situation caused Wellington, who was eighty, to write to Napier: 'If you do not go, I must.'[805] Wellington then informed Dalhousie, in a letter of 5 March 1849, that he had felt obliged by public opinion to replace Gough. 'I was required,' he wrote, 'without loss of time, to submit to Her Majesty, the name of Lieutenant-General Sir Charles Napier as the one most likely by his local experience and the qualities he has manifested in his former services to that country to fulfill the expectations of the country and to carry into execution the views and plans of the Government.'[806] Nevertheless, on Wellington's advice and without consulting the Governor-General, Gough was retained as Commander-in-Chief for the time being.[807]

In the meantime, the second Sikh War had been brought to a close by a resounding British victory at Gujerat on 21 February 1849, the Sikhs being driven to total surrender and their Afghan allies chased out of the Punjab. Dalhousie wrote in jubilation to Couper on 7 March 1849: 'We have taken 53 guns, many standards, his whole camp, stores, baggage, cattle and ammunition. Their loss is stated from 3,000 upwards. We have lost 96 killed of which five are officers, and 700 wounded, many slightly. Thank God for it! I rejoice heartily that the Old Chief [Gough] has been able to close his career with this crowning glory.' [808]

The end of the second Sikh War brought Dalhousie the challenging problem of what his immediate policy for the Punjab should be. The Home Government, the Court of Directors, and the Resident at Lahore were all against annexation by the British. However, Dalhousie believed that, to avoid 'riot and anarchy', swift and firm action was required; and that 'to await four months now for their orders [from London] was impossible'.[809] Dalhousie explained, in a Government of India despatch of 7 April 1849 that 'Experience has shown us that a strong Hindu government, capable of controlling its army and governing its subjects, cannot be formed in the Punjab. The materials for it do not exist.' In order to safeguard the Company's possessions, past policy had to be abandoned. Dalhousie had therefore issued, on 29 March 1849, a Proclamation announcing 'that the Kingdom of the Punjab is at an end, and that all the territories of the Maharaja Dhulip Sing are now and henceforth a portion of the British Empire in India'.[810] Terms to this effect were granted to and accepted by the Maharaja on 29 March 1849, and were ratified by the Governor-General on 5 April 1849. Dalhousie did not hesitate to establish a Board of Administration in Lahore with staffs of civil and military officers under the direction of the brothers John and Henry Lawrence respectively. He also appointed four Commissioners for Lahore, Jhelum, Multan and Leia. His action did not meet with universal approval, for he wrote from Simla on 12 June 1849: 'My letters from home are satisfactory except Hobhouse's [811] who repeats what he has been harping upon – that I should wait orders from home as to what I should do with Punjab. If, after having destroyed the army and destroyed the Government of Lahore, I had hung up the question for four months, I should have been a madman; for I should have thereby proposed a renewed resistance and anarchy and loss of every kind.' [812] However, his annexation of the Punjab met with such acclaim that he was promoted in the peerage to Marquis and Gough to Viscount. As early as 30 March 1849 Dalhousie had pondered, without false modesty, the possibility of his becoming a marquis: 'It is not every day that an officer of their Government adds four millions of subjects to the British Empire, and places the historical jewel of the Mogul Emperor [the Koh-i-noor diamond] in the crown of his sovereign. This I have done.'[813]

Dalhousie next turned his personal attention to organising a military force for the defence of the Punjab. Levies already raised with the approval of the Resident at Lahore (Henry Lawrence), together with some of the Durbar regiments which had remained loyal (some 4,000 in all) were retained under a guarantee of service confirmed by the Governor-General. In addition, Dalhousie had empowered the Punjab Board of Administration to raise an irregular force of five regiments of infantry (about 4,000) and five of cavalry (around 3,000) for the protection of the western frontier, except Peshawar which was to be held by the regular army. To these were to be added the corps of Guides (originally raised in 1846 at the suggestion of Henry Lawrence, and including a company of Gorkhas) with a strength increased to 844, three horse field brigades of artillery, two companies of sappers and miners, and a camel corps. There was considerable opposition, both in India and by the Court of Directors' Secret Committee, to Dalhousie's Punjab irregular force, and, more especially, to raising Sikh regiments in the Punjab. To the criticism, Dalhousie replied that the regiments were not Sikh, and that guarantees given to faithful soldiers of the Lahore State and to levies raised by British officers must be kept.[814]

Among those who objected to the retention of levies and Durbar regiments was the new Commander-in-Chief, about whom Dalhousie had written to Couper on 20 April 1849: 'I am well content to have Sir Charles Napier as Commander-in-Chief'.[815] Dalhousie's apparent contentment with Napier's appointment had evidently diminished by 7 May 1849 (the day after Napier's arrival in Calcutta) when Dalhousie wrote from Simla: 'He shall have full authority and shall have every confidence and support from me in those military duties which belong to him; but, by George, he shall not interfere with me in Civil matters, or touch them with the point of his beard.'[816] By 18 May 1849, Dalhousie's contentment had worn decidedly thin:

Sir Charles Napier is on his way up the country. I do not fear our getting on. He shall have full authority, aid and confidence in his own functions; he shall not stir a hair's breadth beyond them, if he does it designedly. I think I shall not show a want of temper in the management of him. Did you ever know me lose my temper in public? In private I have as much pepper, mustard and vinegar and all other hot and sour ingredients in me as you may choose to allege.[817]

The boundary between civil and military responsibilities had long been a source of argument and friction in India. Dalhousie's explanation to Gough that 'Your Excellency is responsible for the army; I am responsible for the Empire' is far from clear, for in the same letter he had instructed Gough: 'You should not advance without previous communication with me.'[818]

By 25 June 1849, after Dalhousie had met Napier, he seemed reassured: 'I spoke to him very frankly on our relative positions – he seems quite satisfied – so am I, and I do not anticipate any embarrassment from him, or any conflict between us in our respective jurisdictions. He will astonish the Bengal Army before long, and much they need it'.[819]

Napier, almost twice Dalhousie's age and with a fine military reputation, was no stranger to responsibility. Under Ellenborough he had held supreme authority in Sind for both military and civil matters. It did not please him that he had missed the chance of further glory in the second Sikh War; or the possibility of a tour as Governor of the Punjab. However, by some quirk of fate, the very clash of personalities between Napier and Dalhousie was to work to the advantage of the Bengal Army's Gorkha battalions, and to bring about the final recognition of the value of the Gorkha soldier.

Napier's appreciation of the strategic defence of India against potential incursion resembled that of Hardinge, Hastings and Fane. In his 'Memoir on the Defence of India and the military occupation of the Punjaub', Napier stressed the need to pay particular attention to the North-West, i.e. the country between the Jumna and the Sutlej. He wrote:

If an enemy again got these hills as they once had, we might not have

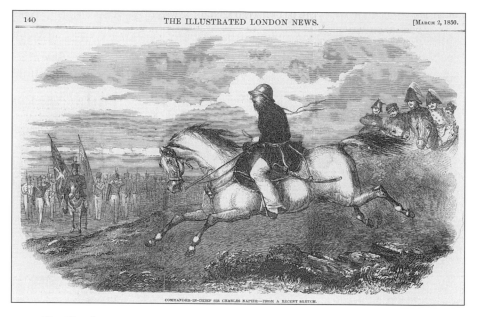

COMMANDER-IN-CHIEF SIR CHARLES NAPIER—FROM A RECENT SKETCH.

19. Sir Charles Napier From the *Illustrated London News*, March 2, 1850.

a second Ochterlony to put them out! The disasters of Kulunga might be repeated. This important mountainous district – the key equally to the Punjaub and to Nepaul – should not be left exposed as it has hitherto been'.[820]

However, Napier was especially alive to the constant threat of insurrection: 'In India peace is never certain for a single day.'[821] Dalhousie agreed: 'In India one is always sitting on a volcano.'[822]

In July 1849, less than a month after Napier's arrival in Simla, 'a mutinous spirit' arose among some of the Bengal Army's Native Infantry. The cause was a reduction in the special allowances (batta) which had been paid to sepoys while in the Punjab during the second Sikh War. Two rupees a month 'hutting money' and one and a half rupees 'marching rates' while on active service had brought a sepoy's monthly pay to twelve rupees. When the Punjab was annexed in April 1849, the Governor-General abolished these former allowances, a decision which was not properly explained to the troops concerned. In July 1849, men of the 22nd and 13th Native Infantry in Rawalpindi refused to accept the reduced pay. Through Napier's prompt action and guidance a serious situation was avoided. However, similar incidents with the 41st Native Infantry at Delhi in November 1849 and 32nd Native Infantry at Wazirabad in December 1849, showed that dissatisfaction was widespread. Indeed by now Napier had reason to believe that twenty-four other battalions might be ready to support a general revolt.[823] It had also been reported to him that a Brahmin havildar had warned a senior officer that, if threatened with disbandment, 'we would all go to our villages and you should not get any more to replace us'.[824] Despite all this, Napier continued to show great patience: 'we must wait; if nothing happens all is right, but if it turns out to be a preconcerted mutiny, force must be met by force; the least concession would cost us India'.[825]

In sharp contrast to the behaviour of sepoys of the regular Bengal Army, Napier was reminded of Gorkhas in the irregular battalions whose pay was considerably less. Napier noted:

When I was at Simla last November [1849], the officer commanding the Gorkha battalion [the Nasiri Battalion close by at Jatogh] told me his men were starving on 4 rupees 8 annas a month; that they were very proud of our service but many had deserted from want of food. He showed me his calculations, by which it appeared clearly that their pay could not support them'.[826]

Of the Gorkhas Napier wrote:

Bravest of Native troops, they, at the battles on the Sutledge, displayed such conspicuous gallantry as to place them on a level with Europeans; and certainly they have a high military spirit, are fierce at war, of unsurpassed activity, and possess great powers of enduring fatigue, and acquaintance with them in no way tended to diminish my opinion of their high character as soldiers.[827]

Napier pointed out to Dalhousie that the time had come 'to win the Goorka's heart by money and the red uniform which he longs to wear':

The Goorka will be faithful, and for low pay we can enlist a large body of soldiers whom our best officers equal in courage to European troops. Even as a matter of economy this will be good; but the great advantage of enlisting these hillmen will be that, with 30,000 or 40,000 Goorkas added to 30,000 Europeans, the possession of India will not 'depend on opinion', but on an Army able with ease to overthrow any combination among Hindoos or Mohamedans, or both together.

Napier went on: 'I asked Lord Dalhousie to take all the Goorka Battalions into the line. He consented. But it was necessary first to ask if they would volunteer for general service.' When this proposition was read and explained to the men and they 'heard the promise of high pay made by the Governor-General to them through the Commander-in-Chief, they volunteered not merely with alacrity but with a joy evinced . . . by extraordinary screams of delight'.[828] In a letter dated 5 January 1850 to Dalhousie, Napier had reiterated his views:

And now I am sure that this most disagreeable affair will open the eyes of the Directors and satisfy them that I am right in wishing for Goorka battalions . . . I do most seriously recommend this subject to your consideration, and whether it ought not to be seriously pressed upon the consideration of the Court [of Directors]. I believe your Lordship's opinion concurs with mine as to the Goorka battalions, and I wish, if so, that you would order their high pay to be issued from the first of January.[829]

In a letter of 18 January 1850 to Napier, Dalhousie had written: 'All testimony has led me to form the same opinion you held of the efficiency and fidelity of the Goorka corps; and if increase of their pay were necessary, to enable you to command the service of these corps in the event of disaffection amongst the native infantry, I should at once issue an order for the increase.' Dalhousie pointed out, however, that the terms of the Gorkhas' contract already entitled Napier to call upon them to move anywhere on emergency. He therefore thought 'it better to wait for the reply from the Court of Directors, which will in another month reach me'.[830] Authority from the Court of Directors did not reach Calcutta until the middle of March, but before then Napier had been overtaken by a far more serious mutiny.[831]

On 25 February 1850, Napier received information that men of the 66th Native Infantry were in open revolt at Govindgarh, and had attempted to seize the fortress, with its immense magazine of gunpowder and vast quantity of Sikh cannon and treasure. The situation was all the more dangerous in that Govindgarh was situated close by the Sikh holy city of Amritsar and in the midst of disbanded and discontented soldiery. With Dalhousie away at sea, and the local commander, Gilbert, having dealt ineptly with the situation, Napier did not hesitate to take far-reaching and decisive action. He issued a General Order on 27 February 1850 using 'the powers entrusted to me by the Governor-General':

> The Native officers, non-commissioned officers and Private Sepoys of the 66th regiment are to be marched to Umballah, and there struck off from the service of the Honorable East India Company; and His Excellency directs that the colors of the 66th are to be delivered over to the brave and loyal men of the Nusseree Goorka Battalion, and that the 66th regiment shall in future be denominated the 66th or Goorka regiment.

Napier intended this action not only to crush the mutiny but to show 'the Brahmins we have another race to rest on for soldiers'.[832] Napier explained his action in a long letter, dated 27 February 1850, addressed to Dalhousie:

> Your Lordship well knows my great objection to the disbanding of regiments. I had that placed in my hands at Scinde, and I used it not. But here hesitation might endanger the safety of the Punjaub, even of India, and I at once issued the general order, copy of which is enclosed, and hope you will approve of it . . . What I have done will put the Company at no expense – things remain the same, and our promise is performed to one of the three Goorka regiments! I mean to repeat the operation if another regiment mutinies, unless your Lordship disapproves.[833]

The reference to 'our promise' relates to a recommendation by Napier to Dalhousie in October 1849 to 'meet Brahmins of Bengal and their bristling prejudices of high caste' by bringing the Goorka regiments into the Bengal line.

On 16 March 1850, having returned to Calcutta from his sea voyage, Dalhousie wrote:

> On my arrival here I was greeted by the news of more mutiny in the Punjab. The whole of the 66th Regiment, the garrison of the fort of Govindgarh, the most important place in all India, perhaps, mutinied almost in a body, and even the guard attempted to close the gates against other troops who fortunately were near. The Commander-in-Chief has acted promptly and well and has disbanded them off his own bat. He has no power to do so, but I should have done the same in his place, and I shall support him in it fully. I hope this strong measure will put down everything of the sort.[834]

However it transpired that, although Dalhousie approved of the disbandment of the 66th Native Infantry, he had some reservation about Napier's decision to replace it by a regular Gorkha regiment. Napier was unrepentent:

> I have had a hasty note from Lord Dalhousie on his landing at Calcutta, in which he regrets my having taken this step without applying for advice to the supreme council. Now, I have no regret and would act precisely in the same way were the work to be done over again . . . I thought everything settled and went on tour; but, when at Hurdwar, to my astonishment received a letter from Lord Dalhousie saying he had no authority to grant the Goorkas increase of pay, but would write to the Court of Directors to recommend it! My answer was that the promises of the Governor-General and the Commander-in-Chief, voluntarily given and gratefully received, could not be withdrawn.[835]

Napier wrote to assure Lord Ellenborough that 'There was no time to hold councils of war! The thing required a blow, heavy and rapid, or the whole effect would have been lost'; and that 'One week, aye! one day would have spread the [mutinous] spirit through the whole Indian army and raised the whole Sikh population against us.'[836] Not unreasonably, Napier had a higher regard of his own experience and abilities than those of the Supreme Council:

He [Dalhousie] was at sea and his Aulic Council so far off that India might have overturned 'ere I could receive the fiat of those sage civilians at Calcutta . . .

My dear coadjutors of the Supreme Council are unfit to form any military opinion, yet are great generals, and form the most decided opinions.

And what could the Supreme Council know about the matter? Which among them knew anything about soldiers? None but [Sir John] Littler, and I am not likely to consult a Major-General on a subject I understand better than he does. I like Littler much but I do not like Councils at all, because I never want to avoid responsibility.[837]

Napier judged, correctly, that Dalhousie would not rescind his General Order of the 27 February 1850.[838] Moreover, the authority received in mid-March 1850 from the Court of Directors was much to Napier's satisfaction.[839] This authority, reflected in the Governor-General's General Order No. 173 dated 22 March 1850, was that:

In recognition of their entire willingness to perform all the duties required of Corps of Native Infantry of the line . . . the Sirmoor and Kemaoon Battalions, as well as the new Nusseree Battalion directed to be raised in the General Order by His Excellency the Commander-in-Chief of the 27th ult. be admitted from the 1st instant. to the pay, batta, pension, and all other advantages enjoyed by regiments of Native Infantry of the line.

In a letter dated 28 March 1850 to Lord Ellenborough, Napier wrote: 'The three Goorka regiments had been ill-used, but that is now made up to them. Lord Dalhousie has given them all Sepoy's pay!' Two days later he wrote to Dalhousie: 'I am quite delighted at the order just come about the Goorkas! It puts an end to Brahmin rule! I cannot express the pleasure it has given me.'[840]

Dalhousie's disagreement with Napier was, perhaps, not so much related to Napier's swift and decisive military action as to his apparent disregard of the Governor-General's rules regarding pay and allowances. Dalhousie stressed the importance he attached to these in a letter dated 16 April 1850 to Couper: 'You know my great object for six months has been to equalise the sepoy's pay in all British provinces, and to withdraw the war allowances in the Punjab. I have done so in the full knowledge of the risk which mutiny in more than one camp has shown not to be visionary.'[841] In dealing with the mutiny of the 32nd Native Infantry at Wazirabad, Napier had allowed himself to be persuaded to suspend a rule introduced on 15 August 1819 reducing the amount payable to sepoys in respect of rises in the cost of their monthly diet.[842] However, in his General Order of 27 February 1850, Napier had taken care to support, or at least to appear to support, the Governor-General's broad aims:

> It is now the Commander-in-Chief's painful duty to remark upon the disobedience of orders committed by Major H. Troup, commanding the 66th Native Infantry.
>
> When the regiment mutinied, the conduct of this Officer was cool, resolute and deserving of the highest praise; but Major Troup had not previously read and explained to the Sepoys of his Regiment, the Governor-General's order dated 25th October 1849, when he received these orders at Lucknow in November.
>
> These orders were issued by the Governor-General through the Commander-in Chief, for the express purpose of preparing the minds of the Sepoys for the just and necessary cessation of a temporary allowance, generously granted to the troops during the war.
>
> To cause the Sepoys to discuss, to consider and thoroughly to understand that reduction was the object of issuing those orders; and they must, from the sound principle on which they were based, have brought a conviction of their justice to the minds of the Sepoys.

Despite Napier's 'unqualified dissatisfaction' with Troup's failure personally to explain the orders to his troops, he was confirmed as substantive commandant of the newly formed 66th or Goorka Regiment on 13 August 1850. In keeping with army tradition (but counter to the normal arrangements for officers to be specially selected for Gorkha regiments) the officers of the 66th Native Infantry were transferred to the 66th or Goorka Regiment. Napier did, however, take the opportunity, in his General Order of 27 February 1850, to express his fervent hope that the young European Officers of this [Bengal] army, who are full of ability, zeal, and of good feeling towards the Natives, will see the necessity of endeavouring to associate as much as possible with the Native Officers, and make them their comrades in every sense of the word. It is thus alone that the European Officer can expect to acquire a thorough knowledge of what passes in his regiment, and of the feelings which exist among those under his command.

Having marched the Nasiri Battalion from Jatogh to Govindgarh to take over 'the arms, accoutrements and colors of the 66th. regiment', Major O'Brien was charged with 'immediately recruiting [i.e. restoring] the Nusseree Battalion to its full strength'. Under a Governor-General's Resolution of 15 July 1850, the Commander-in-Chief was requested, in re-embodying the Nusseree Battalion, 'to transfer to it a proportion of Native commissioned officers, non-commissioned officers, Buglers and Sepoys from the Sirmoor and Kemaoon battalions'. This Resolution, framed 'in obedience to the wishes of the Honorable Court of Directors' established a new individual strength for the Nasiri, Sirmoor and Kumaon Battalions of eight subedars, eight jemadars, forty havildars, forty naiks, sixteen buglers and 640 sepoys, a total of 752 organised in eight companies. In comparison, the complement of the 66th or Goorka Regiment was: one subedar-major, nine subedars, ten jemadars, sixty havildars, sixty naiks, one bugle-major, twenty buglers and 1,000 sepoys, a total of 1,161 men organised in ten companies. The Governor-General's Resolution also conveyed the Court of Directors' wish that 'the nationality of these corps, and of the 66th or Goorka Regiment, shall be kept up by the careful exclusion of men as recruits, who are not Goorkas'. The Court of Directors seem to have been unaware of difficulties in recruitment.

Meanwhile relations between Dalhousie and Napier grew irretrievably worse. For his part Dalhousie realised that he had made a mortal enemy of Napier.[843] The depth of this enmity and the height of Napier's ambition may be judged from entries in his journal:

Lord Dalhousie is always in dread of my interference but he must hear truth: not the whole truth indeed, for I cannot tell him that he is wholly unequal to his position. He is a good, well-meaning man, and I believe honest, but weak as water: his whole treatment of the Punjaub is one great error from beginning to end. [6 February 1850]

Lord Ellenborough tells me he thinks Lord Dalhousie must go home from ill-health, and that I shall be more wanted than ever: he seems quite unaware that I have no power! My resolution is made up, not to stay a moment after Dalhousie goes, unless I am made Governor-General. I was sent out when there was danger, and am as fit, perhaps more so than Hardinge or Dalhousie, to be Governor-General and I will not be made a convenience of again. Events are rising on the horizon which require the hand of a giant, and a pigmy only is present. [6 February 1850]

I am now at war with Lord Dalhousie who is a petulant man, cunning and sly, ill-conditioned, and ready to attack any but those he serves. [7 July 1850] [844]

This situation could not be allowed to continue. When Napier submitted his resignation to the Commander-in-Chief in London, it was accepted. He sailed from India in November 1850, leaving behind him not only a warning of events 'rising on the horizon' (his anticipation of a mutiny of the Bengal Army), but an institution which was to survive and grow stronger: Gorkha battalions as an integral part of the regular army in India.

With the entry of the Nasiri Battalion into the Bengal line as the 66th or Goorka Regiment, and the new Nasiri, Sirmoor and Kumaon battalions given the same terms of service as regular Native Infantry, the full value of the Gorkha soldier had finally been recognised.

Epilogue

Gorkha service with the British was firmly established in 1850, at which point in Indian history the main theme of this book can be brought to a convenient close. However, 1850 was no more than the end of the beginning of Gorkha service with the British. The development of what became the British Indian Army's Gurkha Brigade deserves to be the subject of further scholarly research into relevant strategic, diplomatic, political, economic and social factors from 1850 to Indian Independence in 1947 – and beyond to the British Army's Brigade of Gurkhas. This brief survey of the period 1850 to 1887, in the form of an epilogue, is intended to do no more than point the way.

It took thirty-five years for a Gurkha battalion to be taken into the regular Bengal Army in 1850. It was to take another thirty-five years before the Nepalese Government permitted a form of recruitment of Gorkhas in Nepal. The need for more Gorkha recruits increased in 1850 when the 'loyal and brave men of the Nusseeree Ghoorka Battalion' were denominated the 66th or Goorka Regiment and brought into the Bengal line, with a greatly increased authorised strength. At the same time a new Nasiri Battalion was raised and, together with the Sirmoor and Kumaon Battalions, was given the full terms of service of a regular Bengal Infantry regiment although with a much smaller strength.

An analysis of the returns made by the Commanding Officers of the four Gorkha battalions, in response to a letter dated 29 April 1851 from the Adjutant-General,[845] provides evidence that Dotis (from the far west of Nepal) were being recruited.[846] In their returns, the Commanding Officers of the Sirmoor Battalion and the Kumaon Battalion used the same wording under a heading 'remarks': 'Goorkas (or the inhabitants of Nepal), Doteeallis and Ghurwallis are chiefly recruited for services in the Sirmoor/Kemaon Battalion and are all classed under the head of "Rajpoots"'. By this definition, 'Rajputs' comprised 80 per cent of the actual strength of the Sirmoor Battalion and 88 per cent of that of the Kumaon Battalion. The Commanding Officer of the 66th or Goorka Regiment gave much more detail in his return. From this it may be deduced that out of a total of 1,085 men, 134 (12 per cent) were classed as Rajputs and 677 (62 per cent) as Chhetris, Gurungs and Magars. The return also reveals that 412 men were from Central Nepal and 289 men were 'born in the regiment'.

As the new Nasiri Battalion was still forming at Jatogh, its Commanding Officer, Major O'Brien, was able to give a provisional return only, listing 396 as Nepalese, 75 as descendants of Nepalese – mostly born in British cantonments, 156 other hillmen, and 13 from the plains. A footnote to the effect that other recruits were *en route* to join the battalion suggests that some illicit recruitment was still being successfully conducted in or from Nepal.

In a letter dated 5 May 1851 to the Adjutant-General enclosing his return, the highly experienced Major O'Brien (who had commanded the old Nasiri Battalion until 27 February 1850) wrote: 'I think it is necessary to say a few words regarding the Nepalese tribes, as this is a subject understood by but few officers except those who have served with the "Goorka" corps.'[847] O'Brien stressed that the Khas (Chhetris), Magars and Gurungs were the most valuable class of soldiers. He added that 'children of the old Nasiri soldiers (commonly called Goorkahs) who came into the British service in 1815 – are, in my opinion, excellent soldiers. They consider themselves Goorkas.' He felt nevertheless that it was not desirable to have a regiment composed altogether of Nepalese, and that it was impossible to keep to strength on account of the 'difficulty of getting recruits from Nepaul at all seasons of the year'. O'Brien therefore recommended 'a small proportion (say a third or a fourth) should be of British hill subjects, chiefly Rajputs from our trans-Sutledge [*sic*] possessions and children of the old Goorkas'.

The Governor-General in Council, to whom O'Brien's letter was referred, wrote a minute, dated 5 May 1852 and headed 'Hill Corps and 66th Regiment'. In this he noted that 'real Goorkhas cannot be got in any numbers' and that 'the Rajah of Nepal and his Ministers will not openly oppose but they will secretly thwart attempts to obtain recruits openly through the Resident at the capital' (Kathmandu).[848] Dalhousie added: 'If we could get them I would not have the corps all Goorkhas first because I don't think it expedient to have these corps all foreigners and second because our own hill subjects are as good soldiers and have a claim on us to be employed.' Accepting O'Brien's recommendation, he decided that 'as nearly as possible of the four as [sic] called Goorkha regiments a third shall be real Goorkhas, and the remaining two thirds shall be made up of the descendents of Goorkhas bred amongst ourselves and "Paharrees" (hillmen) from the hills now belonging to the British Government between the Indus and Nepal'. The Secretary to the Military Department informed the Adjutant-General of this decision in a letter dated 11 May 1852.[849]

In 1852, Sir Charles Napier gave evidence before the Select Committee of the House of Lords:

> The other point to which I referred was one that I think very important; the employment of the Goorkah race; they are excellent soldiers, as Lord Gough can testify much better than I can, for he has seen them engaged and I have not, but everybody says that their courage is equal to that of our own men; they have no caste, so there is no difficulty as to their food; they mess and do everything without causing any difficulty, and they are excessively attached to the European troops; they feel the greatest possible pride in the British uniform. When I turned a Goorkah regiment into the 66th, their delight at wearing a red coat was great.[850]

Napier went on 'they are very fine soldiers; if we had 30,000 of them in addition to 30,000 of our own Europeans, we should have a force in India that could do what we liked; we should no longer hold India by opinion, but by actual force'.[851]

Asked by Lord Elphinstone 'Is there not an immense advantage in raising Sikh regiments?' Napier replied:

> Yes, but you do not know the Sikhs are true. In India we must take

broad views; while we are victorious all goes smooth, but if we had a reverse what would the Sikh regiments do? After Kabul they were quite ready to attack us; Lord Ellenborough's force at Ferozpore, and the still existing policy of Runjeet Singh hardly kept the Sikhs in check;- they have fought us twice since, and both times run us hard; they may be faithful, but they are not fond of our rule.

Napier was firmly of the opinion that 'the Sikhs may be good soldiers, but the Goorkahs are as good, and are devoted to us'.[852]

In answer to a leading question from Viscount Gough: 'Do you think it rather unfortunate that our Goorkah regiments, including the one that is now transferred to the line, were paid only at the rate of five rupees a month?', Napier said: 'Yes, so much so that I got their pay increased.' And to Gough's further question: 'Was that confined to that regiment?', Napier seized the opportunity to pronounce:

> I begged for the others too, and I have Lord Dalhousie's promise to give it them, dated about November 1849. Those people are absolutely starving in the hills, yet they said they would not desert while they could live; when I obtained a promise of an increase of pay for them, I heard that their yell of joy was something extraordinary: if they have not the increase in pay, the public faith has been broken with them: I do hope this is not the case.[853]

Shortly before he left India, Dalhousie recommended, in a minute dated 5 February 1854 that the strength of each of the three irregular Gorkha battalions (the Nasiris, Sirmoor and Kumaon) be brought up to 800 and that they be armed with the best rifles.[854] However, the recommendation was not put into effect. Nor was his belated urging, one of his last acts as Governor-General, that an increase in the Gorkha force was essential to the security of India.[855] The Government in India were to realise, too late, the importance of Dalhousie's appeal.

As has already been pointed out (see page 197), in 1857, the year of the Mutiny, Hodgson wrote: 'It is infinitely to be regretted that the opinions of Sir H. Fane, of Sir Charles Napier, and of Sir H. Lawrence, as to the high expediency of recruiting largely from this source [the Gorkhas] was not acted upon long ago.'[856]

However, Hodgson went on working discreetly in retirement in an attempt to establish congenial relations with Nepal through his friendship with the Nepalese Prime Minister Jang Bahadur Rana. His hopes of persuading Jang Bahadur to allow the recruitment of Gorkhas in Nepal were doomed to failure. A master opportunist faced with stabilising a country torn by centuries of internecine feuds, Jang Bahadur promised much but delivered very little. His visit to England in 1850, when he was received by Queen Victoria, seems to have caused him to take an even firmer line. Hodgson did, however, persuade Jang Bahadur to provide, and Lord Canning to accept, a contingent of the Nepalese Army to fight for the British against the rebels in the Mutiny.[857] This was not altruism on Jang Bahadur's part but a calculated political and economic move. Apart from the gratitude of the British Government and field training for Nepalese troops, Nepal gained more than 4,000 cartloads of loot from Lucknow, 10,000 rifles of the latest model, and substantial financial reward. Not even the Queen's bestowal of the GCB, which pleased Jang Bahadur greatly, nor the return to Nepal of land in the Western Terai could deflect him from an iron resolve not to allow the recruitment of Gorkhas. Right up to his death in 1877 he did his utmost to thwart British attempts at illicit recruitment.[858]

Hodgson did, nevertheless, influence Lord Canning to increase the number of Gorkha battalions.[859] In 1857, during the Mutiny, an Extra Gurkha Regiment was raised at Pithoragarh (a Gorkha recruiting depot near Almora – see map 2) by Lieutenant Donald MacIntyre of the 66th or Goorka Regiment from a nucleus of Gorkha officers, and non-commissioned officers and sepoys of his Regiment.[860] The following year, the 25th Punjab Infantry or Hazara Battalion was raised from 'Goorkhas' from other units of the Punjab Irregular Force.[861]

On 1 November 1858, Queen Victoria became Empress of India and the Governor-General, Lord Canning, became the first Viceroy. The change of administration, with a Secretary of State for India, was followed by a comprehensive reform of what was now the Indian Army. The new Nasiri Battalion was disbanded and its men dispersed among the other Gorkha battalions. At the same time the five Gorkha Regiments were brought into a new line as the 11th, 17th, 18th, 19th

Regiments of Native Infantry, and the 7th Regiment of Infantry (or Hazara Goorkha Battalion) of the Punjab Irregular Force.[862] Less than six months later the five Gorkha regiments were brought into a separate line as, respectively, the 1st Goorkha Regiment, the 2nd Goorkha (the Sirmoor Rifle) Regiment, the 3rd Goorkha (the Kumaon) Regiment, the 4th Goorkha Regiment and the 5th Goorkha Regiment (the Hazara Goorkha Battalion: attached to the Punjab Irregular Force).[863] This laid the basis to what was to become until 1947, the Indian Army's Gurkha Brigade. By one means or another, the recruitment of Gorkhas continued, supplemented by the intake of other hillmen, throughout Jang Bahadur's rule and that of his successor Ranodip Singh, whose opposition to British recruitment of Gorkhas was no less. However, in 1885, following the assassination of Ranodip, Bir Shamsher, the new Prime Minister, found himself in urgent need of British support. He therefore agreed to send his own recruiting teams throughout Nepal to seek volunteers for service with the British. Weekly progress reports were made to the Resident at Kathmandu. This arrangement proved so successful that a second battalion was raised for each of the five British Gorkha regiments in the period 1886–7.[864]

Appendices

Descriptive detail of men engaged in the Affair of the 21st instant with the loss sustained by subsequent desertions (26th February 1815)[865]

	Total Raised by the different Sirdars	Men Engaged	Desertions from the different bodies	Killed	Wounded
Kishen Singh, Low Country	419	430	365	55	10
Puharees	481	431	—	2	—
Duraz Khan Patan, mixed troops Low Country	554	150	481	21	6
Sunnow Khan, mixed troops Low Country	300	250	266	21	13
Hurkdad Khan, mixed troops Low Country	400	400	77	34	17
Bhodie Khan, Mewattee	600	100	*40	14	1
Khyrattee Khan, Patan, mixed troops Low Country	78	78	67	8	3
Gammee Khan mixed troops Low Country	128	128	37	4	7
Mooltaza Khan mixed troops Low Country	62	62	62	—	—
Kundaz, formerly an Officer of the Sirmore family	60	60	56	3	1
Nujeeb Singh formerly an Officer of the Sirmore family	223	223	—	18	25
TOTAL	3305	2312	1451	180	83

N.B Men, all of the low country people, have applied for discharge

* The Mewattees had deserted before the action, none went off subsequent to it

Signed: F. Young Lieut
Commanding Irregular Corps

Signed: W Fraser
1st Assistant

Memo. of Wm. Fraser's questions with Lt. Young's replies and Wm. Fraser's consequent remarks respecting the Irregular Corps [866]

1. The Corps of irregulars is formed of different bodies of men, remarkably distinguished by cast, religion, sect and local situation of their native soil. Which so distinguished are judged by you most proper for the service thay are likely to be engaged in?

I consider the Puharees [hillmen] the best and indeed the only people fit for the service in which we are likely to be engaged. I have observed none of the others are equal to the fatigue or capable of bearing the cold to which we must so often be exposed. Besides the Puharees are much more easily fed in the hills than any other description of people

I am generally speaking inclined to coincide with Lt. Young's opinions. For Irregular service I think Highlanders best adapted but for actual fighting in battle I prefer Patans or Mewattees who are supposed to be people most remarkable for resolute bravery and courage; therefore it appears advisable that the Irregular Corps should be formed of men of both descriptions, the one to support a distant desultory fight and the latter to sustain the onset of compact bodies attacking with the sword.

2. Which amongst the above have evinced the greatest or indeed any degree of bravery or devotion? Which are most remarkable for any opposite line of conduct?

In the unfortunate affair of the 21st I did not observe bravery or devotion in any particular body or description of men

No remark can be offered on this reply. There is however a great difference of opinion in the account given of the numbers of the enemy opposed to the detachment of irregulars engaged. I have never been able to obtain a higher result than 400. Lt. Young is of the opinion that the numbers amount to 7 or 800 and Kishen Sing, upon whose imformation Lt. Young acted, asserts that there was not less than 12 or 1400 men opposed to us. Major Stevenson whose intelligence ought to be the most correct (estimates) the force the enemy

3. What nature of service do you consider the Corps under your command adequate to?

I do not look on the Corps as it is presently formed equal to meet the enemy in open action in the hills. It may be employed usefully in holding fortified posts, in distressing the enemy by eating up supplies in the country, taking all escort duties, cutting off supplies, drawing off the attention of the enemy from other points or even undertaking assistance to regular troops in action by covering their flanks on Gools [867] but without assistance of Regulars. I do not now expect anything from them by reason of their want of confidence in each other and proper native officers to command them.

attacked with at 750 or 800 men.

The Corps although principally intended to act upon the auxiliary and partisan system may I think be opposed to small detachments of the enemy in open action affording to them the numerical majority required. They are as Lt. Young justly observes fully equal to the subservient duties of war. I believe the various bodies that did compose the Corps had not sufficient dependence one upon the other but that the defeat of the 21st did not wholly spring from this cause when so considerable a body of Asiatick Troops raised in a space of two months it is not to be expected that they shall act with unanimity and confidence. By repeated trials those best adapted to the Service will shew themselves, the unworthy be removed and the daring retained. I would therefore instead of witholding the men from action take every opportunity of opposing them to the enemy and accustom them to the warfare of attack and not exclusively to the defensive system; although such may be not followed as the most prudent it is not always the best or the most successful plan and an enemy who has been accustomed for twenty-five years to an uninterrupted course of success and conquest whose troops are brave and enterprising merits and requires a corresponding system of offensive warfare.

4. If from the different description of men of which it is formed an efficient force be made of that most approved by you, in such an event what numerical superiority do you consider necessary to ensure a probable advantage over the enemy who are supposed to be possessed of a greater degree of personal bravery and activity and to act upon principles which incite and sustain this superiority, to possess moreover some degree of Military skill and enterprise supported by a long course of victory and conquest?

Allowing the Corps to be formed of Puharees regularly trained to the use of the matchlock which at present they seem to know little of, the advantage in favour of the enemy would still be 2 to 1 on account of their having musquets against our matchlocks, and when you add to this the want of discipline in our men and the superior strength and courage of the enemy the odds will still be more.

I do not altogether coincide with Lt. Young's opinion. The Goorkah musquet is not very superior to the matchlock and they never, I believe, use the bayonet. Their flints are bad and the locks very indifferent the piece in consequence very frequently misses fire and the only superiority they possess is the faculty of loading which a musquet charged by cartridge has over the horn and ball of the matchlock, the aim is by no means so certain but the ball is thrown with more force to a greater distance in consequence of the greater quantity of powder used by them.

The Goorkahs are generally as deficient in tactical intelligence as others but more obedient to and more under the command of their officers; they are superior in courage but not in physical strength. Their situation completely cut off from their native soil, surrounded by enemies and embittered by the reflection of what they have been, contrasted with the degradation of the people they have conquered and the long course of success and tyranny they have pursued acts in the twofold manner of blinding them to danger and forcing the resistance of despair. The last success stimulates, misfortune creates resolution. Arguing thus their moral superiority in battle is doubtless great, because their irregular opponents are actuated by principles generally of a nature almost directly opposite, they are preceded by inexperience, swayed by scattered interests, guided by a growling spirit consequent to slavery, depressed in mind, awed by uncertainty of result, deterred by fear of defeat and of its consequences, wavering and indefinite propects for the future and ignorant indecision stifling hope by fear. But conciliatory, kind and just conduct and above all success will operate to remove these impressions and results.

5. Are you of the opinion that any superiority less than in proportion to 4 to 1 is sufficient to ensure the advantage in open action supposing your corps formed of the description of men you most approve?

The corps at present being formed of different bodies of men all of whom have separate interests and prejudices and the greater of whom being of low country and in my opinion unfit for hard service in the hills I do not think a superiority of less than 3 to 1 sufficient to ensure success in an open action with the Goorkahs.

I am of the same opinion with Lt. Young perhaps not assenting to the necessity of so great a superiority, for instant [*sic*] the remark applies to small numbers, but not to large.

6. Be pleased to answer this question with the alterations of having the corps formed as it is at the present of men of various descriptions?

If formed of trained Puharees I conceive 2 to 1 ought to ensure success even with the matchlocks

I acquiesce with Lt. Young's opinion.

7. Are you of the opinion that the Irregular Corps under any circumstances are unequal to oppose the enemy in the field and only equal to retaining fortified posts?

I do not think under any circumstances the Irregulars should be opposed to the enemy without the assistance of regular troops. I think they might be employed in annoying the enemy as much as possible without risking an action.

On this point I differ entirely with Lt. Young and he acknowledges in the two preceding replies that a specific numerical superiority is adequate to ensure the general probability of success.

8. Do you possess any ground on which you can give an opinion of the character and value of the inhabitants of the Hills as soldiers?

I understand the Goorkahs began to recruit in Sirmore but discontinued that practice in consequence of finding the people neither brave nor faithful. Many of the Goorkah soldiers are inhabitants of Gurhwaul

I differ also on this point from Lt. Young. I entertain a high opinion of the character of the inhabitants of Jounsar, Puchad and Joobul. I have not been able to ascertain that the inhabitants of Gurhwaul are superior to them. The number of men raised in the service of Nepaul raised in Guhrwaul arises, I think, from the circumstances of that Province having been reduced 11 or 12 years ago and the country on this side of the Jumna only. This remark appies even more strongly to Kumaon.

9. What number of men do you consider yourself able to command personally with reference to the character, habits and prejudices of the men?

I do not feel equal to the duty of commanding and doing justice to more than 1000 men. At the same time I am convinced a body of Irregulars of that strength properly managed would answer the expected wishes of Government better than twice their numbers when they were under natives through whose hands their pay passed. Indeed if officers could be spared I think two to every 1,000 men would render them a serviceable body.

The justice of Lt. Young's reply to this question is obvious and could his proposal be put into execution the arrangement is desirable. It is not however even now necessary that the men should be paid through the medium of their officers.

10. Do you approve of the present plan under which the corps is organised, or can you suggest any means by which discipline could be improved and devotion excited?

For the reasons before stated I do not approve of the present plan in which the corps is organised and the only mode I can immediately suggest for improving it is to divide it into smaller bodies and give more European officers to the present men till Puharees can be procured and trained. If Goverment could make it convenient to raise a local corps of Puharees and arm them them with fusils I am convinced 2 European officers would in the course of 6 months make it superior for Hill service to our regular Sepoys.

As many British officers as can be procured properly selected, with reference to the duties they are intended to discharge and their knowledge of the Asiatick character are obviously desirable. An intemperate hasty boisterous person would do more harm than good. It is therefore plain that the expediency of employing British officers must depend on the practicability of procuring people calculated for the service. It will be entirely at Lt. Young's desire to divide the men into bodies to the extent he may deem most manageable and convenient. To raise a corps and arm them with fusils or musquets in the event of protracted warfare being possible would be an expedient and desirable plan, otherwise an unnecessary trouble.

Signed W. Fraser 1st Asst.

The whole signed as a true copy

W. Fraser
1st Asst.

Translation of a Convention executed by Lieutenant-Colonel Gardner (authorised for that purpose by the Honourable E. Gardner and Colonel Nicolls, acting on the part of the British Government) on one side, and by Bum Sah Choutra, Chamoo Bundaree Kajee, Ungut Sirdar, and Jasmun Dan Thapa, for the Nepaul Government on the other side [27 April 1815]⁸⁶⁸

The Rajah's name at the top of the paper "Gurbhun Jat Bekram Sah".

In the year 1872 Sumbut [AD 1815], on thursday the 4th of Bysak, the following Convention has been written by the Choutra Bum Sah, Kajee Chamoo Bundaree, Captain [*sic*] Ungut Sing Sirdar and Jasmun Dan Thappa; and Lieutenant-Colonel Gardner, on the part of the General [*sic*] Colonel Nicolls, and the Honourable Edward Gardner acting for the Governor-General; in which the Choutra Bum Sah and the Goorka Sirdars, on the part of the Rajah of Nepaul (here a space is left for the Rajah's name inserted at the top of the paper), agree:

That the fort of Almora, and the province of Kamaon, with all its fortified places shall be evacuated. The garrison with their property (namely private effects), ammunition (namely ball, powder, and flints, with all musquets and accoutrements, and eleven guns) shall be allowed to march across the Kalee unmolested, by a convenient road, being supplied with provisions and carriers who are to be collected and sent to such part as may be pointed out. The fort of Lalmaudi shall be evacuated this day, and possession given to the British troops.

                              (L.S.) The Seal of Colonel GARDNER.
(L.S.) BUM SAH's Seal.   (L.S.) W. L. GARDNER.
(L.S.) The Seal of KAJEE CHAMOO THAPA.
(L.S.) Ditto of JASMUN DAN THAPA.

Ratified and confirmed by us, this twenty-seventh of April 1815.
        (Signed) J. NICOLLS, Colonel.
                E. GARDNER.
Second Assistant to Resident of Delhi.

Memorandum of four propositions offered by Messrs Jaykissen [*sic*] bearing the seal and signature of General Ochterlony under date the 24th January 1815[869]

1. Every man who shall join the British from the Goorkha army with his musket shall obtain a reward of 10 rupees and in future receive the pay of his rank agreeably to the Goorkha standards.

   Each man will receive 10 rupees as the price and in lieu of his arms and be retained in service on the Goorkha rates of pay.

2. Subedars, Jemadars and other officers on their arrival in the first instance shall receive the pay of their ranks for one month as a reward and afterwards be retained and receive their fixed allowances.

   Approved.

3. Whatever agreements shall be made with Killadars during negotiations exclusive of rewards to Sepahees shall be reported and your orders shall fix the extent of their reward.

   Approved.

4. Whatever you have in consideration as in reward for my services and please to commit to paper. But I am anxious to obtain a Jageer of a village in Kashipoor or Roodurpoor.

   Your reward will be thus effected: for every man that shall come over thro' you, you will receive one rupee. If a whole company should come over you will receive the pay of a subedar viz. 60 rupees for life. If less than one company, your pay will be regulated agreeably to the account of Puttee (or parties of 25) and should 5 companies come over you will receive 150 per month. If a battalion your pay will be that of a commandant viz. 300 per month. With regard to the Jageer the fact is that it is unknown to me to what government Kashipoor and Roodurpoor appertain, besides I have not authority to grant a Jageer but I shall report your wishes for the consideration of the Right Honourable the Governor-General and if approved it will afford you satisfaction and be pleasing to me also. But whatever has been written above you may rely upon as being adjusted for life.

Note: The words in the right hand column are as such on the folio and are obviously Ochterlony's decisions.

Letter from Lieutenant Ross to Captain Birch (20 April 1815)[870]

My dear Birch

On the night of the 14th, 2 Light Companies and a party of irregulars with Lawtie ascended unperceived a height in front of our camp and about 1/2 hour before day break. A fire from thence apprised us that with them all was well. On this preconcerted signal the Grenr. Bn. with 2 guns under Major Innes, and the 3d, the Lt. Bn., the Pioneers and 2 guns under Colonel Thompson moved from this camp into the bed of the Gumrola which runs between Malown Doab and our positions thus:

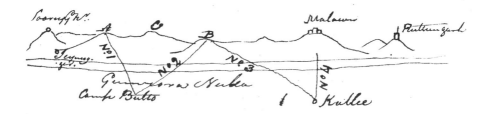

On the preceding day 400 regulars and 300 irregulars under Captain Bowyer had marched from Colonel Arnold's camp at Ruttungurh and encamped at Kallee. These also on the signal above-mentioned moved into the Gumrora [Gumrola] and at the first dawn of day the whole began to ascend the opposite Range as follows:

Major Innes' Dett. by route No.1; Colonel Thompson's No.2; Major Lawrie's by No.3; Captain Bowyer's by No.4. 4 Companies under Captain Hamilton at the same hour from Jeynuggur to Ryla marked A and 300 regulars under Captain Showers from Ruttungurh towards the Malown Cantonment. The object was to establish posts at A and B cutting off Malown from Soorujgurh. The post A was established with little or no opposition. 3 or 4 men only were wounded. Colonel Thompson's and Major Lawrie's columns arrived at B at the very same instant without the loss of a man; though the latter sustained in his advance a considerable fire from a jungle on his left. The detachments of Captains Bowyer and Showers were destined to threaten the Cantonment of Malown to prevent any parties being detached thence to the annoyance of Major Lawrie's advance, but were instructed to sieze and maintain any good position which the enemy might evacuate or greatly weaken for that purpose.

The heads of our columns had scarcely reached B when the Goorkhas came down on them; though thanks to the demonstrations made on Malown not in great numbers. A sharp fire ensued from both sides. The Goorkhas gained excellent cover within 30 yards of B behind rocks etc. and remained there during the whole day keeping up a very galling fire by which we had Ensn. Bagot, a Serjt. of Pioneers and an artilleryman killed, Gable slightly wounded and about 70 natives killed and wounded. During this time we were employed in erecting a stockade. In the quarter of Malown Captain Showers was killed after slaying the Chief opposed to him in single combat and his detachment having suffered severely fell back on Ruttungurh. Captain Bowyer pushed on towards the cantonment but finding their stockades all manned he fulfilled the principal object of his instructions by drawing and keeping their attention on him for upwards of 4 hours and then retired in excellent order and with little loss and the enemy was then relieved from apprehension in that quarter.

This morning at the very first break of day the Goorkhas from Malown headed by Bhugtee Thappa made a grand attack on B which lasted nearly two hours, and during which they sustained the hardest fire of grape and musquetry I have ever heard. They returned there several times to the charge with most unparalleled intrepidity and endeavoured sword in hand to cut in upon our guns, during which attempt as fast as one set of men were knocked down others springing up from behind rocks rushed forward to supply their places. They were finally however driven back from all quarters with a loss which though not ascertained must have been very great. Bhugtee Thappa the most renowned Chief of their army fell just before their final retreat covered with wounds and glory, bayonetted, scabred and shot. Besides him they have lost Juskurrum Kajee and Jehr Sing, officers of note, whose bodies, originally brought into the camp, the General has sent to Ummer Sing wrapped in shawls and with every mark of honour (Bhugtee's particularly) which their rank and valour merited. The approach of the dark hour will not allow me to say more. Offer to Salter and Mrs. Salter my congratulations on this further success of the General, the results of arrangements which well merited it.

Ever sincerely yours,
R. Ross

P.S. Captain Showers fell in personal conflict with a sirdar whom he slew. Our loss on both days (inclusive of Captain Showers' detachment) is about 100 killed and wounded. That of the enemy is estimated at 300 killed and wounded.

Convention or Agreement entered into between Kajee Ummer Sing Thapa and Major-General Ochterlony, on the 15th May 1815[871]

In consideration of the high rank and character of Kajee Ummer Sing Thappa, and of the skill, bravery, and fidelity with which he has defended the country committed to his charge, it is agreed:

1. That Kajee Ummer Sing Thappa, with the troops now in Raujgurh [Malaun], shall march out and retain their arms and accoutrements, the colours of their respective corps, two guns and all private property, which shall be duly respected and preserved, and every attention and delicacy observed in respect to the Zenana of the Kajee, and every person under his authority.

2. In consideration, also, of the gallant conduct of Kajee Runjore Sing Thappa, it is agreed that he shall likewise march out of the fort of Jeytuck with two hundred men, who are to retain their arms, colours and one gun, with the Bharadars [chief officers] and their followers, about three hundred more in number, unarmed, with his own and their private property, which shall be respected, and the sanctity of the Zenana preserved.

3. Kajee Ummer Sing Thappa and Kajee Runjore Sing Thappa, with their property and followers, are at liberty to proceed by the route of Thaneisur, Hurdwar, and Nujeebabad, to join the troops eastward of the river Surjoo (or Kalee), or by whichever route they determine to proceed to that destination. Conveyance shall be provided for the transportation of their property to the confines of the Nepaul territory.

4. Kajee Ummer Sing Thappa and Kajee Runjore Sing Thappa shall be at liberty to meet wherever they please.

5. All the troops in the service of Nepaul, with the exception of those granted to the personal honour of the Kajees, Ummer Sing and Runjore Sing, will be at liberty to enter into the service of the British Government, if it is agreeable to themselves and the British Government choose to accept their services, and those who are not employed will be maintained on a specific allowance by the British Government, till peace is concluded between the two states.

6. Kajee Sing Thappa, on his part, agrees to leave the fort of Malown, whenever bearers and other conveyance are prepared for his private property.

7. Kajee Ummer Sing Thappa also agrees to send immediate orders for the evacuation and delivery, to persons properly authorised, of the forts of Bhylee (Irkee), Subbatoo, Mornee, Jeytuck, Juggutgurh, Rowaheen, and all other forts and fortresses now held by the Nepaul troops between the Jumna and Sutleje rivers. The garrisons of all which forts, strong holds, etc., shall enjoy their private property unmolested, and the arms and warlike stores in each shall be left in deposit, for the future decision of the Right Honourable the Governor-General; with exception to such among them as are related to Kajee Ummer Sing Thappa by kindred, about eighty-three men, shall be at liberty to retain their arms and accoutrements.

8. Kajee Ummer Sing Thappa also agrees to send immediate orders to Kajee Bukhtour Sing for the evacuation of the territory of Ghurwall, to deliver over the forts, etc. in that district to the officers of the British Government, and to proceed to Nepaul by the Kamaon route, with their garrisons, all public and private property including warlike stores, accompanied by a Chuprassie with a pass, on the part of the British Government.

Separate Article. – Kajee Ummer Sing Thappa wishes it to be understood, that he shall give immediate orders for the instant surrender of the distant forts, in the hope that it may lead to an early renewal of the relations of amity which have subsisted between the two states for these sixty years, and by the advice of Bum Sah and the Bharadars of Kamaon.

The Treaty of Segauli (4 March 1816) and translation of a related engagement[872]

Treaty of peace between the Honourable East India Company and Maha Raja Bickram Sah, Raja of Nipal, settled between Lieutenant-Colonel Bradshaw, on the part of the Honourable Company, in virtue of the full powers vested in him by his Excellency the Right Honourable Francis, Earl of Moira, Knight of the Most Noble Order of the Garter, one of His Majesty's Most Honourable Privy Council, appointed by the Court of Directors of the said Honourable Company to direct and control all the affairs in the East Indies, and by Sree Gooroo Gujraj Missur, and Chunder Seekur Opadheea, on the part of Maharaja Kurman Jodh Bickram Sah Behaudur Shumsheer Jung, in virtue of the powers to that effect vested in them by the said Raja of Nipal.

Whereas war has arisen between the Honourable East India Company and the Raja of Nipal, and whereas the parties are mutually disposed to restore the relations of peace and amity, which, previously to the occurrence of the late differences, had long subsisted between the two states, the following terms of peace have been agreed upon.

Article 1st. – There shall be perpetual peace and friendship between the Honourable East India Company, and the Raja of Nipal.

Article 2d. – The Raja of Nipal renounces all claim to the lands which were the subject of discussion between the two states before the war; and acknowledges the right of the Honourable Company to the sovereignty of those lands.

Article 3d. – The Raja of Nipal hereby cedes to the Honourable the East India Company, in perpetuity, all the undermentioned territories, namely. –

First, – The whole of the low lands between the rivers Kali and Raptee.

Secondly, – The whole of the low lands (with the exception of Bootwul Khas) lying between the Raptee and the Gunduk.

Thirdly, – the whole of the low lands between the Gunduk and Koosee, in which the authority of the British Government has been introduced, or is in actual course of introduction.

Fourthly, – All the low lands between the river Mechee and the Teesta.

Fifthly, – All the territories within the hills, eastward of the river Mechee, including the fort and lands of Nagree, and the pass of Nagarcote, leading from Morung into the hills, together with the territory lying between that pass and Nagree. The aforesaid territory shall be evacuated by the Goorkha troops within forty days from this date.

Article 4th. – With a view to indemnify the chiefs and barahdars of the state of Nipal, whose interests will suffer by the alienation of the lands ceded by the foregoing article, the British government agrees to settle pensions, to the aggregate amount of two lakhs of rupees per annum, on such chiefs as may be selected by the Raja of Nipal, and in the proportions which the Raja may fix. As soon as the selection is made, Sunuds shall be granted under the seal and signature of the Governor-General for the pensions respectively.

Article 5th. – The Raja of Nipal renounces for himself, his heirs and successors, all claim to, or connexion with, the countries lying to the west of the river Kalee; and engages never to have any concern with those countries or the inhabitants thereof.

Article 6th. – The Raja of Nipal engages never to molest or disturb the Raja of Sikkim in the possession of his territories; but agrees, if any differences arise between the state of Nipal and the Raja of Sikkim, or the subjects of either, that such differences shall be referred to the arbitration of the British government, by whose award the Raja of Nipal engages to abide.

Article 7th. – The Raja of Nipal hereby engages never to take or retain in his service any British subject, nor the subject of any European or American state, without the consent of the British government.

Article 8th. – In order to secure and improve the relations of amity and peace hereby established between the two states, it is agreed that accredited ministers from each shall reside at the court of the other.

Article 9th. – This treaty, consisting of nine articles. shall be ratified by the Raja of Nipal within fifteen days from this date; and the ratification shall be delivered to Lieutenant-Colonel Bradshaw, who engages to obtain and deliver to the Raja the ratification of the Governor-General within twenty days, or sooner, if practicable.

Done at Segoulee, on the 2d. day of December 1815.

(L.S.) (Signed) Paris Bradshaw, Lt.-Col. P.A.
(L.S.) (Signed) Gujraj Misur.
(L.S.) (Signed) Chundur Seekhur Opadheea.

Received this treaty from Chundur Seekhur Opadheea, agent on the part of the Raja of Nipal, in the valley of Muckwanpoor, at half-past two o'clock on the 4th of March, 1816, and delivered to him the counterpart treaty on behalf of the British government.

(Signed) D.Ochterlony,
Agt. Governor-General.

Translation of an engagement (Ikrarnama) in the Hindee language, executed at Mukwanpoor Mandee, by Kajee Bukhtawur Singh Thapa, and Chundur Seekhur Opadheea, Plenipotentiaries on the part of the Raja of Nipal, and forwarded by General Sir David Ochterlony along with the above treaty.

At the time of delivering the treaty, Major-General Sir David Ochterlony was pleased to observe, that the Right Honourable the Governor-General had not authorised him to accept the treaty, and that he could not encourage any hope of those indulgences of which a prospect had been held out by Lieutenant- Colonel Bradshaw, being granted in addition to the treaty; that his Lordship indeed would not grant them, and that he (the General) would not recommend him to do so; that nothing beyond what was stated in the treaty would be allowed. Accordingly, we, Sree Kajee Bukhtawar Singh Thappa, and Chundur Seekhur Opadheea, have agreed to what Sir D. Ochterlony has required; in testimony whereof, we have executed this Razeenama, and delivered it to the Major-General, dated 5th of Soodee Phagun, 1872, Sumbut, corresponding with Tuesday thc 4th of March, 1816.

A true translation.
(Signed) J. Monckton,
Persn. Secretary to Government.

Return of Hillmen Natives of Kumaon and Garhwal who were to accompany Soobah Jey Kishen Plassea, May 26th 1815[873]

	Furnished from										
	Lall Sahi's company	Jey Kishen's company	Munni Raj Rana's company	Chumaso Rana's company	Pursram Gurung's puttees	Bahadur Sahi's puttees	Bagburn Soobah's puttees	Rehersin Thappa	Subber Sing's Puttees	From men under Munni Raj Rana not formed	Total
Jem.	—	8	—	—	1	—	—	—	—	—	9
Adj.	—	2	—	—	—	—	—	—	—	—	2
Majors	—	3	—	1	—	—	—	—	—	—	4
Kote Hav.	—	4	—	—	—	—	—	—	—	—	4
Hav.	3	16	—	2	1	1	—	—	—	—	23
Nks.	4	10	1	1	2	4	—	—	—	1	23
Nishaunchees	—	8	—	—	—	—	—	—	—	—	8
Sepoys	115	244	31	47	31	93	8	7	10	28	614
Total Fighting men	122	295	32	51	35	98	8	7	10	29	679 + 8 Nish.
Musicians	3	3	—	—	—	—	—	—	—	—	6
Clashees	1	24	—	10	4	7	—	3	—	1	50
Bheestees	2	—	—	4	—	—	—	—	—	—	6
Total of Estab.	6	27	—	14	4	7	—	3	—	1	62
GRAND TOTAL	128	322	32	65	39	105	8	10	10	30	749

N.B. the total number of muskets viz. Hav., Nks., Sepoys 670 (excl. Jems & Nish)

Signed R. Ross Lt. Commanding Nusseeree Battalion

Sir Henry Fane's return of the strength of the Nipal Army (undated)[874]

Artillery

No.	and Calibre	How disposed	Where quartered
6	4 pounders	Light Regiment	Catmandhu
6	4 do	Srinath Regnt	do do
2	4 do	Deri dutt Regnt	do do
2	4 do	Kali Bux. Reg	do do
2	4 do	Sing dul Reg.	Mukwanpoor
2	4 do	Birjolani Reg	Catmandhu
2	4 do	New Ghora Reg	Salliana
2	4 do	Old Ghora Reg	Catmandhu
4	4 do	Sri Mehur Reg	East Frontier
1	4 do	Run Dul. Reg	Duri Dulak
1	4 do	Goor. Bux Reg	Putana
1	4 do	Run Seil Reg	Catmandhu
6	4 do	Subuj Pultun	Palpa
4	4 do	Buruk Regnt	Doti
8	9 do	Garrison Guns	Cheshaghur
8	9 do	do do	Mukwanpoor
2	9 do	do do	Hurriarpoor
6	9 do	do do	Sinduli
4	9 do	do do	Hamgur Sikim
4	9 do	do do	Pokra near Gorkha
4	9 do	do do	Salliana
4	9 do	do do	Puttanah
12	9 do	do do	Doti
12	3 do	In store	Katmandhu
1	24 do	In store	Katmandhu
59	6 do	In store	Katmandhu

165 Total Guns

Nipal Infantry

Stations of Corps 1838	Captains	Lieutenants	Subadars	Jemadars	Havildars	Amildars	Hurdars	Majors	Adjutants	Privates	Names of Regiments
Doti	1	1	1	6	12	24	1	1	1	600	Barat
Doti	1	1	1	6	12	21	1	1	1	300	Adgam
Doti	—	1	1	4	8	8	1	—	—	200	Maya Bux
Doti	—	1	1	3	6	8	1	—	—	150	Bora Nath
Salliana	1	1	1	6	12	24	1	1	1	600	Nya Gora
Pokra	—	1	1	6	12	12	1	—	—	300	Kali Jung
Toomla	—	1	1	6	12	12	1	—	—	300	Bhowani Bux
Toomla	—	1	1	4	8	8	1	—	—	200	Cundum Persa
Durdilak	1	1	1	3	6	12	1	1	1	300	Rundul
do.	—	1	1	2	4	4	1	—	—	100	Nya Sri Nath
Piuthana	1	1	1	4	8	16	1	1	1	200	Joroo Bux
Palpa	1	1	5	10	20	40	1	2	1	1500	Subuj
Palpa	1	2	1	6	12	24	1	1	1	500	Sher
Palpa	—	1	1	3	6	6	1	—	—	150	Bulum dul
Palpa	—	1	1	3	6	6	1	—	—	150	Saloo Jumg
Pythana	—	1	1	2	4	4	1	—	—	100	Sheo dul
Catmandhu	5	5	5	10	20	40	1	2	1	1100	Light
do	5	5	5	10	20	40	1	2	1	1100	Sri Nath
do	1	1	1	6	12	26	1	1	1	600	Purana Gora
	18	28	31	100	200	335	19	13	10	8450	

Infantry continued

Stations of Corps	Captains	Lieutenants	Subadars	Jemadars	Havildars	Amildars	Hurdars	Majors	Adjutants	Privates	Names of Regiments
Cathmandu	1	1	1	6	12	24	1	1	1	600	Hunuman dull
do	1	1	1	6	12	24	1	1	1	600	Kali Bux
do	1	1	1	6	12	24	1	1	1	600	Devi dutt
do	1	1	1	6	12	24	1	1	1	600	Birjobani
Mukanpoor	1	2	2	8	16	24	1	3	1	800	Sing Nath
Chesagur	—	1	1	2	4	4	1	—	—	120	Butook dul
Hurripoor	—	1	1	4	8	8	1	—	—	200	Bhiroo
Sindalgur	—	1	1	3	6	6	1	—	—	150	Dirga Bux
Hamghur	1	1	1	4	8	12	1	1	1	500	Sri Mhur
Dunkosla	—	1	1	6	12	12	1	1	—	600	Sri Jung
E Terai	—	1	1	3	6	6	1	—	—	150	Run Seth
	6	12	12	54	108	168	11	9	6	4920	

Artillerymen and Gun Lascars 1700
Cavalry none, useless in so mountainous a country

This formidable force which can be trebled in a very short time on the principle of the Landueler is principally cantonned within 200 miles of both Patna and Benares

Bibliography

1. MANUSCRIPT SOURCES

(1) *Private papers*

The Fraser of Reelig family papers, Inverness-shire; catalogued (Survey no. 2696) by the National Register of Archives (Scotland), Scottish Record Office, Edinburgh [Fraser papers]

Papers of the Ochterlony family owned by Ean Ramsay, of Dorset, direct descendant of Major-General Sir David Ochterlony, Bart., GCB [Ramsay papers]

Records of Sir Henry Fane, Commander-in-Chief India (1835–9) owned by Mrs H.W. Fane and held in the Lincolnshire Archives. [Fane Collection]

(2) *India Office Records:* British Library, Oriental and India Office Collections, 96 Euston Road, London, NW1 2DB:

Bengal Political Consultations
Bengal Political Letters
Bengal Secret and Military Consultations
Bengal Secret and Political Consultations
Despatches to Bengal
Home Miscellaneous Series
Indian Military Proceedings
Military Department Records
Political and Secret Department Records

(3) *India Office Library Manuscripts:* British Library, Oriental and India Office Collections:

Nicolls, Major-General Jasper, Eur. MS F/175/31.
[Nicolls papers]
Kinloch, Captain George, Eur. MS F/128/140.
[Kinloch diary]
Munro, Sir Thomas, Eur. MS F/151/72.
[Munro papers]

(4) *British Library*, 96 Euston Road, London, NW1 2DB:

Richard, Marquess Wellesley, Add. MS 13578.
[Wellesley papers]
William, Earl Amherst, Add. MS 48225.
[Morley papers]

(5) *National Library of Scotland*, Edinburgh :

Ochterlony, Lieutenant-Colonel D, MS 591, 1841.
(Letter)

2. OFFICIAL PUBLICATIONS

(1) *Report of the Select Committee of the House of Commons, 1831–2, XIV, Minutes of Evidence taken before the Select Committee on the Affairs of the East India Company, Feb. 18th to May 10th 1832:*

printed by order of the Court of Directors, London 1833.
[*Parliamentary Papers*]

(2) 1st Report of the Select Committee of the House of Lords, 1852–3, xxxi.

[*Parliamentary Papers*]

(3) *Papers Respecting the Nepaul War.* Printed in conformity to the Resolution of the Court of Proprietors of East-India Stock, of the 3 March 1824, London, 1824.
[*PRNW*]

(4) *Punjab Government Records*

Records of the Delhi Residency and Agency, i, Lahore, 1911.
Records of the Ludhiana Agency, ii, Lahore, 1911.
Punjab Gazetteer of the Kangra District, i (Kangra Proper), 1883–4.

(5) *Selections from the Records of the Government of Bengal.*

Hodgson, B.H., 'On the Origin and Classification of the Military Tribes of Nepal, Papers Relative to the Colonisation, Commerce, Physical Geography, Ethnography etc., of the Himalaya Mountains and Nepal', xxvii, Calcutta, 1857.

3. OTHER PRIMARY SOURCES

Aspinall, A. (ed.), *The letters of King George IV, 1812–1830*, 2 vols., London, 1938.

Baird, J.G.A. (ed.), *Private letters of the Marquess of Dalhousie*, London, 1910.

Bute, Marchioness of (ed.), *The Private Journal of the Marquis of Hastings K.G.*, 2 vols., London, 1858.

Colchester, Lord (ed.), *A Political Diary 1828–1830 by Edward Law, Lord Ellenborough*, 2 vols., London, 1881.

Forrest, G.W., *Selections from the Minutes and other official writings of the Hon. Mountstuart Elphinstone*, London, 1889.

Hardinge, Charles Viscount, *The War in India: despatches of Hardinge and others*, London, 1846.

Kaye, J.W., *The Life and Correspondence of Charles, Lord Metcalfe*, 2 vols., London, 1854.

Napier, W. (ed.), *Defects Civil and Military of the Indian Government, by Lt. General Sir Charles James Napier G.C.B.*, London, 1853.

Philips, C.H. (ed.), *The Correspondence of Lord William Cavendish Bentinck, Governor-General of India 1828–1835*, 2 vols., Oxford, 1977.

4. ARTICLES AND PAPERS

Alavi, Seema, 'The Company Army and Rural Society: The Invalid Thanah 1780–1830', *Modern Asian Studies*, xxvii, 1993, pp. 152, 153.

Bingle, R.J., "Administration leadership: the Governor-General, the Bengal Council, and the Civil Service, 1800–1835", in Robb P.G. and Tayler D. 'Rule, protest, identity: aspects of modern South Asia', *School of Oriental and African Studies, collected papers on South Asia*, no.1, 1978, p. 17.

Caplan, L., ' "Bravest of the Brave". Representations of "The Gurkha" in British Military Writings', *Modern Asian Studies*, xxv, 1991, p. 563.

Cross, J.P., 'Four and four-squared: Gurung origins and identity', *The Regimental Journal of the 7th Duke of Edinburgh's Own Gurkha Rifles*, no.45, 1991.

Fürer-Haimendorf, C. von, 'Contributions to the Anthropology of Nepal', London University School of Oriental and African Studies; contribution to Symposium, June-July 1973.

Hodgson, B.H., 'On the Origin and Classification of the Military Tribes of Nepal', *Journal of the Asiatic Society of Bengal*, ii, 1833, pp. 217–24.

—— 'On the Physical Geography of the Himalayas' in *Essays on the Language, Literature and Religion of Nepal and Tibet*, 1874.

Kohli, S.R., 'The army of Maharaja Ranjit Singh', *Journal of Indian History*, i (2), 1921–22, pp. 210, 212, 219, 402.

Marshall, P.J., 'British Expansion in India in the Eighteenth Century: A Historical Revision', *History*, 60, 1975, pp. 36, 41, 42.

Moorcroft, W., 'Journal of a journey to Lake Manasarova in Un-des, a province of little Tibet', *Asiatick Researches*, xii, 1816, pp. 375–534.

Pant, M.R., 'Bir Bhakti Thapa', *Purnima*, no. 16, 1968, p. 390.

Wagner, Anthony R., 'An Eighteenth Century King of Arms' Collection of American Pedigrees', *New England Historical and Genealogical Register*, xcv, 1941, p. 24.

5. UNPUBLISHED THESIS

Bingle, R.J., 'The Governor-Generalship of the Marquess of Hastings, 1813–1823, with special reference to the Supreme Council and Secretariat, the Residents with Native States, Military Policy, and the Transactions of the Palmer Company', D.Phil., Oxford, 1965.

6. OTHER THESES

Alavi, Seema., 'North Indian Military Culture in Transition *c.* 1770–1860', Ph.D., Cambridge, 1991.

Peers, D. M., 'Between Mars and Mammon: the military and political economy of British India at the time of the First Burma War, 1824–1826', Ph. D., London 1988.

Pemble, J., 'The Invasion of Nepal: John Company at War', Ph. D., London, 1968.

7. OTHER WORKS

Adhikari, K.K., *Nepal under Jang Bahadur 1846–1877*, 2 vols., Kathmandu, 1984.

Archer, M. and Falk, T., *India Revealed: the Art and Adventures of James and William Fraser 1801–35*, London, 1989.

Atkinson, Edwin T., *The Himalayan Districts of the North West Provinces of India*, 2 vols., Allahabad, 1884.

Badenach, Walter, *An Inquiry into the State of the Indian Army, with suggestions for its improvement and the establishment of a Military Police in India*, London, 1826.

Bajwa, F.S., *The Military System of the Sikhs 1799–1849*, Delhi, 1964.

Banskota P, *The Gurkha Connection: a History of the Gurkha Recruitment in the British Indian Army*, Jaipur, 1994.

Bista, Dor Bahadur, *People of Nepal*, second edition, Kathmandu, 1972.

Chapple, J. *The Lineages and Composition of Gurkha Regiments in British Service*, Gurkha Museum, Winchester, 1984

Colebrooke, T.E., *Life of the Honourable Mountstuart Elphinstone*, 2 vols, London, 1884.

Cunningham, J.D., *History of the Sikhs*, Reprint, Delhi, 1955.

Dalrymple, W., *City of Djinns: a year in Delhi*, London, 1993.

Edwardes, H.B. and Merivale, H., *Life of Sir Henry Lawrence*, 2 vols., London, 1872.

Elphinstone, M., *An Account of the Kingdom of Caubul*, 2 vols., London, 1815.

Fane, H.E., *Five years in India*, 2 vols., London, 1842.

Fraser, J.B., *Journal of a Tour through Part of the Snowy Range of the Himala Mountains and to the sources of the Rivers Jumna and Ganges*, London, 1820.

Ghosh, B., *British Policy towards the Pathans and the Pindaris in Central India, 1805–18*, Calcutta, 1966.

Grey, C., Garrett, H.L.O. (ed.), *European Adventurers of Northern India 1785–1849*, Lahore, 1929.

Gupta, N., *Delhi Between Two Empires 1803–1931*, Delhi, 1981.

Gyawali, S.B. (alternatively quoted as jNavali, S.V.), *Amar Singh Thapa 1748–1816*, Darjeeling, 1943.

Hamilton, F.B., *An Account of the Kingdom of Nepaul, and of the Territories annexed to this Dominion by the House of Gurkha*, Edinburgh, 1819.

Harding, D.F., *Smallarms of the East India Company 1600–1856*, 4 vols., London, 1997 and 1999.

Hardinge, Charles Viscount, *Viscount Hardinge: by his son and Private Secretary in India*, Oxford, 1891.

Hasrat, B.J., *Anglo-Sikh Relations, 1799–1849*, Hoshiarpur, 1968.

Heber, Reginald D.D., *Narrative of a Journey through the Upper Provinces of India from Calcutta to Bombay, 1824–1825*, 2 vols., London, 1844.

Hodson, V.C.P., *A List of the Officers of the Bengal Army 1758–1834*, 4 vols., London, 1927–46.

Hughes, B.F., *Firepower*, London, 1974.

Hunter, W.W., *Life of Brian Houghton Hodgson*, London, 1896.

Jenkins, L. Hadow, *General Frederick Young*, London, 1923.

Kirkpatrick, W., *An Account of the Kingdom of Nepaul, being the substance of observations made during a mission to that country in the year 1793*, London, 1811.

Lee-Warner, W., *The Life of the Marquess of Dalhousie KT*, 2 vols., London, 1904.

Mackenzie, Alexander, *History of the Frasers of Lovat*, Inverness, 1896.

Mason, Philip, *A Matter of Honour: an account of the Indian Army, its officers and men*, London, 1974.

Minto, Countess of (ed.), *Lord Minto in India, 1807–1814*, London, 1880.

Moon, Penderell, *The British Conquest and Dominion of India*, London, 1989.

Napier, W., *The Life and Opinions of General Sir Charles James Napier, GCB*, 4 vols., London, 1857.

Northey, W.B. and Morris, C.J., *The Gurkhas*, London, 1928.

Nugent, Maria Lady, *A Journal from the year 1811 to the year 1815*, 2 vols., London, 1839.

Oldfield, H.A., *Sketches from Nipal*, 2 vols., London, 1880.

Osborne, W., *Court and Camp of Runjeet Singh*, Lahore, 1895.

Panikkar, K.N., *British Diplomacy in North India*, New Delhi, 1968.

Peers, D.M., *Between Mars and Mammon: Colonial Armies and the Garrison State in Early Nineteenth-century India*, London, 1995.

Pemble, John, *The Invasion of Nepal: John Company at War*, Oxford, 1971.

Petre, F.L., *The 1st King George's Own Gurkha Rifles*, London, 1925.

Praval, K.C., *Valour Triumphs: A history of the Kumaon regiment*, Faridabad, 1976.

Prinsep, H.T., *History of the Political and Military Transactions in India during the Administration of the Marquess of Hastings 1813–1823*, 2 vols., London, 1825.

Rathaur, K.R.S., *The British and the Brave, a History of the Gurkha Recruitment in the British Army*, Jaipur, 1987.

Royal Nepalese Army Headquarters, *Royal Nepalese Army Colours: a short history*, Kathmandu, 1991.

Shaha, R., *Heroes and Builders of Nepal*, Oxford, 1965.

—— *Modern Nepal, a Political History 1769–1955*, 2 vols., New Delhi, 1990.

Sharma, S.P. et al. (eds), *Military History of Nepal*, Kathmandu, 1992.

Shipp, John, *The Path of Glory, being the Memoirs of the Extraordinary Career of John Shipp*, edited by C.J.Stranks, London, 1969.

Singh, A.K.J., *Himalayan Triangle, a historical survey of British India's relations with Tibet, Sikkim and Bhutan 1765–1950*, London, 1988.

Sinha, N.K., *Ranjit Singh*, Calcutta, 1933.

Stiller, L.F., *Nepal; Growth of a Nation*, Kathmandu, 1993.

—— *Prithvinarayan Shah in the light of Dibya Upadesh*, Kathmandu, 1989.

—— *The Rise of the House of Gorkha: a study in the unification of Nepal 1768–1816*, Patna, 1973.

—— *The Silent Cry: the People of Nepal 1816–1839*, Kathmandu, 1976.

Stubbs, F.W., *History of the Bengal Artillery*, 2 vols., London, 1877–95.

Tucci, Guiseppi, *Nepal, The Discovery of the Mallas*, translated by Lovett Edwards, London, 1962.

Wilkinson-Latham, R., *British Artillery on Land and Sea 1790–1820*, Newton Abbott, 1973.

Wilson, C.R. (ed.), *List of Inscriptions on Tombs and Monuments in Bengal possessing historical or architectural interest*, Calcutta, 1896.

Yapp, M.E., *Strategies of British India: Britain, Iran and Afghanistan 1798–1850*, Oxford, 1980.

Abbreviations

Add.MS	Additional Manuscript(s)
Add.Or.	Additional Oriental
BL	British Library
BMC	Bengal Military Consulations
BPC	Bengal Political Consultations
BPL	Bengal Political Letters
BSMC	Bengal Secret and Military Consultations
BSPC	Bengal Secret and Political Consultations
DRA	Delhi Residency and Agency
Eur.MS	European Manuscript(s)
H	Home Miscellaneous Series
IHR	Institute of Historical Research
IMP	Indian Military Proceedings
IOL	India Office Library
IOR	India Office Records
LA	Ludhiana Agency
MDR	Military Department Records
PP	Parliamentary Papers
PRNW	*Papers Respecting the Nepaul War*
PSDR	Political and Secret Department Records

} Now the British Library, Oriental and India Office Collections

Notes and References

1. The Parbatiya hill tribes of western Nepal.
2. Chiefly Kumaonis and Garhwalis.
3. E. Thompson, *The Making of the Indian Princes*, Oxford, 1943, p. 288.
4. University of London, 1968. His book with the same title was published by the Clarendon Press in 1971.
5. F.B. Hamilton, *An Account of the Kingdom of Nepaul, and of Territories annexed to this Dominion by the House of Gurkha*, Edinburgh, 1819, pp. 61–100.
6. B.H. Hodgson, 'On the Physical Geography of the Himalayas' in *Essays on the Language, Literature and Religion of Nepal and Tibet*, London, 1874, p. 21.
7. The epicanthus is a fold of skin over the inner canthus (junction of the eyelids) of the eye, characteristic of the Mongolian race.
8. J.P. Cross, 'Four and four-squared: Gurung origins and identity', *The Regimental Journal of the 7th Duke of Edinburgh's Own Gurkha Rifles*, no.45, 1991, p. 115.
9. An excellent introduction to this is given in Dor Bahadur Bista's *People of Nepal*, second edition, Kathmandu, 1972. Pemble also gives an account of the early history of Nepal and its people in his *The Invasion of Nepal: John Company at War*, chapter 1. See also C. von Fürer-Haimendorf, 'Contributions to the Anthropology of Nepal', London University School of Oriental and African Studies; contribution to Symposium, June-July 1973. In his *Nepal, The Discovery of the Mallas*, translated by Lovett Edwards, London, 1962, p. 76, Guiseppi Tucci wrote: 'the ethnographical study of Nepal, despite the many researches undertaken is still one of the most complex in the world'.
10. G. Tucci, *Nepal, the Discovery of the Mallas*, pp. 60–1, 68.
11. B.H. Hodgson, 'On the Origin and Classification of the Military Tribes of Nepal', Papers Relative to the Colonisation, Commerce, Physical Geography. Ethnography etc., of the Himalaya Mountains and Nepal, vii of *Selections from the Records of the Government of Bengal*, xxvii, Calcutta, 1857, pp. 653–61.
12. Originally in what are now the hill districts of Lumbini, Rapti and Bheri zones in western Nepal. In the seventeenth and early eighteenth centuries, the Magar kingdom was concentrated in and around Palpa district (see Map 1). Dor Bahadur Bista, *People of Nepal*, pp. 62, 63.
13. B.H. Hodgson, 'On the Origin and Classification of the Military Tribes of Nepal', *Journal of the Asiatic Society of Bengal*, 1833, ii, pp. 217–24.
14. The redoubtable Nepalese Army commander, Kaji Amar Singh Thapa and his son Ranjor Singh Thapa, who confronted the Bengal Army during the Anglo-Nepal war of 1814–16, were Chhetri-Thapas.
15. Dor Bahadur Bista, *People of Nepal*, p. 75.

16. B.H. Hodgson, 'On the Origin and Classification of the Military Tribes of Nepal', *Selections from the Records of the Government of Bengal*, xxvii, p. 656.
17. In 1482, on the death of Yaksha Malla, his Kathmandu-valley kingdom was divided between his three sons into three kingdoms which extended to the south, east and west of the valley. The lack of fixed boundaries gave rise to quarrels between the three sovereigns.
18. The Rai and Limbu tribes, of Mongolian ancestry, are believed to have descended from the Kiratas who inhabited the Kathmandu valley around the eighth or seventh centuries BC.
19. The five companies were named Shree Nath, Kali Buksh, Barda Bani, Sabuj and Gorakh; the first four were raised in Sept. 1762; the Gorakh in Feb. 1763. These original companies founded what was to become the Royal Nepalese Army. Royal Nepalese Army Headquarters, *Royal Nepalese Army Colours: a short history*, Kathmandu, 1991.
20. Pemble gives a detailed account of Himalayan trade in *The Invasion of Nepal: John Company at War*, chapter 3, pp. 54–89.
21. H.A. Oldfield, *Sketches from Nipal*, 2 vols., London, 1880, i, pp. 267–8.
22. IOR, H/515, ff.543–7.
23. IOL, Eur.MS, F.128/140, 2 vols.
24. Royal Nepalese Army Headquarters, *Royal Nepalese Army Colours, a short history*, pp. 22, 24, 30, 34, 38.
25. L.F. Stiller, *Prithwinarayan Shah in the light of Dibya Upadesh*, Kathmandu, 1989, pp. 36, 49.
26. Ibid., p. 37.
27. Ibid., p. 38.
28. K.R.S. Rathaur, *The British and the Brave. A History of the Gorkha Recruitment in the British Army*, Jaipur, 1987, p. 24. See also L.F. Stiller, *Prithwinarayan Shah in the light of Dibya Upadesh*, p. 42.
29. L.F. Stiller, *Prithwinarayan Shah in the light of Dibya Upadesh*, p. 43.
30. Ibid., pp. 44, 67.
31. Ibid., p. 46.
32. P.J. Marshall, 'British Expansion in India in the Eighteenth Century: A Historical Revision', *History*, 60, 1975, pp. 36, 41.
33. British tactics on the plains were to fire muskets parallel to the ground usually in volleys. In the smoke of battle this ensured that rounds were delivered at a lethal height. Cannons too were designed generally to fire level on flat ground. D.F. Harding, *Smallarms of the East India Company 1600–1856*, 4 vols, London, 1999, 3, chapter 26.
34. P.J. Marshall, 'British Expansion in India in the Eighteenth Century: A Historical Revision', p. 42.
35. Ibid., p. 36.
36. Ibid., p. 41.
37. J. Pemble, *The Invasion of Nepal: John Company at War*, pp. 16–18, gives an account of the succession and of palace intrigues during the 30 years following Prithvi Narayan Shah's death in 1775.

38. IOR, Despatch to Bengal, E/4/620, 10 Apr. 1771, f. 541.
39. IOR, H/219, 16 Feb. 1768, f. 325.
40. A.K.J. Singh, *Himalayan Triangle, a historical survey of British India's relations with Tibet, Sikkim and Bhutan, 1765–1950*, London, 1988, p. 294.
41. 13 Geo. III c.63.
42. A.K.J. Singh, *Himalayan Triangle, a historical survey of British India's relations with Tibet, Sikkim and Bhutan, 1765–1950*, p. 294.
43. 24 Geo. III, c.25, s.2.
44. Royal Nepalese Army Headquarters, *Royal Nepalese Army Colours, a short history*. Two additional companies were raised in 1779–80, eight in 1783, two in 1784, eleven in 1785 and one in 1786.
45. Dor Bahadur Bista, *The People of Nepal*, pp. 62, 74.
46. W.B. Northey and C.J. Morris, *The Gurkhas*, London, 1928, p. 41; K.R.S. Rathaur, *The British and the Brave. A History of the Gurkha Recruitment in the British Army*, p. 26.
47. Seven of the eleven new companies were raised in 1791.
48. W. Kirkpatrick, *An Account of the Kingdom of Nepaul, being the substance of observations made during a mission to that country in the year 1793*, London, 1811.
49. Ibid., p. 123. The Maugurs (Magars) to whom Kirkpatrick refers are the Chhetri-Magars and Magar-Thapas resulting from the inter-marriage of Khas men and Magar women.
50. Ibid., p. 123.
51. Ibid., p. 214. The Royal Nepalese Army Headquarters, *Royal Nepalese Army Colours, a short history*, lists 40 companies as at 1792.
52. W. Kirkpatrick, *An Account of the Kingdom of Nepaul*, p. 215. This probably referred to the Kali Buksh company raised by Prithvi Narayan Shah in 1762. See *Royal Nepalese Army Colours, a short history*, p. 27.
53. W. Kirkpatrick, *An Account of the Kingdom of Nepaul*, p. 213.
54. Ibid., p. 215.
55. Ibid.
56. W. Kirkpatrick, *An Account of the Kingdom of Nepaul*, p. 118. (from which comes Figure 1, The Khookeri).
57. J.P. Cross, a polyglot of unrivalled experience both as a linguist living in Nepal and as a former Recruiting Officer for the British Army's Brigade of Gurkhas, points out that the far western people in modern Nepal still speak a language quite different from the Nepali of the western hills. His view is corroborated by his godson, Buddhiman Gurung.
58. J. Pemble, *The Invasion of Nepal: John Company at War*, pp. 14–15.
59. K.K. Adhikari, *Nepal under Jang Bahadur 1846–1877*, 2 vols., Kathmandu, 1984, i, pp. 19–20.
60. L.F. Stiller, *The Rise of the House of Gorkha: a Study in the Unification of Nepal 1768–1816*, Patna, 1973, pp. 298–9.
61. Ibid., pp. 301–3.

62. Extract from Minute of the Governor-General dated 16 May 1801: IOR, H/515, ff. 287–8.

63. IOR, H/515, ff. 464–8.

64. Ibid., ff. 314–19.

65. F.B. Hamilton, *An Account of the Kingdom of Nepaul and of the Territories annexed to this Dominion by the House of Gurkha*, Edinburgh, 1819, p. 110.

66. Ibid., p. 111.

67. Report by William Fraser: *PRNW*, pp. 240–1; Lieutenant R. Ross, 'Memoir on the Hill States between the Tonse and Sutleje': IOR, BSPC, P/Ben/Sec/273, 27 Sept. 1815, no.41; J.B. Fraser, *Journal of a Tour through Part of the Snowy Range of the Himala Mountains and to the sources of the Rivers Jumna and Ganges*, London, 1820, pp. 383–4; Edwin T. Atkinson, *The Himalayan Districts of the North West Provinces of India*, 2 vols., Allahabad, 1884, ii, pp. 615–16.

68. L.F. Stiller, *The Rise of the House of Gorkha: a Study in the Unification of Nepal 1768–1816*, Kathmandu, 1973, pp. 310.

69. R. Shaha, *Modern Nepal: a Political History 1769–1955*, 2 vols., New Delhi, 1990, i, p. 107.

70. L.F. Stiller, *The Rise of the House of Gorkha*, pp. 322–3.

71. J.D. Cunningham, *History of the Sikhs*, Reprint, Delhi, 1955, p. 122 fn.

72. Acting Resident at Kathmandu to Political Secretary to Government, 18 Apr. 1818: IOR, BPC, P/120/43, 4 May 1816, no. 54.

73. The names of the Bara Thakuri, given by Lieutenant Robert Ross in his 'Memoir on the Hill States between the Tonse and the Sutleje', are as follows:

Kionthal	Baghat	Baghal	Kothar
Kumarharasin	Bhajji	Mailog	Dhami
Kiari	Kunhiar	Mangal	Koti

74. J. Pemble, *The Invasion of Nepal: John Company at War*, Oxford, 1971, p. 21; J.B. Fraser, *Journal of a Tour through Part of the Snowy Range of the Himala Mountains*, p. 271.

75. J. Pemble, ibid., p. 22.

76. Ibid.

77. Ibid., p. 23; S.B. Gyawali (alternatively quoted as S.V. jNavali), *Amar Singh Thapa 1748–1816*, Darjeeling, 1943, p. 38. The fortress of Kangra was captured in 1620 by Shah Jehan.

78. Royal Nepalese Army Headquarters, *Royal Nepalese Army Colours: a short history*, Kathmandu, 1991. The Companies were:

Barda Bani	Singhnath	Jabarjang	Sabuj
Rana Bhim	Ramdal	Purano Gorakh	Naya Shreenath
Rana Shah	Naya Gorakh	Jwalidal	Kaliparshad
Devidutta	Taradal		

The Kaliparshad was raised in 1806 for the 'western campaign'.

79. Ibid. Durga Bhanjan (1805) and Nandabuksh (1806).

80. K.K. Adhikari, *Nepal under Jang Bahadur 1846–1877*, 2 vols., Kathmandu, 1984, i, p. 151, fn. 6.

81. S.P. Sharma et al. (eds), *Military History of Nepal*, Kathmandu, 1992, pp. 71, 81, 82, 83.

82. K.K. Adhikari, *Nepal under Jang Bahadur 1846–1877*, i, p. 160.

83. See pp. 158–9.

84. Major F. Young, Comdg. Sirmoor Battalion, to Adjutant-General, 29 Dec. 1829: IOR, BMC, P/33/57, 1 Oct. 1830, nos. 34 to 37.

85. Ibid.

86. K.C. Praval, *Valour Triumphs: A history of the Kumaon regiment*, Faridabad, 1976, pp. 398–401.

87. Governor-General to Secret Committee of the Court of Directors of the East India Company, 12 Apr. 1804: IOR, H/492, f. 203.

88. Lord Lake to Governor-General, 8 Aug. 1803: IOR, H/492, f. 287.

89. Lord Lake to Governor-General, 23 Sept. 1803: ibid., ff. 351–2.

90. N. Gupta, *Delhi Between Two Empires, 1803–1931*, Delhi, 1981, p. 13 fn.

91. Anthony R. Wagner, 'An Eighteenth-Century King of Arms' Collection of American Pedigrees', *New England Historical and Genealogical Register*, xcv (1941), p. 24.

92. V.C.P. Hodson, *A List of the Officers of the Bengal Army 1758–1834*, 4 vols., London, 1927–46.

93. Ochterlony to Yale, 13 Aug. 1804: National Library of Scotland, Edinburgh, MS 591, 1841.

94. The young men were Lieutenants Birch and Woodville. Lord Lake to Governor-General, 23 Sept. 1803: IOR, H/492, f. 352.

95. Ochterlony to Yale, 13 Aug. 1804: National Library of Scotland, Edinburgh, MS 591, 1841.

96. William Burn was senior to Ochterlony as a Lieutenant-Colonel but subordinate to him in his capacity as Acting Resident. The overall responsibility was Ochterlony's.

97. Birch later became one of Ochterlony's Assistants.

98. BL, Add. MS 13578, ff. 18–20.

99. IOR, BSPC, P/Ben/Sec/151, 31 Jan. 1805, no. 243. An extract from this letter was sent to all other Residents at Native Courts on 24 Jan. 1805.

100. Ibid., para.5.

101. IOR, H/637, ff. 591–2.

102. He also won third prizes in Bengali and Arabic in 1805, and was ninth in the first class for Persian. An original pass list of the Fifth Examination held in Jan. 1805 is in bundle 76 of the Fraser papers.

103. Alexander Mackenzie, *History of the Frasers of Lovat*, Inverness, 1896, pp. 710–15.

104. His collection of about 200 manuscripts, mostly Persian, are now in the Bodleian Library, Oxford.

105. An excellent account of James' career and artistry is given in M. Archer and T. Falk, *India Revealed, the Art and Adventures of James and William Fraser 1801–35*, London, 1989.

106. These private family papers, carefully preserved by Edward Satchwell Fraser

and most recently by Malcolm Fraser (20th of Reelig) and his wife Kathy, have been catalogued by the Scottish Record Office, Edinburgh. The papers are referred to in William Dalrymple's *City of Djinns: a Year in Delhi*, London, 1993; and also in M. Archer and T. Falk, *India Revealed*.

107. William Fraser to his father, 23 Jan. 1805: Fraser papers, bundle 76.
108. William Fraser to his father, 21 Aug. 1804: ibid.
109. William Fraser to his father, May 1805: ibid.
110. Edward Satchwell Fraser to his son William, 3 Mar. 1806: ibid.
111. William Fraser to his father, May 1805: ibid.
112. William Fraser to his father, 21 Aug, 1804: ibid.
113. Letter dated 16 Oct. 1805: Fraser papers, vol. 29, p. 51.
114. Ibid.
115. William Fraser's diary entry for 15 Jan. 1806: Fraser papers, vol. 29. An account of William's journey from Calcutta to Delhi is given in this volume.
116. Edward Satchwell Fraser to William Fraser, 3 Mar. 1806: Fraser papers, bundle 331.
117. Letter dated 11 Aug. 1810: Fraser papers, vol. 33, p. 186.
118. Letter dated 20 Oct. 1811: Fraser papers, bundle 335.
119. Letter dated 23 Sept. 1813: Fraser papers, bundle 14.
120. Fraser papers, vol. 29, p. 304.
121. Letter dated 12 May 1815: Fraser papers, bundle 80.
122. Letter dated 1 Dec. 1814: Fraser papers, vol. 34, p. 150.
123. William Fraser to his brother James, 6 Apr. 1819: Fraser papers, vol. 29, pp. 339–44.
124. William Fraser to his father, 2 Sept. 1817: Fraser papers, vol. 29, p. 316.
125. To James Fraser from his father, 10 Aug. 1815: Fraser papers, bundle 40.
126. Letter dated 19 July 1815: Fraser papers, vol. 29, p. 309.
127. Fraser papers, bundle 11.
128. Ochterlony to William Fraser, 17 Sept. 1815: Fraser papers, bundle 25.
129. Letter dated 18 Sept. 1817: Fraser papers, vol. 29.
130. Charles Metcalfe to William Fraser, 14 Oct. 1817: Fraser papers, bundle 326.
131. Letter dated 31 Dec. 1817: Fraser papers, vol. 23, p. 37.
132. William Fraser to his brother James, 5 Jan. 1818: Fraser papers, vol. 56.
133. George Fraser to his father, 22 Nov. 1818: Fraser papers, bundle 20.
134. Fraser papers, vol. 34, p. 60.
135. William Fraser to Thomas Fortescue, Civil Commissioner in Delhi, 30 Sept. 1819: IHR, DRA, *Punjab Government Records*, Lahore, 1911, p. 201. Ochterlony, then again Resident at Delhi, disliked Fortescue intensely.
136. Adam to Ochterlony, 27 Jan. 1806: BL, Add.MS 13578, f. 83. The Governor-General at the time was Sir George Barlow.
137. Letter dated 7 Nov. 1806: Fraser papers, vol. 20, p. 117.
138. Governor-General's minute dated 5 June 1806: IOR, BSPC, P/Ben/Sec/189, 5 June 1806, no. 46.
139. Correspondence dated 1 Mar. 1785 and 20 Apr. 1785 between the officiating

Governor-General and Major James Browne: IOR, BSMC, P/B/6, ff. 505–6, and P/B/7, ff. 761–2.

140. IOR, H/326, ff. 829–52.
141. Letter dated 19 Feb. 1806: BL, Add. MS 13578, f. 89.
142. Ibid., ff. 91–8.
143. General Order of the Governor-General in Council dated 5 June 1806: IOR, MDR, L/MIL/5/423, no. 403, f. 279.
144. Letter dated 20 Dec. 1820: Fraser papers, bundle 349.
145. Diary entry 6 Sept. 1805: Fraser papers, vol. 29.
146. Reginald Heber, D.D., *Narrative of a Journey through the Upper Provinces of India from Calcutta to Bombay, 1824–1825*, 2 vols., London, 1844, i, pp. 187–8.
147. Letter dated 7 Nov. 1806: Fraser papers, vol. 29, p. 117.
148. Letter dated 7 Nov. 1806: Fraser papers, vol. 29.
149. Even during the battle of Jaithak in 1815, Major-General Martindell handed letters from Ochterlony to William Fraser: Fraser papers, bundle 446.
150. Letter dated 5 Jan. 1818: Fraser papers, vol. 56.
151. Letter undated but probably written in 1819: Ramsay papers.
152. Fraser papers. vol. 29, p. 330.
153. Fraser papers, bundle 427.
154. Mountstuart Elphinstone to Villiers, 19 Aug. 1832: T.E. Colebrooke, *Life of Mountstuart Elphinstone*, 2 vols., London, 1884, ii, p. 320.
155. Fraser papers, vol. 33, pp. 162, 163. See also Philip Mason, *A Matter of Honour: an account of the Indian Army, its officers and men*, London, 1974, p. 179.
156. Letter dated 28 Feb. 1812: Fraser papers, bundle 352.
157. Maria, Lady Nugent, *A Journal from the year 1811 to the year 1815*, 2 vols., London, 1839, ii, p. 35.
158. Reference to all four missions is made in M.E. Yapp, *Strategies of British India: Britain, Iran and Afghanistan, 1798–1850*, Oxford, 1980.
159. Edmonstone to Elphinstone, 19 Aug. 1808: IOR, H/657, ff. 1, 2.
160. Fraser papers, vol. 30, pp. 171–2.
161. Fraser papers, ibid., p. 110.
162. Fraser papers, vol. 29, p. 146.
163. Fraser papers, ibid., p. 145.
164. Fraser papers, ibid., p. 150.
165. Fraser papers, vol. 30, p. 74.
166. Fraser papers, vol. 29, p. 148.
167. Letter dated 8 Apr. 1809, Fraser papers, vol. 29, p. 167.
168. IOR, H/657, f. 189.
169. Fraser papers, vol. 30, p. 132.
170. Fraser papers, ibid., pp. 171–2.
171. Fraser papers, ibid., p. 168.
172. Fraser papers, ibid., p. 201.
173. Fraser papers, ibid., p. 204.
174. Fraser papers, vol. 29, p. 146.
175. Fraser papers, vol. 30, p. 132.

176. Fraser papers, vol. 29, p. 180.
177. Fraser papers, ibid., p. 152.
178. Fraser papers, ibid., p. 100.
179. Fraser papers, vol. 30, p. 34.
180. Fraser papers, ibid., p. 206.
181. Fraser papers, ibid., p. 81.
182. Fraser papers, ibid., p. 214.
183. M. Elphinstone, *An Account of the Kingdom of Caubul*, 2 vols., London, 1815.
184. Fraser papers, vol. 33, pp. 108–9.
185. Fraser papers, ibid., p. 140.
186. Fraser papers, bundle 351.
187. IOR, H/657, f. 5. Minto signified this by the size of the respective military escorts. Each had two companies of native infantry, but Elphinstone had a full troop of cavalry whereas Metcalfe had only twenty troopers.
188. G.W. Forrest, *Selections from the Minutes and other official writings of the Hon. Mountstuart Elphinstone*, London, 1889, p. 27.
189. R.J. Bingle, "Administrative leadership: the Governor-General, the Bengal Council and the civil service, 1800–1835", in P.G. Robb and D. Taylor, 'Rule, protest, identity: aspects of modern South Asia', *School of Oriental and African Studies, Collected papers on South Asia*, no. 1, 1978.
190. IOR, H/506a, ff. 1–24.
191. Ibid., f. 22.
192. IOR, H/595, ff. 43–5.
193. IOR, H/637, ff. 591–2.
194. IOR, BSPC, P/Ben/Sec/197, 2 Nov. 1806, no. 1.
195. Seton to Edmonstone, 3 Apr. 1808: IOR, BSPC, P/Ben./Sec/206, 18 Apr. 1808, no. 8, para. 5.
196. Countess of Minto (ed.), *Lord Minto in India, 1807–1814*, London, 1880, p. 158.
197. IOR, H/511, f. 42.
198. Ibid., f. 37.
199. Ibid., f. 43.
200. Ibid., ff. 45–6.
201. IOR, H/593, ff. 265–6.
202. Edmonstone to Ochterlony, 18 Nov. 1808: ibid., ff. 273–4.
203. Edmonstone to Ochterlony, 27 Dec. 1808: IOR, H/594, ff. 137–50.
204. IOR, H/511, f. 70.
205. IOR, H/595, ff. 247–53.
206. Adjutant-General to Ochterlony, 23 Mar. 1809: ibid., f. 251.
207. Ochterlony to Adjutant-General, 26 Mar. 1809: IOR, H/595, ff. 254–6.
208. Ibid., ff. 289–303.
209. Ibid., f. 318.
210. Ochterlony to Edmonstone: IOR, H/594, ff. 665–7.
211. Ibid., f. 670.
212. Edmonstone to Ochterlony, 10 Apr. 1809: ibid., ff. 679–87.
213. IOR, H/638, ff. 25–7.

214. Ibid., f. 85.
215. B.J. Hasrat, *Anglo-Sikh Relations, 1799–1849*, Hoshiarpur, 1968, p. 109.
216. Ochterlony to Lushington, 5 May 1810: quoted in K.N. Panikkar, *British Diplomacy in North India*, New Delhi, 1968, p. 113.
217. Edmonstone to Ochterlony, 13 June 1809: IHR, LA, *Punjab Government Records*, ii, Lahore, 1911, p. 125, para. 5.
218. Metcalfe to Edmonstone, 2 June 1809: IOR, H/595, f. 509.
219. Ibid., ff. 510, 527.
220. Ibid., f. 579.
221. See p. 21.
222. IOR, *Punjab Gazetteer of the Kangra District*, i: *Kangra Proper 1883–84*, pp. 39, 40.
223. See p. 22.
224. The Bara Thakuri were twelve very small states in high, wild and inaccessible terrain.
225. The fourteen included five of the seven most senior companies of the Nepalese Army. There may have been other regular units: the services of some companies with the western army have so far not been linked to specific battle zones.
226. F.V. Raper, 'Memoir of Gurwall and Kumaon': *PRNW*, pp. 145–6. Bhakti Thapa had been instructed to engage such militia in 1795 for local defence in Kumaon; M.R. Pant., 'Bir Bhakti Thapa', *Purnima*, 1968, no. 16, p. 390.
227. Wade to Secretary to Government: IOR, BPC, P/126/30, 1 July 1831, no. 43.
228. Ochterlony to Secretary to Government, 20 Dec. 1813: IHR, LA, *Punjab Government Records*, ii, Lahore, 1911, p. 360.
229. IOR, BPC, P/118/53, 9 Jan. 1810, no. 4.
230. Ibid., no. 3.
231. Ibid., no. 4., The Royal Nepalese Army Headquarters, *Royal Nepalese Army Colours: a short history*, lists three extra companies: Chandannath, Kalijung and Aridaman which, with the Jwaladal, fought at Panthajada in 1810 against the Bara Thakuri.
232. See pp. 7, 8 9.
233. C.P. Kennedy, 'Report of the Protected Sikh and Hill States', dated 6 July 1824: IHR, DRA, *Punjab Government Records*, i, Lahore, 1911, pp. 258–68.
234. IOR, BPC, P/119/38, 4 Oct. 1811, no. 18.
235. IHR, LA, *Punjab Government Records*, ii, p. 195. Also referred to in a letter from the Governor-General to the Raja of Nepal dated 15 May 1813: IOR, BPC, P/119/53, 15 May 1813, no. 39.
236. IOR, BSPC, P/Ben/Sec/192, 17 July 1806, no. 89.
237. IOR, BPC, P/118/33, 16 Jan. 1809, no. 77.
238. IOR, BPC, P/118/41, 13 June 1809, no. 72.
239. IOR, BPC, P/119/16, 12 Oct. 1810, nos. 151, 173.
240. IOR, BPC, P/119/44, 13 Mar. 1812, nos. 38, 39.
241. L.F. Stiller, *The Silent Cry: The People of Nepal 1816–39*, Kathmandu, 1976, pp. 91–3.
242. K.K. Adhikari, *Nepal under Jang Bahadur*, i, pp. 176–7, 183.

243. L.F. Stiller, *The Silent Cry: The People of Nepal 1816–39*, pp. 93, 251.

244. IHR, LA, *Punjab Government Records*, ii, p. 279.

245. Such recruits to the Raja of Lahore's army came to be known as 'Lahuris'.

246. Ibid., pp. 219–20.

247. See pp. 6, 13, 16. David Ochterlony served with Lt. Col. William Kirkpatrick in the 2nd Battalion 12th Bengal Native Infantry, and took command in 1803 when Kirkpatrick went on furlough.

248. W. Moorcroft, 'Journal of a journey to Lake Manasarova in Un-des, a province of little Tibet', *Asiatick Researches*, xii, 1816, pp. 375–534; an unauthorised mission, for which Moorcroft was reproved by Minto: Political Secretary's letter to Moorcroft, 18 Dec. 1812: IOR, BPC, P/119/44, 18 Dec. 1812, no. 31.

249. W. Moorcroft, ibid., p. 512.

250. W. Fraser to his father, 10 Apr. 1810: Fraser papers, bundle 12.

251. Seton to W. Fraser, undated; Fraser papers, bundle 78.

252. Ibid.

253. Seton to W. Fraser 1 October 1812; Fraser papers, bundle 79.

254. Fraser papers, vol. 33, p. 218.

255. Ibid.

256. Maria, Lady Nugent, *A Journal from the Year 1811 to the Year 1815*, 2 vols., London, 1839: i, pp. 415, 428; ii, pp. 2, 9, 29, 30.

257. Ibid., ii, p. 31, (8 Jan. 1813).

258. Ibid., ii, p. 43, (16 Jan. 1813).

259. Ibid., ii, p. 52.

260. Extract letter from Charles Metcalfe dated 19 Feb. 1813; IOR, H/511, f. 639.

261. Extract letter from Ochterlony dated 4 Mar. 1813; ibid., f. 640.

262. A. Aspinall (ed.), *The letters of King George IV, 1812–1830*, 2 vols., London, 1938, i, pp. 179–83.

263. R.J. Bingle, "Administrative leadership: The Governor-General, the Bengal Council, and the civil service, 1800–1835"; P.G. Robb and D. Taylor, 'Rule, protest, identity: aspects of modern South Asia', *School of Oriental and African Studies, collected papers on South Asia*, no.1, London, 1978, p. 17; see also R.J. Bingle, 'The Governor-Generalship of the Marquess of Hastings, 1813–1823, with special reference to the Supreme Council and Secretariat, the Residents with Native States, Military Policy, and the transactions of the Palmer Company', unpublished D.Phil. thesis, Oxford 1965, especially chapter ii, part 2, pp. 121–59, and chapter v, pp. 328–413.

264. Adam to Charles Metcalfe, 20 Aug. 1813, IHR, LA, *Punjab Government Records*, ii, p. 342.

265. Marchioness of Bute (ed.), *The Private Journal of the Marquess of Hastings, K.G.*, 2 vols., London, 1858, i, p. 47 (1 Feb. 1814).

266. Ibid., p. 54 (6 Feb. 1814).

267. Ibid., pp. 54–5.

268. B. Ghosh, *British Policy towards the Pathans and the Pindaris in Central India, 1805–18*, Calcutta, 1966, pp. 191–202.

269. J.W. Kaye, *The Life and Correspondence of Charles, Lord Metcalfe*, 2 vols., London, 1854, i, p. 382.

270. Hastings to Court of Directors, 1 Dec. 1815: IOR, H/603, f. 136, para. 130

271. ibid. f. 92, para. 83.

272. L.F. Stiller, *The Silent Cry: The People of Nepal 1816–39*, pp. 220–1.

273. A general account is given in some detail in Pemble's *The Invasion of Nepal: John Company at War*, Oxford 1971, chapter 2.

274. See p. 55.

275. See p. 50.

276. Minto to Bikram Shah, 7 May 1813: IOR, BPC, P/119/53, 15 May 1813, no. 30.

277. Bikram Shah to Minto, letter received on 5 Aug. 1813 : IOR, BPC, P/120/3, 1 Oct. 1813, no. 39.

278. IHR, LA, *Punjab Government Records*, ii, p. 338: Captain H.Y. Hearsey to J. Adam, 24 Aug. 1814: *PRNW*, p. 49.

279. Adam to Ochterlony, 20 Aug. 1813: IHR, LA, *Punjab Government Records*, ii, p. 343.

280. Ibid., p. 345.

281. Kalka lies where the plains of Sirhind meet the hills of Hindur south of Kaji Amar Singh Thapa's Headquarters at Arki and his fort at Subathu. It became the railhead for the Simla narrow gauge railway.

282. Ochterlony to Adam, 18 Dec. 1813: IHR, LA, *Punjab Government Records*, ii, p. 347.

283. Alexander Fraser to his father, 1 Jan. 1815; Fraser papers, vol. 34, p. 166.

284. Alexander Fraser to his father, 20 Jan. 1815; Fraser papers, ibid., pp. 191, 192.

285. Alexander Fraser to his mother, 3 Apr. 1815: Fraser papers, ibid., p. 342.

286. Marchioness of Bute (ed.), *The Private Journal of the Marquess of Hastings K.G.*, 2 vols., London, 1858, i, p. 342.

287. Political letters to Bengal, 18 Feb. 1814: IOR, BPL, vol. 3, ff. 202–3.

288. Alexander Fraser to his mother, 1 Dec. 1814: Fraser papers, vol. 34, p. 150.

289. Fraser papers, vol. 33, p. 280.

290. Alexander Fraser to Jane Anne Fraser: Fraser papers, vol. 34, p. 100.

291. Fraser papers, vol. 33, pp. 197, 239, 276.

292. Undated letters: Fraser papers, bundles 327, 328.

293. Fraser papers, bundle 336.

294. Fraser papers, vol. 29, pp. 238, 239.

295. Letter dated 25 May 1814: Fraser papers, bundle 345.

296. William Fraser to his brother Alexander, 7 Feb. 1814: Fraser papers, bundle 428.

297. Letter dated 4 April 1814: Fraser papers, bundle 13.

298. IOR, BPC, P/120/1, 20 Aug. 1813, no. 34.

299. IHR, LA, *Punjab Government Records*, ii, pp. 393–400, 401.

300. Ibid., p. 401.

301. See p. 20.

302. Ibid., p. 404.

303. Ochterlony to Adam, 9 July 1814: *PRNW*, p. 16, para. 7.

304. IHR, LA, *Punjab Government Records*, ii, pp. 405, 406.
305. Ibid., p. 406.
306. Ibid., p. 402.
307. See p. 19.
308. H.T. Prinsep, *History of the Political and Military Transactions in India during the Administration of the Marquess of Hastings 1813–1823*, 2 vols., London, 1825, i, pp. 68–70.
309. *PRNW*, pp. 683–4, 688–9.
310. J. Pemble, *The Invasion of Nepal: John Company at War*, pp. 44–7.
311. *PRNW*, p. 696.
312. Ibid., p. 701.
313. Marchioness of Bute (ed.), *The Private Journal of the Marquis of Hastings K.G.*, i, p. 170.
314. F.W. Stubbs, *History of the Bengal Artillery*, 2 vols., London, 1877–95, ii, p. 140.
315. Pemble, *The Invasion of Nepal: John Company at War*, p. 133 fn. 7.
316. Alexander Fraser to his father, 20 Jan. 1815: Fraser papers, vol. 34, p. 191.
317. *PRNW*, pp. 37–46, 267–9.
318. Ibid., pp. 31, 76–93, 285–7.
319. Maria, Lady Nugent, *A Journal from the Year 1811 to the Year 1815*, ii, p. 70.
320. Adam to Hearsey 30 July 1814, *PRNW*, p. 13, para. 3.
321. *PRNW*, pp. 47–9.
322. Ibid., pp. 49–50.
323. Ibid., p. 50.
324. Ibid., pp. 18, 19.
325. Bradshaw to Adam 25 Nov. 1813, IOR, BPC, P/120/5, 10 Dec. 1813, no. 87.
326. *PRNW*, p 701.
327. *PRNW*, pp. 41, 55.
328. Moira (Hastings) to the Secret Committee of the Court of Directors, 2 Aug. 1814: *PRNW*, p. 701.
329. Captain Hearsey to Political Secretary, 24 Aug. 1814, *PRNW*, p. 50; further evidence of the composition of the Nepalese Army is given by Kaji Amar Singh Thapa in a letter to the Raja of Nepal dated 2 Mar. 1815: *PRNW*, p. 556.
330. Memoir by Captain F. N. Raper, undated: *PRNW*, p. 146.
331. *PRNW*, p. 146.
332. Adj. Gen. to Maj. Gen. Gillespie, 13 Sept. 1814: *PRNW*, p. 124.
333. The original watercolour painting from which this reproduction was made is in the Prints and Drawings section of the British Library (Oriental and India Office Collections): Add.Or.1260. The two figures on the left of the group, and the figures second and third from the right also appear in M. Archer and T. Falk, *India Revealed, the Art and Adventures of James and William Fraser 1801–35*, London, 1989, pp. 96 and 130 respectively.
334. *PRNW*, pp. 702–17.
335. See p. 76.
336. *PRNW*, p. 702.

337. Moira (Hastings) to the Secret Committee of the Court of Directors, 2 Aug. 1814: *PRNW*, p. 702.
338. Ibid.
339. *PRNW*, p. 718.
340. *PRNW*, pp. 704–7.
341. *PRNW*, pp. 709–10.
342. *PRNW*, pp. 710–12.
343. *PRNW*, p. 713.
344. *PRNW*, pp. 718–22.
345. Pol. Sec. to Bradshaw, 8 Oct. 1814: *PRNW*, p. 94.
346. Bradshaw to Marley, Nov. 1814: *PRNW*, p. 310; a statement at *PRNW*, p. 309 refers to 23 prisoners, whereas a Return at *PRNW*, p. 482, lists twelve prisoners and eighteen wounded and in hospital.
347. Ochterlony to Adjutant-General, 6 Nov. 1814: *PRNW*, pp. 453, 454. The 95 included:

1 Subedar	1 Adjutant
8 Jemadars	1 Writer
14 Havildars	5 Musicians
9 Naiks	1 Colourman
52 Sepoys	2 Blacksmiths
1 Belt-maker.	

348. Ochterlony to Adj.-Gen., 6 Nov. 1814: *PRNW*, p. 453.
349. Ochterlony to Adj.-Gen., 7 Nov. 1814: *PRNW*, p. 457.
350. Adj.-Gen. to Ochterlony, 21 Nov. 1814: *PRNW*, pp. 230, 231; the term 'Goorka Proper' was used by the British to denote the country of Nepal as distinct from the district of Gorkha and the Nepalese Empire: see *PRNW*, p. 721.
351. Ludlow to Mawby, 2 Dec. 1814: *PRNW*, pp. 496–7.
352. *PRNW*, p. 146.
353. Bute, Marchioness of (ed.), *The Private Journal of the Marquis of Hastings K.G.*, 2 vols., London, 1858, i, p. 274.
354. *PRNW*, p. 231.
355. Pp. 47, 51, 59, 102, 105, 110.
356. K.R.S. Rathaur, *The British and the Brave: a History of the Gurkha Recruitment in the British Indian Army*, Jaipur, 1987, p. 35.
357. J. Pemble, *The Invasion of Nepal: John Company at War*, pp. 204, 205 fn. 6.
358. *PRNW*, pp. 530–31.
359. *PRNW*, pp. 521–2.
360. *PRNW*, pp. 538–40.
361. Adj.-Gen. to George Wood, 3 Mar., 4 Mar. 1815, IOR, H/652, f. 63.
362. Acting Collector Gorakhpur, to Pol. Sec., 11 Nov. 1814; *PRNW*, p. 177.
363. Adj.-Gen. to Deputy Adj.-Gen., 30 Sept. 1814: *PRNW*, p. 185.
364. The Nepalese called it Nalapani.
365. Fraser papers, vol. 29, p. 304.
366. Letter to Alexander Fraser dated 31 Oct. 1814; Fraser papers, vol. 29, p. 304. An account of the battle, no doubt based on information supplied by William

Fraser, is given in James Fraser's diary; Fraser papers, vol. 8, entries for 18–21 Nov. 1814.

367. Letter to Alexander Fraser dated 5 Nov. 1814; Fraser papers, bundle 80.

368. Letter to Adam dated 31 Oct. 1814 from Camp Dehra; ibid.

369. Fraser papers, bundle 341.

370. William Fraser to Alexander Fraser, 17 Feb. 1815; Fraser papers, vol. 34, p. 259.

371. Pol. Sec. to Adj.-Gen., 22 Oct. 1814: *PRNW*, p. 136.

372. Pol. Sec. to Metcalfe, 22 Oct. 1814: *PRNW*, pp. 137–8; Lord Moira to the Secret Committee, 2 Aug. 1815: *PRNW*, p. 709.

373. Pol. Sec. to Adj.-Gen., 23 Oct. 1814: *PRNW*, p. 142.

374. Adj.-Gen. to Pol. Sec., 24 Oct. 1814: *PRNW*, p. 178.

375. Adj.-Gen. to Gillespie, 24 Oct. 1814: *PRNW*, p. 180.

376. Adj.-Gen. to Gillespie, 26 Oct. 1814: *PRNW*, p. 182.

377. Adj.-Gen.to Martindell, 6 Dec. 1814: *PRNW*, p. 290.

378. Adj.-Gen.to Ochterlony, 5 Dec. 1814: *PRNW*, p. 290; Adj.-Gen.to Martindell 13 Dec. 1814: *PRNW*, p. 312.

379. The capital of Kumaon, Fraser to Pol. Sec., 20 Oct. 1814: *PRNW*, p. 239.

380. Fraser to Pol. Sec., 30 Oct 1814: *PRNW*, pp. 247–8.

381. Pol. Sec. to Ochterlony, 2 Oct. 1814: *PRNW*, p. 73.

382. Pol. Sec. to Fraser, 30 Nov. 1814: *PRNW*, p. 278.

383. Hearsey to Pol. Sec., 24 Aug. 1814: *PRNW*, p. 48.

384. Ochterlony to Mawby, 16 Nov. 1814: *PRNW*, p. 475; Martindell did not take over command of the Second division until 19 Dec. 1814.

385. *PRNW*, pp. 274–8.

386. *PRNW*, pp. 276, 277.

387. *PRNW*, p. 274.

388. *PRNW*, p. 275.

389. Ibid.

390. *PRNW*, p. 276.

391. Ibid.

392. *PRNW*, pp. 278–9.

393. Pol. Sec. to Ochterlony, 18 Dec. 1814: *PRNW*, p. 284.

394. Fraser to Pol. Sec., 8 Dec. 1814: *PRNW*, p. 293.

395. Pol. Sec. to Fraser, 13 Dec. 1814: *PRNW*, pp. 296–7.

396. Fraser papers, vol. 34, p. 166.

397. Fraser papers, ibid., p. 190.

398. Fraser papers, bundle 455. These abstracts, numbered 6–10, are signed by William Fraser and Lieutenant Frederick Young, and countersigned by Lieutenant-Colonel H. Imlach, Military Auditor-General.

399. *PRNW*, p. 708, para. 133.

400. Fraser papers, bundle 437, p. 100.

401. IOR, H/652, f. 200.

402. Fraser papers, bundle 357.

403. L. Hadow Jenkins, *General Frederick Young*, London, 1923, pp. 47–9.

404. IOR, H/652, ff. 199–200.

405. Ibid., f. 326.
406. Ibid., ff. 303–25.
407. For the rest of the first campaign of the Anglo-Nepal War, Young was engaged in reforming an irregular force before assuming command of the Sirmoor Battalion. Neither he nor his battalion was involved in the second campaign of the War.
408. IOR, H/652, ff. 300–2.
409. Ibid., ff. 199–200.
410. Unsigned letter from Fraser to Major Stevenson. Fraser papers, bundle 437, ff. 1, 2.
411. Ibid.
412. Fraser papers, bundle 437, ff. 36–9.
413. Martindell to Stevenson, undated; Fraser papers, bundle 437, ff. 53–4.
414. Fraser papers, bundle 437, f. 100.
415. Fraser papers, bundle 446.
416. Ibid.
417. Ibid.
418. Pay abstracts and abstracts of muster rolls, numbered 11–13. Fraser papers, bundle 455.
419. James Fraser to Alexander Fraser, 31 Mar. 1815. Fraser papers, bundle 337.
420. Fraser papers, vol. 56.
421. Fraser papers, bundle 437, f. 31. The rounded figure of 7,000 is substantiated in table 1 and in Hastings' letter of 2 Aug. 1815 to the Secret Committee of the Court of Directors: *PRNW*, p. 708, para. 133, fn. where a figure of 6,668 is given for irregulars of all descriptions.
422. Fraser papers, vol. 8, p. 400.
423. William Fraser to his brother Alexander, 4 Mar. 1815: Fraser papers, vol. 29, p. 307.
424. Fraser papers, vol. 8, p. 417 (10 Apr. 1815). The reference to 'regular Ghoorka company' suggests that the Nepalese soldiers were regulars.
425. Fraser papers, vol. 8, pp. 415, 416.
426. Ibid., p. 436.
427. Fraser papers, bundle 455, abstracts numbers 1–3.
428. Ibid., number 3.
429. Fraser to Ochterlony, 31 Mar. 1815: IOR, BSPC, P/Ben./Sec./269, 16 May 1815, no. 37.
430. Fraser to Pol. Sec., 5 Apr. 1815, no. 37.
431. Fraser to Ochterlony, 31 Mar 1815: IOR, BSPC, P/Ben./Sec./269, 16 May 1815, no. 37.
432. Fraser papers, vol. 8, pp. 396, 398.
433. An account is given by James (J.B.) Fraser in his *Journal of a Tour through Part of the Snowy Range of the Himala Mountains and to the sources of the Rivers Jumna and Ganges*, London, 1820. See also M. Archer and T. Falk, *India Revealed: the Art and Adventures of James and William Fraser 1801–35*, chapter 3. It is worthy of note that James Fraser did not join William (near Jaithak)

until 17 Mar. 1815. He spent much of his time sketching until they left on their tour on 6 May 1815.

434. Fraser papers, bundle 455: Pay abstract and abstract of muster roll for the period 17 Apr. to 25 May 1815.

435. Fraser papers, vol. 63, p. 307.

436. *PRNW*, pp. 742–6.

437. Pol. Sec. to Edward Gardner, 14 Dec. 1814: *PRNW*, pp. 301–3.

438. H.T. Prinsep, *History of the Political and Military Transactions in India during the Administration of the Marquess of Hastings 1813–1823*, 2 vols., London, 1825, i, p. 142.

439. Adj.-Gen. to Lt. Col. Gardner, 21 Dec. 1814: *PRNW*, pp. 329–32; *PRNW*, pp. 187–92.

440. Pol. Sec. to Adj.-Gen., 14 Nov. 1814: *PRNW*, pp. 192–3.

441. *PRNW*, pp. 190–1.

442. *PRNW*, pp. 188–9.

443. *PRNW*, p. 191.

444. *PRNW*, p. 192.

445. Hearsey to Pol. Sec., 24 Aug. 1814: *PRNW*, p. 48.

446. Pol. Sec. to Edward Gardner, 14 Dec. 1814: *PRNW*, p. 302.

447. William Martindell, son of Major-General Martindell by an Indian woman, conducted the siege against hopeless odds only to be deserted by his men.

448. *PRNW*, p. 751.

449. H.T. Prinsep, *History of the Political and Military Transactions in India during the Administration of the Marquess of Hastings 1813–1823*, i, p. 153.

450. Fraser papers, vol. 34, pp. 253–4.

451. *PRNW*, pp. 752–4.

452. *PRNW*, pp. 753–74.

453. Fraser papers, vol. 34, p. 231.

454. Pemble, *The Invasion of Nepal: John Company at War*, Oxford, 1971, p. 252.

455. R. Wilkinson-Latham, *British Artillery on Land and Sea 1790–1820*, Newton Abbott, 1973. Maj. Gen. B.P. Hughes *Firepower*, London, 1974.

456. Letter dated 27 Dec. 1814: *PRNW*, p. 443, para. 4.

457. Ochterlony to Adj.-Gen., 7 Nov. 1814: *PRNW*, p. 457.

458. Letter dated 4 Nov. 1814: *PRNW*, p. 458.

459. Adjutant-General to Ochterlony, 19 Nov. 1814: *PRNW*, p. 459.

460. 'Sketch of Ummer Singh's position at Rhamghur, 1814', signed by H. Watkins. National Army Museum, London, ref. no. 6807–183–8–7.

461. Ochterlony to Adj.-Gen, 17 Nov. 1814: *PRNW*, p. 473.

462. Ochterlony to Adj.-Gen., 27 Nov. 1814: *PRNW*, pp. 478–9.

463. Ochterlony to Adj.-Gen., 26 Nov. 1814: *PRNW*, pp. 476–7.

464. Adj.-Gen. to Pol. Sec., 8 Jan 1815: IOR H/649, f. 86.

465. Ochterlony to Adj.-Gen., 31 Dec. 1814: IOR H/649, f. 102

466. Ochterlony to Adj.-Gen., 29 Dec. 1814: *PRNW*, p. 507.

467. Fraser papers, bundle 341.

468. Fraser papers, bundle 357. See also J. Pemble, *The Invasion of Nepal: John Company at War*, pp. 268–70.
469. *PRNW*, pp. 449–50.
470. *PRNW*, p. 453.
471. Fraser papers, bundle 341.
472. IOR, H/653, f. 140, Paper no.1.
473. Ochterlony to Adj.-Gen., 6 Apr. 1815: IOR, H/653, f. 136, para. 7.
474. Kirthi Rana was in charge of troops scattered to the north.
475. Adj.-Gen. to Ochterlony, 20 Apr. 1815: IOR, H/653, ff. 146–8.
476. IOR, H/653, ff. 138–9.
477. Dr. M.I. Waley, Curator for Persian and Turkish, British Library, Oriental and India Office Collections, has confirmed this.
478. PRNW, opposite p. 584.
479. Fraser papers, vol. 8, p. 398.
480. Ramsay papers.
481. Undated letter: Fraser papers, bundle 341. The sketch is missing.
482. IOR, MDR, L/Mil/5/391, f. 275.
483. Lawtie to Ochterlony, 10 Apr. 1815 – an obvious error for what was probably 18 Apr. 1815: IOR, BSPC, P/Ben./Sec./270, 23 May 1815, no.30; IOR, MDR, L/Mil./5/391, ff. 275–6.
484. IOR, BSPC, P/Ben./Sec./270, 23 May 1815, no.30: IOR, MDR, L/Mil./5/391, f. 276.
485. IOR, BSPC, P/Ben./Sec./270, 23 May 1815, no.30: IOR, MDR, L/Mil./5/391, ff. 276–7.
486. Fraser papers, vol. 8, p. 426.
487. Undated note: Fraser papers, bundle 446.
488. Fraser papers, bundle 453.
489. Fraser papers, bundle 453.
490. Letter dated 25th, probably of Apr. 1815: Fraser papers, bundle 437.
491. Fraser to Pol. Sec., 27 Apr. 1815: IOR, H/653, ff. 612–19.
492. Pol. Sec. to Fraser, 8 May 1815; IOR, BSPC, P/Ben./Sec./270, 6 Jun. 1815: IOR, MDR, L/Mil./5/391, 6 Jun. 1815, no. 3.
493. Ochterlony to Ross, Commanding Nusseeree Battalion, 3 May 1815: *PRNW*, p. 406.
494. Ross to Ochterlony, 3 May 1815: *PRNW*, pp. 604–5.
495. Fraser papers, bundle 345.
496. *PRNW*, pp. 605–6.
497. *PRNW*, pp. 607–8.
498. Pol. Sec. to Ochterlony, 21 May 1815: *PRNW*, pp. 608–9.
499. Pol. Sec. to Edward Gardner, 3 May 1815: *PRNW*, pp. 570–1.
500. *PRNW*, p. 570.
501. *PRNW*, p. 607.
502. Nicolls to Pol. Sec., 1 May 1815: IOR, BSPC, P/Ben./Sec./270, 6 June 1815, no.41.
503. *PRNW*, p. 755.
504. *PRNW*, p. 760.

505. Adj.-Gen. to Pol. Sec., 25 July 1815: IOR, BSPC, P/Ben./Sec./272, 30 Aug. 1815, no. 18.
506. Moira to the Secret Committee, 2 Aug. 1815: *PRNW*, p. 759, para. 313.
507. Ibid., p. 763.
508. Pol. Sec. to Major-General Wood, 31 Oct. 1814: *PRNW*, p. 155, para. 21.
509. Pol. Sec. to Bradshaw, 26 Nov. 1814: *PRNW*, p. 255, para. 11.
510. *PRNW*, pp. 262–5.
511. Pol. Sec. to Bradshaw, 27 Dec. 1814: *PRNW*, p. 254, para. 5.
512. Vice-President in Council to the Court of Directors, 21 June 1815: *PRNW*, pp. 635–6.
513. The four were Chandra Sekher Opadeia, Guru Gujraj Misser, Bum Sah and Amar Singh Thapa; Moira (Hastings) to the Secret Committee of the Court of Directors, 5 Aug. 1815: *PRNW*, pp. 763–80.
514. Moira (Hastings) to the Secret Committee of the Court of Directors, 20 July 1815: *PRNW*, p. 673, para. 4.
515. Moira (Hastings) to Raja of Nepal, 22 July 1815: *PRNW*, pp. 812–13.
516. Moira (Hastings) to the Secret Committee of the Court of Directors, 2 Aug. 1815: *PRNW*, p. 762, para. 321.
517. B.J. Hasrat, *Anglo-Sikh Relations 1799–1849*, Hoshiarpur, 1968, p. 12.
518. Fraser papers, bundle 351.
519. Kaji Amar Singh Thapa to Raja of Nepal, 2 Mar. 1815: *PRNW*, pp. 553–7; C.T. Metcalfe to Pol. Sec., 21 May 1815: *PRNW*, p. 559.
520. Pol. Sec. to Elliott, 9 Dec. 1815: *PRNW*, p. 856.
521. Moira (Hastings) to Raja of Nepal, 13 Jan. 1816: *PRNW*, pp. 894–5.
522. Fraser papers, bundle 47.
523. Letter dated 17 Feb. 1816: Fraser papers, bundle 47.
524. *PRNW*, p. 842, paras. 32 and 33; see also Pol. Sec. to Ochterlony, 5 Jan. 1816: *PRNW*, pp. 860–1.
525. Ochterlony to Bradshaw, 25 Jan. 1816: *PRNW*, pp. 904–5.
526. Pol. Sec. to Ochterlony, 13 Jan. 1816: *PRNW*, pp. 888–94.
527. Ibid. p. 890, para. 17.
528. *PRNW*, p. 914.
529. *PRNW*, pp. 863–4.
530. L.F. Stiller, *The Silent Cry: the People of Nepal 1816–1839*, Kathmandu, 1976, p. 99.
531. R. Shaha, *Heroes and Builders of Nepal*, Oxford, 1965, p. 70. Perhaps shocked at his government's eventual capitulation, Kaji Amar Singh Thapa withdrew into the mountains at Gosainkund where in 1816 he died.
532. H.T. Prinsep, *History of the Political and Military Transactions in India during the administration of the Marquess of Hastings, 1813–1823*, i, p. 203; see also *PRNW*, p. 940, postscript to Kelly's letter of 2 Mar. 1816 to Ochterlony.
533. S.P. Sharma et al. (eds.), *Military History of Nepal*, Kathmandu, 1992, p. 106.
534. *PRNW*, p. 724, para. 182.
535. *PRNW*, pp. 870–87.
536. Not Colonel Jasper Nicolls, who commanded the troops at Almora.

537. Ochterlony to Acting Adj.-Gen., 9 Feb. 1816: *PRNW*, p. 867.
538. John Shipp, *The Path of Glory, being the Memoirs of the Extraordinary Career of John Shipp*, edited by C.J. Stranks, London, 1969, pp. 109, 110.
539. Ochterlony to Acting Adj.-Gen., 19 Feb. 1816: *PRNW*, pp. 933–4.
540. Ibid.
541. Ochterlony to Acting Adj.-Gen., 28 Feb. 1816: *PRNW*, p. 937.
542. *PRNW*, p. 939.
543. Governor-General in Council to the Secret Committee of the Court of Directors, 30 Mar. 1816: *PRNW*, p. 948, para. 5.
544. Kelly to Ochterlony, 2 Mar. 1816: *PRNW*, p. 940; Governor-General in Council to Secret Committee of the Court of Directors, 30 Mar. 1816: *PRNW*, p. 947, para. 2.
545. Ochterlony to Acting Adj.-Gen., 5 Mar. 1816: *PRNW*, p. 955.
546. Ochterlony to Adam, 5 Mar. 1816: *PRNW*, pp. 953–4.
547. Adj.-Gen. to Pol. Sec., 28 Nov. 1815: *PRNW*, p. 878.The detachment comprised 1 Subaltern, 1 Assistant Surgeon, 1 Adjutant, 1 Staff Serjeant, 6 Subadars, 23 Jemadars, 50 Havildars, 11 buglers and drummers, and 516 sepoys: *PRNW*, pp. 884–5.
548. Governor-General in Council to Secret Committee of the Court of Directors, 30 Mar. 1816: *PRNW*, pp. 948–9.
549. Pol. Sec. to Ochterlony, 13 Jan. 1816: *PRNW*, p. 889.
550. Ochterlony to Adj.-Gen., 29 Jan. 1816: *PRNW*, pp. 873–4.
551. Acting Adj.-Gen. to Ochterlony, 12 Feb. 1816: *PRNW*, p. 874. The Champaran Light Infantry Local Battalion comprised 912 all ranks in Dec. 1814 and 1,397 all ranks (a third of Colonel Kelly's 1st Brigade) in Jan. 1816: see *PRNW*, pp. 519, 883.
552. Ibid.
553. Ochterlony to Adam, 5 Mar. 1816: *PRNW*, p. 953.
554. Ibid.
555. Governor-General in Council to Secret Committee of the Court of Directors, 30 Mar. 1816: *PRNW*, p. 948, para. 7.
556. Adam to Ochterlony, 16 Mar. 1816: *PRNW*, p. 965–7.
557. *PRNW*, p. 948, paras. 6 and 11.
558. L.F. Stiller, *The Silent Cry: The People of Nepal 1816–39*, p. 99.
559. Ibid., p. 101.
560. Ibid., pp. 106–7.
561. Ibid., p. 216.
562. Ibid. pp. 48, 49; L.F. Stiller, *Nepal; Growth of a Nation*, Kathmandu, 1993, p. 36 (note 3), p. 39 (fn.1).
563. L.F. Stiller, *Nepal; Growth of a Nation*, p. 60, para. 6.
564. The indigenous Tharu people were immune to the 'owl', a deadly form of malaria.
565. H.T. Prinsep, *History of the Political and Military Transactions in India during the Administration of the Marquess of Hastings 1813–1823*, i, p. 207.
566. Ibid., pp. 464–5.

567. Letter dated 30 Mar. 1816: Fraser Papers, vol. 34, p. 305. Alexander Fraser died at Delhi on 14 June 1816.

568. Governor-General in Council to the Secret Committee of the Court of Directors, 30 Mar. 1816: *PRNW*, pp. 949–51, paras. 13, 18; Adam to Ochterlony, 16 Mar. 1816: ibid., p. 966, para. 7.

569. Governor-General in Council to Secret Committee, 30 Mar. 1816: *PRNW*, 950, para. 14; Adam to Ochterlony, 16 Mar. 1816: ibid., p. 966, paras. 8–10; Adam to Ochterlony, 20 Mar. 1816: ibid., p. 971.

570. Governor-General in Council to the Secret Committee of the Court of Directors, 30 Mar. 1816: *PRNW*, p. 951, para. 22.

571. Adam to Edward Gardner, 16 Mar. 1816: *PRNW*, p. 968, para. 4.

572. Ibid., para. 5.

573. L.F. Stiller, *Nepal; Growth of a Nation*, p. 64.

574. W. W. Hunter, *Life of Brian Houghton Hodgson*, London, 1896, p. 101.

575. ibid., p. 128.

576. This excludes the 300 said to be at Almora.

577. It has to be remembered that Ochterlony obtained post-facto authority from the Governor-General both for his Agreement with Jeykishen and his Convention with Kaji Amar Singh Thapa.

578. Evidence of comparative costs will be given in the next chapter.

579. Moira (Hastings) to the Secret Committee of the Court of Directors, 1 June 1815: *PRNW*, p. 566.

580. *PRNW*, p. 566.

581. Fraser papers, vol. 29, p. 309.

582. *PRNW*, p. 760.

583. Pol. Sec. to Ochterlony, 21 May 1815: *PRNW*, pp. 608–9; General Order of the Governor-General dated 21 May 1815: *PRNW*, pp. 605–6.

584. Adj.-Gen. to Pol. Sec., 28 June 1815: IOR, BSPC, P/Ben./Sec./271, 9 Aug. 1815, no. 24.

585. P. Banskota, *The Gurkha Connection: a History of the Gurkha Recruitment in the British Indian Army*, Jaipur, 1994, Preface.

586. In contrast, the British awarded a battle honour to the 2nd Battalion 42nd Royal Highlanders and the 8th Bombay Native Infantry, for their heroic but unavailing defence of Mangalore against overwhelming odds in 1783–84. Philip Mason, *A Matter of Honour: an account of the Indian Army, its officers and men*, London, 1974, p. 127.

587. p. 416.

588. *PRNW*, pp. 339, 340.

589. Royal Nepalese Army Headquarters, *Royal Nepalese Army Colours: a short history*, p. 54.

590. Ibid., p. 340.

591. Hearsey to Pol. Sec., 24 Aug. 1814: *PRNW*, p. 50. The Palpese came from a district in central Nepal which stretched from the southern borders of Tibet. The Jumlese were from the high hills of far western Nepal. Both were therefore

Nepalese hillmen. However Hearsey did not regard them as Gorkhas as they were not from the western hills.

592. *PRNW*, p. 191.

593. *PRNW*, p. 556.

594. Ochterlony to Adj.-Gen., 5 Feb. 1815: IOR, BSPC, P/Ben./Sec./271, 9 Aug. 1815, no. 24.

595. *Asiatick Researches*, vol. xii, p. 513.

596. IOR, BSPC, P/Ben./Sec./ 271, 9 Aug. 1815, no. 25.

597. IOR, BSPC, P/Ben./Sec./328, 4 Mar. 1825, no. 16, para. 15.

598. *PRNW*, p. 702, para. 110.

599. IOR, H/653, ff. 133, 140. Dor Bahadur Bista's *People of Nepal*, Kathmandu, 1972 (second edition), lists, at p. 6, Sahi as a Thakuri (Chhetri) clan name. A map in the same book shows the district of Piuthan.

600. IOR, BSPC, P/Ben/Sec/271, 9 Aug. 1815, no. 24. This return has been inserted out of sequence i.e. after Consultations dated 23 Aug. 1815.

601. Extract enclosed with letter from Adj.-Gen. to Pol. Sec., 28 June 1815: IOR, BSPC, P/Ben./Sec./271, 9 Aug. 1815, no. 24.

602. Adj.-Gen. to Secretary to Government, 25 July 1815: IOR, BSPC, P/Ben./Sec./ 272, 30 Aug. 1815, no. 18.

603. A Gorkha chief of similar name is depicted in figure 3.

604. IOR, H/653, ff. 612–19.

605. Pol. Sec.to Fraser, 8 May 1815: IOR, MDR, L/Mil./5/391, pp. 279–80.

606. Adj.-Gen. to Pol. Sec., 28 June 1815: IOR, BSPC, P/Ben./Sec./271, 9 Aug. 1815, no. 24.

607. Moira (Hastings) to Secret Committee of the Court of Directors, 1 June 1815, *PRNW*, p. 566.

608. Adj.-Gen. to Pol. Sec., 28 June 1815: IOR, BSPC, P/Ben./Sec./271, 9 Aug. 1815, no. 24.

609. Ibid.

610. Pol. Sec. to Adj.-Gen., 9 July 1815: IOR, BSPC, P/Ben./Sec./271, 9 Aug. 1815, no. 25.

611. Prinsep was wrong in asserting that all three were called 'Nuseeree battalions': H.T. Prinsep, *History of the Political and Military Transactions in India during the Administration of the Marquess of Hastings 1813–1823*, i, p. 175.

612. It was finally decided to raise two extra Pioneer companies.

613. Pol. Sec. to Adj.-Gen., 9 July 1815: IOR, BSPC, P/Ben./Sec./271, 9 Aug. 1815, no. 25.

614. Close green jacket without facings, red cuffs and collar and trimmings, blue loose trousers and a bonnet.

615. Adj.-Gen. to Pol. Sec., 25 July 1815: IOR, BSPC, P/Ben./Sec./272, 26 Aug. 1815, no. 18.

616. Ibid.

617. Pol. Sec. to Adj.-Gen., 3 Aug. 1815: IOR, MDR, L/Mil./5/391, 26 Aug.1815, no. 41.

618. Fraser papers, bundle 351.

619. IOR, BSPC, P/Ben./Sec./271, 9 Aug. 1815, no. 24.

620. IOR, BMC, P/27/5, 26 Aug. 1815, no. 43. F.L. Petre in his *The 1st King George's Own Gurkha Rifles*, London, 1925, p. 5, refers to a Governor-General's Order of 24 April 1815, directing the constitution of the first battalions, as 'not now traceable at Simla'. It seems doubtful whether this order ever existed. As Hastings was then on tour, any such order would have been published by the Vice-President in Council. It seems likely that the General Order of the Vice-President in Council published on 26 August 1815 authorised the formation of the Gorkha battalions. The date of formation of the 1st and 2nd Nusseri (Gorkha) Battalions (and the Sirmoor and Kemaon Battalions) is given as 24 April 1815 in the General Abstracts with the General Orders of the Governor-General in Council dated 2 May 1823: IOR, MDR, L/Mil./17/2/272, ff. 141a, *et seq.*

621. Moira (Hastings) to the Secret Committee of the Court of Directors, 2 Aug. 1815: *PRNW*, pp. 675–763.

622. *PRNW*, p. 699, para. 99.

623. Alexander Fraser to his father, 16 June 1815: Fraser papers, bundle 47.

624. *PRNW*, p. 700, para. 100.

625. *PRNW*, p. 757, para. 304.

626. *PRNW*, p. 760, paras. 316–18.

627. S. Alavi, 'North Indian Military Culture in Transition c. 1770–1860', unpublished Ph.D. thesis, University of Cambridge, 1991, p. 197. See also S. Alavi, 'The Company Army and Rural Society: The Invalid Thanah 1780–1830', *Modern Asian Studies*, xxvii, 1993, p. 153.

628. Extract from Military letter to Bengal, dated 16 Apr. 1816: IOR, MDR, L/MIL/5/391, f. 294.

629. IOR, H/653, ff. 612–19, para. 6.

630. S.R. Kohli, 'The army of Maharaja Ranjit Singh', *Journal of Indian History*, i (2), 1921–2, p. 212.

631. N.K. Sinha, *Ranjit Singh*, Calcutta, 1933, p. 207.

632. F.S. Bajwa, *The Military System of the Sikhs 1799–1849*, Delhi, 1964, p. 58.

633. IOR, BSPC, P/Ben/Sec/280, 25 May 1816, no. 2.

634. The agent in both cases seems to have been sent from Bilaspur by Seodat Rau.

635. R. Shaha, *Heroes and Builders of Nepal*, Oxford, 1965, pp. 75–6. The British erected a monument at Kalanga inscribed 'As a tribute of respect for our adversary Bulbudder, Commander of the Fort, and his brave Gurkhas, who were afterwards, while in the service of Ranjit Singh, shot down in their ranks to the last man by Afghan artillery'.

636. S.R. Kohli, 'The army of Maharaja Ranjit Singh', *Journal of Indian History*, i (2), 1921–2, p. 219. Kohli thought it probable that Ranjit Singh raised his first infantry battalion in about 1805. Ibid., p. 210.

637. W. Osborne, *Court and Camp of Runjeet Singh*, Lahore, 1895, p. 165.

638. S.R. Kohli, 'The army of Maharaja Ranjit Singh', *Journal of Indian History*, i (3), 1921–2, p. 402.

639. C. Grey (H.L.O. Garrett, ed.), *European Adventurers of Northern India 1785–1849*, Lahore 1929, pp. 25, 27, 59–60, 71–2.

640. F.S. Bajwa, *The Military System of the Sikhs 1799–1849*, pp. 64–6.

641. It remained so until 1885.

642. Letter from Bengal to the Court of Directors, 6 Nov.1830, enclosures nos. 36 and 37. IOR, MDR, L/MIL/3/32 no. 32. The details were submitted by the respective Commanding Officers in statements to the Adj.-Gen. and were given in relation to retirements. Some of the recruits may have been Garhwalis.

643. L.F. Stiller, *The Silent Cry: the People of Nepal 1816–39*, Kathmandu, 1976, pp. 56–64.

644. IOR, BMC, P/33/57, 1 Oct. 1830, no. 35, para. 16.

645. Ibid., no. 36, para. 6.

646. L. Caplan ' "Bravest of the Brave". Representations of "The Gurkha" in British Military Writings', *Modern Asian Studies*, xxv, 1991, p. 563.

647. Order attached to Enclosure no. 37 of Military Letter from Bengal to the Court of Directors: IOR, MDR, L/MIL/3/332, no.52 of 6 Nov. 1830. Captain Kennedy succeeded Ross as Commandant of the 1st Nasiris in 1822 and held the appointment until his retirement in 1836. Lieutenant Nicholson was Adjutant of the 1st Nasiris from 1815 to 1826.

648. Data taken from IOR, MDR, L/MIL/17/2/272, f. 141a and associated General Abstracts. The date of 24 April 1815 is doubtful: see note 620 above. The last four units in the list are shown as 'in the Civil Department'.

649. Ibid., f. 141d.

650. Unpublished Ph.D. thesis, University of Cambridge, 1991

651. Ibid., p. 142.

652. See p. 148.

653. From a memorial to Cleveland erected in Bhagalpur by the Governor-General in Council: C.R. Wilson (ed.), *List of Inscriptions on Tombs and Monuments in Bengal possessing historical or architectural interest*, Calcutta, 1896.

654. Maria, Lady Nugent, *A Journal from the Year 1811 to the Year 1815*, 2 vols., London, 1839, i, pp. 203–5.

655. S. Alavi, 'The Company Army and Rural Society: The Invalid Thanah 1780–1830', *Modern Asian Studies*, xxvii, 1993, p. 152.

656. The invasion did not take place, owing to the speed of Ochterlony's advance on Makwanpur.

657. Ochterlony's division had been held in reserve. William Fraser had also served under Ochterlony as a Major in Skinner's Horse.

658. Ochterlony's Nasiris were in action in April 1815, but were not then part of a British Gorkha battalion.

659. Young to Adj.-Gen. 25 Aug. 1830: IOR, BMC, P/33/57, 1 Oct. 1830, no. 36, paras. 12, 13.

660. BL, Add. MS 48225, f. 120. (Morley Papers).

661. Adam died in 1825 at sea *en route* for England.

662. Data extracted from *PP*, Appendix (A), Returns nos. 10, 24, 26, 28, 30, 32.

663. Reginald Heber, D.D., *Narrative of a Journey through the Upper Provinces of India from Calcutta to Bombay, 1824–1825*, London, 1844, 2 vols., i, p. 125.

664. S. Alavi, 'North Indian Military Culture in Transition c. 1770–1860', unpublished Ph.D. thesis, University of Cambridge, 1991, p. 56.
665. Ibid., pp. 57, 58, 67.
666. Ibid., p. 67.
667. D.M. Peers, 'Between Mars and Mammon: the military and political economy of British India at the time of the First Burma War, 1824–1826', Ph.D. thesis, University of London, 1988, p. 74.
668. Young to Adj.-Gen. 29 Dec. 1829 IOR, BMC, P/33/57, nos. 35–37 of 1 Oct. 1830.
669. Ibid. The reference to 'most others' is to Indian Infantry. Arrangements in the Nasiri battalions were similar to those of the Sirmoor Battalion.
670. Young to Adj.-Gen., 25 Aug. 1830: IOR, BMC, P/33/57, no.36 of 1 Oct. 1830
671. See pp. 83, 110.
672. See p- 168.
673. See pp. 98, 259.
674. See p. 140.
675. IOR, H/665, ff. 233–5.
676. Lawrence to Adjutant-General, 8 Dec. 1824: IOR, H/665, extracts at ff. 222–4.
677. Lawrence quoted figures of 1,500 to 2,000 unemployed Nepalese soldiers in Dhoti province annually: Ibid., f. 223.
678. Adj.-Gen. to Swinton, 8 Jan. 1825: IOR, H/665, f. 219.
679. IOR, H/665, ff. 233–5.
680. Letter dated 20 Nov. 1824, ibid., ff. 237–44.
681. General Sir Stapleton Cotton became Lord Combermere in 1825.
682. Attached to Enclosure no.37 of Military Letter from Bengal to the Court of Directors: IOR, MDR, L/MIL/3/32, no.52 of 6 Nov. 1830.
683. Ibid., item 5. 'Bhurtpore' was awarded as a battle honour to the two Gorkha battalions.
684. General Return showing numbers present. *PRNW*, pp. 882–3.
685. *PP*, House of Commons, 1831–2, xiv, v (Military), Appendix (A), no.46; per military statement of 1830. Gross totals include clothing, proportion of pensions and, where appropriate, recruiting charges, cost of passage ,etc.
686. Ibid., para. 2281.
687. Ibid., Appendix (A), nos.24, 25, 38, 39.
688. Butterworth Bayley, the Senior Councillor, had acted as Governor-General from 13 Feb. 1828 following Amherst's departure for England.
689. Lord Ellenborough was appointed President of the Board of Control in September 1828.
690. Lord Colchester (ed.), *A Political Diary 1828–1830 by Edward Law, Lord Ellenborough*, 2 vols., London, 1881, i, p. 273. 11 Dec. 1829.
691. Data taken from *PP*, House of Commons, 1831–2, xiv, v (Military), Appendix (A), no.1.
692. Ibid., xii.
693. Ibid., Extract from Appendix (A), no.1.
694. Bengal General Order no.251 of 4 Dec. 1829; B.G.Os dated 15 Feb. and 12 Mar. 1830 show that 95 men transferred to the Indian infantry.

695. IOR, MDR, L/MIL/8/37.
696. IOR, MDR, L/MIL/8/38.
697. IOR, MDR, L/MIL/8/43.
698. Here it should be noted that, at this stage of its evolution, the Kumaon Battalion was comprised mainly of Kumaonis and came under the Civil Department.
699. Lord Colchester (ed.), *A Political Diary 1828–1830 by Edward Law, Lord Ellenborough*, 2 vols., London, 1881, ii, pp. 92–3, 3 Sept. 1829.
700. Ibid., 13 Nov. 1829, p. 131.
701. M.E. Yapp, *Strategies of British India – Britain, Iran and Afghanistan 1798–1850*, p. 205.
702. C.H. Philips (ed.), *The Correspondence of Lord William Cavendish Bentinck, Governor-General of India 1828–1835*, 2 vols., Oxford, 1977, ii, pp. 1440–2.
703. Hastings to Court of Directors, 6 Jan. 1820: IOR, MDR, L/MIL/5/386/98.
704. J.W. Kaye, *The Life and Correspondence of Charles, Lord Metcalfe*, London, 1854, p. 149.
705. Major-General Nicolls, *Diary*, 5 July 1824: IOR, Eur.MS, F/175/31 (Nicolls Papers).
706. D.M. Peers, 'Between Mars and Mammon: the Military and Political Economy of British India at the time of the First Burma War, 1824–1826', Ph. D. thesis, London, 1988, pp. 118–19. See also Peers, D.M., *Between Mars and Mammon, Colonial Armies and the Garrison State in Early Nineteenth-Century India*, London, 1995, pp. 52, 53.
707. Ibid. Ph. D. thesis, pp. 103–4.
708. Charles Wynn (President of the Board of Control) to Munro, 29 May 1826: IOR, Eur. MS, F/151/72 (Munro Papers).
709. W. Badenach, *An Inquiry into the State of the Indian Army, with suggestions for its improvement and the establishment of a Military Police in India*, London, 1826. Despite the title, Badenach confined himself to the Bengal army both because of his experience and because it represented more than half the Indian army in size.
710. Ibid., p. 28.
711. Ibid., pp. 21, 31–4.
712. Ibid., p. 146.
713. Ibid., p. 115.
714. Ibid., p. 117.
715. W. W. Hunter, *Life of Brian Houghton Hodgson*, London, 1896, pp. 107, 108.
716. *PP*, House of Commons, 1831–2, xiv, v (Military), para. 2268.
717. IOR, BSPC, P/Ben/Sec/ 328, 4 Mar. 1825, no. 16, para. 6.
718. Ibid., para. 33.
719. A reference to Swiss mercenary forces employed in European wars.
720. IOR, Hodgson papers, MSS. 9, ff. 177, 178.
721. R. Shaha, *Modern Nepal: a Political History 1769–1955*, i, pp. 155–7. Bhim Sen Thapa's powers gradually diminished. Eventually he was imprisoned, and committed suicide in 1839.

722. B.H. Hodgson, 'On the Origin and Classification of the Military Tribes of Nepal', *Selections from the Records of the Government of Bengal*, xxvii, Calcutta, 1857, pp. 657, 658.

723. Ibid.

724. R. Shaha, *Modern Nepal, a Political History 1769–1955*, 2 vols., New Delhi, 1990, i, p. 155.

725. C.H. Philips (ed.), *The Correspondence of Lord William Cavendish Bentinck*, ii, p. 1442.

726. Ibid., p. 1450.

727. IOR, BMC, P/33/55, no. 11, 25 July–13 Aug. 1830.

728. Kennedy to Adj.-Gen. 4 Sept. 1830 and Young to Adj.-Gen. 29 Dec. 1830: IOR, BMC, P/33/57, nos. 34–7 of 1 Oct. 1830.

729. Kennedy to Adj.-Gen. 4 Sept. 1830 and Young to Adj.-Gen. 25 Aug. 1830: IOR, BMC, P/33/57 nos. 36 and 37 of 1 Oct. 1830.

730. Bengal Military letter dated 6 Nov. 1830 to the Court of Directors: IOR, MDR, L/MIL/3/32 no. 52 of 1830. See also Mil. Sec. to Adj.-Gen. 30 July 1830: IOR, BMC, P/33/55 no. 12.

731. Kennedy to Adj.-Gen., 4 Sept. 1830 and Young to Adj.-Gen., 25 Aug. 1830: IOR, BMC, P/33/57, nos 36 and 37 of 1 Oct. 1830.

732. IOR, MDR, L/MIL/3/32 letter no. 52 of 6 Nov. 1830.

733. Dor Bahadur Bista, *People of Nepal*, Kathmandu, 1972, p. 111.

734. Kennedy to Adj.-Gen., 4 Sept. 1830, para. 6: IOR, BMC, P/33/57, no. 37 of 1 Oct. 1830.

735. Young to Adj.-Gen., BMC, P/33/57, no.35 of 1 Oct. 1830.

736. D.M. Peers, 'Between Mars and Mammon', Ph.D. thesis, University of London, 1988, p. 73.

737. Extract from *PP*, House of Commons, 1831–2, xiv, v (Military), Appendix (A), no. 55.

738. Ibid., paras. 2265, 2268.

739. Ibid., para 2279.

740. Ibid., paras. 2278, 2284.

741. Ibid., paras. 2282, 2283.

742. Ibid., para. 265.

743. Ibid., paras. 4, 264, 2316.

744. See pp. 186, 188, 189, 191, 195.

745. In P. Banskota, *The Gurkha Connection: a History of the Gurkha Recruitment in the British Indian Army*, Jaipur, 1994, p. 46.

746. *PP*, House of Commons, 1831–2, xiv, v (Military), para. 2269. This policy probably delayed the recruitment of Gorkhas into the Kumaon Battalion.

747. *Selections from the Records of the Government of Bengal*, xxvii, p. 658 fn.

748. Anon. letter published in *United Services Journal*, 8 (1832), p. 32.

749. See pp 116–17, 122.

750. See p. 168.

751. General Order no. 38 dated 8 Feb. 1836.

752. Sir Henry Fane's Journal, Fane Collection 6/6/1.

753. Sir Henry Fane's Journal provides evidence of this; Fane Collection 6/6/1.

754. Fane Collection 6/6/4.

755. H.E. Fane, *Five years in India*, 2 vols., London, 1842, i, p. 194.

756. Ibid., p. 219. 'Captain M' was probably Captain (later Lieutenant-General) J.K. McCausland, the second-in-command, officiating in the absence of the Commandant, Colonel H.T. Tapp.

757. Fane Collection 6/6/7, ff. 287–95.

758. Ibid., f. 311.

759. Fane Collection 6/6/1, ff. 29–33.

760. J.D. Cunningham, *History of the Sikhs*, London, 1849, p. 227.

761. Fane Collection, 6/6/7, ff. 295–6.

762. *Selections from the Records of the Government of Bengal*, no. xxvii, 1833; see also W.W. Hunter, *Life of Brian Houghton Hodgson*, London, 1896, p. 105.

763. Fane Collection, 6/6/1, ff. 64–5.

764. W.W. Hunter, *Life of Brian Houghton Hodgson*, London, 1896, p. 110.

765. Fane Collection, 6/6/9, f. 874.

766. Fane left India on 1 Jan. 1840 and died on the voyage home. Nicolls had been involved in the war with Nepal in 1815–16 and at Ochterlony's instigation had helped to found the Kumaun Battalion.

767. Fane Collection, 6/6/9, ff. 828, 894.

768. W.W. Hunter, *Life of Brian Houghton Hodgson*, London, 1896, p. 177.

769. Ibid., p. 184

770. Ibid., pp. 200–1.

771. Letter from the Governor-General to the King of Nepal, dated 22 Jan. 1842; Auckland MSS. Quoted in W.W. Hunter, *Life of Brian Houghton Hodgson*, London, 1896, p. 201.

772. IOR, L/MIL/17/2/289.

773. The 4th Regiment is the Gorkha battalion to which Penderell Moon refers in his *The British Conquest and Dominion of India*, London, 1989, p. 536. Eldred Pottinger, Political Officer in Kohistan had escaped to Charikar when his home was attacked, only to leave for Kabul when the garrison was forced to evacuate the town. Pottinger was taken prisoner but released by Sir George Pollock's troops. See also Field Marshal Sir John Chapple, *The Lineages and Composition of Gorkha Regiments in British Service*, Gurkha Museum, Winchester, 1984, p. 10.

774. Undated letter to a Secretary of the Governor-General, probably written in 1837. H.B. Edwardes and H. Merivale, *Life of Sir Henry Lawrence*, 2 vols., London, 1872, i, p. 170.

775. Ibid., p. 200.

776. W.W. Hunter, *Life of Brian Houghton Hodgson*, London, 1896, p. 233.

777. Letter dated 18 November 1843. H.B. Edwardes and H. Merivale, *Life of Sir Henry Lawrence*, London, 1872, i, pp. 459–61.

778. P. Banskota, *The Gurkha Connection, a History of the British Recruitment to the British Indian Army*, Jaipur, 1994, p. 50.

779. From Lawrence's 'defence' of Macnaghton. H.B. Edwardes and H. Merivale, *Life of Sir Henry Lawrence*, London, 1872, i, p. 448.

780. Letter dated 17 June 1844. H.B. Edwardes and H. Merivale, *Life of Sir Henry Lawrence*, London, 1872, ii, p. 5.

781. W.W. Hunter, *Life of Brian Houghton Hodgson*, London, 1896, p. 237.

782. Charles Viscount Hardinge, *Viscount Hardinge: by his son and Private Secretary in India*, Oxford, 1891, pp. 49–50.

783. Letter dated 25 May 1845. H.B. Edwardes and H. Merivale, *Life of Sir Henry Lawrence*, London, 1870, i, p. 482.

784. Ibid., p. 88. The President of the Board of Control wrote to instruct Hardinge to direct military as well as civil affairs as necessary. However, the Sikh War ended before a formal authority could be despatched: Ibid., pp. 104, 105.

785. Penderell Moon, *The British Conquest and Dominion of India*, London, 1989, p. 598.

786. A scholarly account of the Kot Massacre is given in K.K. Adhikari, *Nepal under Jang Bahadur 1846–1877*, Kathmandu, 1984, i, pp. 29–38.

787. P. Banskota, *The Gurkha Connection: A History of the Gurkha Recruitment in the British Indian Army*, Jaipur, 1994, pp. 53–5.

788. Despatch to Adj.-Gen. of the Army dated 30 January 1846; Viscount Hardinge, *The War in India: despatches of Hardinge and others*, London, 1846, p. 76.

789. Ibid., p. 102.

790. Ibid., p. 63.

791. Ibid., pp. 93–4.

792. Charles Viscount Hardinge, *Viscount Hardinge: by his son and Private Secretary in India*, Oxford, 1891, p. 120.

793. H.B. Edwardes and H. Merivale, *Life of Sir Henry Lawrence*, London, 1872, ii, p. 59.

794. F.S. Bajwa, *Military System of the Sikhs*, Delhi, 1964, p. 141.

795. J.D. Cunningham, *A History of the Sikhs*, London, 1849, p. 333.

796. W.W. Hunter, *Life of Brian Houghton Hodgson*, London, 1896, p. 105.

797. Letter dated 7 Mar. 1849 from Dalhousie to Sir George Couper, his oldest and dearest friend; J.G.A. Baird (ed.), *Private Letters of the Marquess of Dalhousie*, London, 1910, p. 58.

798. Sir W. Lee-Warner, *The Life of the Marquis of Dalhousie, K.T.*, 2 vols., London, 1904, i, pp. 154–6.

799. Lt. General W. Napier (ed.), *Defects Civil and Military of the Indian Government, by Lt.-General Sir Charles James Napier, GCB*, 2nd. edition, London, 1853, pp. 24, 25.

800. The Duke of Wellington commented: 'I never could understand why he [Hardinge] was in such a damned hurry'. Sir W Lee-Warner, *The Life of the Marquis of Dalhousie, K.T.*, London, 1904, i, p. 63.

801. Ibid., i, p. 206.

802. J.G.A. Baird (ed.), *Private Letters of the Marquess of Dalhousie*, London, 1910, p. 210.

803. Ibid., p. 207.

804. Ibid., p. 47.
805. Lt-General Sir W. Napier, *The Life and Opinions of General Sir Charles James Napier, GCB*, 4 vols., London, 1857, iv, p. 266.
806. Ibid., pp. 226, 227.
807. Ibid., p. 159.
808. Ibid., p. 56.
809. Letter dated 13 April 1849 from Dalhousie to his cousin Fox Maule. Sir W. Lee-Warner, *The Life of the Marquis of Dalhousie, K.T.*, London, 1904, i, pp. 241, 242.
810. Ibid., pp. 240, 241.
811. Hobhouse was President of the Board of Trade.
812. J.G.A. Baird (ed.), *Private Letters of the Marquess of Dalhousie*, London, 1910, p. 80.
813. Ibid., pp. 61–5.
814. The number of Sikhs involved soon rose, from a total originally planned at 400, to 2,000.
815. J.G.A. Baird (ed.), *Private Letters of the Marquis of Dalhousie*, London, 1910, p. 66.
816. Ibid., p. 70.
817. Ibid., p. 76.
818. Letter dated 17 Dec. 1848. Sir W. Lee-Warner, *The Life of the Marquis of Dalhousie, K.T.*, London, 1904, i, pp. 200–1.
819. Ibid., p. 81.
820. Lt.-General Sir W. Napier (ed.), *Defects Civil and Military of the Indian Government, by Lt.-General Sir Charles James Napier, GCB.*, London, 1853, pp. 365, 375.
821. Ibid., p. 221.
822. Letter dated 10 May 1848: J.G.A. Baird (ed.), *Private Letters of the Marquess of Dalhousie*, London, 1910, p. 24.
823. Napier's Journal, Meerut, 9 Nov. 1849; Letter from Napier to Dalhousie dated 5 Jan. 1850; Letter from Napier to Lord Ellenborough dated 11 May 1850. All in Lt.-General Sir W Napier, *The Life and Opinions of General Sir Charles James Napier, GCB*, London, 1857, 4 vols., iv, pp. 217, 220, 250.
824. Ibid., pp. 220, 250.
825. Letter from Napier to Dalhousie dated 5 Jan. 1850. Lt.-General Sir W. Napier (ed.), *Defects Civil and Military of the Indian Government, by Lt.-General Sir Charles James Napier, GCB*, London, 1853, p. 182.
826. Letter from Napier dated 28 March 1850. Lt.-General Sir W. Napier, *The Life and Opinions of General Sir Charles James Napier, GCB.*, London, 1857, 4 vols., iv, p. 248. The officer was probably Major C. O'Brien who was Commandant of the Nasiri Battalion at Jatogh from 1843 to 1850.
827. Lt.-General Sir W. Napier (ed.), *Defects Civil and Military of the Indian Government, by Lt.-General Sir Charles James Napier, GCB*, London, 1853, p. 28.
828. Ibid., pp. 29–31.

829. Ibid., p. 221.
830. Lt.-General Sir W. Napier (ed.), *Defects Civil and Military of the Indian Government, by Lt.-General Sir Charles James Napier, GCB*, London, 1853, p. 185.
831. Lt.-General Sir W Napier, *The Life and Opinions of General Sir Charles James Napier, GCB*, London, 1857, 4 vols., iv, p. 270.
832. Ibid., p. 247.
833. Lt.-General Sir W. Napier (ed.), *Defects Civil and Military of the Indian Government, by Lt.-General Sir Charles James Napier, GCB*, London, 1853, pp. 129, 130.
834. J.G.A. Baird (ed.), *Private Letters of the Marquess of Dalhousie*, London, 1910, p. 113.
835. Lt.-General Sir W. Napier, *The Life and Opinions of General Sir Charles James Napier, GCB*, London, 1857, 4 vols., iv, pp. 248, 249.
836. Ibid., pp. 251, 263.
837. Ibid., pp. 268, 245, 251.
838. Ibid., p. 247.
839. Ibid., p. 270.
840. Ibid., pp. 150, 251.
841. J.G.A. Baird (ed.), *Private Letters of the Marquess of Dalhousie*, London, 1910, p. 120.
842. Sir W. Lee-Warner, *The Life of the Marquis of Dalhousie, K.T.*, London, 1904, i, pp. 328–9.
843. Letter dated 22 July 1850. J.G.A. Baird (ed.), *Private letters of the Marquess of Dalhousie*, London, 1910, p. 132.
844. Lt.General Sir W. Napier, *The Life and Opinions of General Sir Charles James Napier, GCB*, London, 1857, 4 vols., iv, pp. 225, 271.
845. IOR, MDR, P/43/38 no. 135.
846. This adds weight to the suggestion that a recruitment depot existed in eastern Kumaon, probably at Lohughat. P. Banskota. *The Gurkha Connection: a History of the British Recruitment in the British Indian Army.* Jaipur, 1994.
847. IOR, MDR, P/43/38 no. 135.
848. Erskine, the Resident there, had tried, without success, to obtain recruits on the establishment of the 66th or Goorka Regiment.
849. IOR, MDR, P/43/38.
850. The 'lal kurti paltan' (the red coat regiment) attracted recruits with its red coats and white facings.
851. 1st Report of the Select Committee of the House of Lords 1852–3, *Parliamentary Papers*, 1852–3, xxxi, para. 949. Napier had earlier pointed this out to Dalhousie. See p. 228.
852. Ibid., paras. 951, 952.
853. Ibid., paras. 954–55.
854. Sir W. Lee-Warner, *The Life of the Marquis of Dalhousie, K.T.*, London, 1904, ii, p. 282.
855. Sir W.W. Hunter, *Life of Brian Houghton Hodgson*, London 1896, p. 109.

856. Ibid., p. 110.
857. Ibid, pp. 255–8.
858. L. F. Stiller, S.J., *Nepal, Growth of a Nation*, Kathmandu, 1993, Chapters 7 and 8. P. Banskota, *The Gurkha Connection: A History of the Gurkha Recruitment in the British Indian Army*. Jaipur, 1994, pp. 53–74.
859. Sir W.W. Hunter, *Life of Brian Houghton Hodgson*, London, 1896, pp. 256, 258.
860. The Extra Goorkha Regiment later became the 1st Battalion, 4th Gurkha Rifles.
861. This Battalion later became the 1st Battalion, 5th Gurkha Rifles.
862. Formerly the 66th or Gorkha Regiment, the Sirmoor (Rifle) Battalion, the Kemaon Battalion, the Extra Goorkha Regiment and the 25th Punjab Infantry or Harzara Battalion, respectively: Governor General's Order No. 400 dated 3 May 1861.
863. Governor-General's Order No. 990 dated 29 Oct. 1861.
864. P. Banskota, *The Gurkha Connection: A History of the Gurkha Recruitment in the British Army*, Jaipur, 1994, pp. 88–94.
865. IOR, H/652, f. 326.
866. IOR, H/652, ff. 303–25.
867. Detached bodies acting separately without discipline.
868. *PRNW* p. 570.
869. IOR, H/453, f. 140, Paper no. 1.
870. Ramsay papers.
871. *PRNW*, pp. 607–8.
872. *PRNW*, pp. 835–6. The treaty was executed on 2 December 1815 and ratified by the Governor-General on 12 January 1816. Ibid., p. 852.
873. IOR, BSPC, P/Ben/Sec/271, 9 Aug. 1815, no.24.
874. Fane Collection, FANE 6/6/1, ff. 66, 65. Spellings are as in the original.

Index

308   *A Special Corps*